# Discovering Free Will
# and Personal Responsibility

# Discovering
# Free Will
# and
# Personal
# Responsibility

JOSEPH F. RYCHLAK
DEPARTMENT OF PSYCHOLOGICAL SCIENCES
PURDUE UNIVERSITY

New York     Oxford
OXFORD UNIVERSITY PRESS
1979

Library of Congress Cataloging in Publication Data

Rychlak, Joseph F
Discovering free will and personal responsibility.

Includes indexes.
1. Free will and determinism.
2. Responsibility. I. Title.
BF621.R93      155.2'34      78-31709
ISBN 0-19-502580-6

Acknowledgment is made for permission to reprint materials from the
following publications:

*Mach's Philosophy of Science* by J. Bradley. Copyright © 1971 by J. Bradley. Reprinted by permission of Athlone Press of the University of London.

*How To Win Friends and Influence People* by Dale Carnegie. Copyright © 1936 by Dale Carnegie, renewed copyright © 1964 by Dorothy Carnegie. Reprinted by permission of Simon & Schuster, A Division of Gulf & Western Corporation.

*The Origins of Psycho-Analysis: Letters to Wilhelm Fliess* by Sigmund Freud, edited by Marie Bonaparte, Anna Freud, and Ernst Kris, authorized translation by Eric Mosbacher and James Strachey. Copyright © 1954 by Basic Books, Inc., Publishers, New York; also the Hogarth Press Ltd., London, for British rights. Reprinted by permission of Basic Books and The Hogarth Press.

*Psycho-cybernetics and Self-fulfillment* by Maxwell Maltz. Copyright © 1970 by Maxwell Maltz. Reprinted by permission of Grosset and Dunlap, Inc.

*Experimenter Effects in Behavioral Research* (enlarged edition) by Robert Rosenthal. Copyright © 1976 by Irvington Publishers, Inc. Reprinted by permission of Irvington Publishers.

*The Psychology of Rigorous Humanism* by Joseph F. Rychlak. Copyright © 1977 by John Wiley & Sons, Inc. Reprinted by permission of John Wiley & Sons.

*The Human Use of Human Beings* by Norbert Wiener. Copyright © 1950, 1954 by Norbert Wiener. Reprinted by permission of Houghton Mifflin Publishers.

*An Essay Concerning Human Understanding* by John Locke, edited by A. S. Pringle-Pattison. Copyright © 1924 by Oxford University Press. Reprinted by permission of Oxford University Press.

Permission for the following by Harper & Row:

*est: 60 Hours That Transform Your Life* by Adelaide Bry, 1976.
*Your Erroneous Zones* by Wayne Dyer, 1976.
*I'm OK—You're OK* by T. A. Harris, 1967.

Printed in the United States of America

To Stef and Ron,
in hopes that you will never forget who
you are and how you must always be . . .

# Preface

I wrote this book because I sincerely believe that the average person has an unclear grasp of his or her humanity. Though we are routinely told by our religions and the popular media that we have free wills, with the capacity to take responsibility for our lives, there are no books which purport to explain just how this takes place. Most of us can describe in general terms how our stomach or heart works, but we haven't the foggiest notion of how to describe the workings of our free will. If we turn to scientific texts we are sure to be disappointed because the going assumption in science is that we are *not* really free but mechanistically determined. Even though there is growing scientific evidence in support of a free-will conception of human behavior, the public never gets this message because such findings are put through a mechanistic wringer before they are presented to us as "facts." This book is my effort to set the record straight and to offer the reader another—equally scientific! —view of such facts, one which puts humanity back into the human image.

J. F. R.

*West Lafayette, Indiana, USA*
*February 1979*

# Contents

# Discovering Free Will
# and Personal Responsibility

# ONE

# The Search for Personal Freedom
# and Responsibility

We live in a time of specialization and expertise. There are technical advisers today for everything, from how to manage our stock portfolio to how to manage our sex life. What used to be the province of priests, rabbis, and ministers is now the province of psychologists and psychiatrists. There are scores of specialists today who promise to raise our consciousness or to shake us loose from our unimaginative existence and generate something of real significance in our lives. If we look carefully we usually find that at the heart of these advisory services there is a scientific claim being made. Many people today have great faith in this scientific know-how, and look to those approaches which rely on its tenets and research procedures for helpful direction.

And yet, there is an area of the greatest possible significance for human beings about which science has thus far been unable to offer advice. We refer to free will and personal responsibility. These two aspects of the human condition must necessarily go together, for only when a person is initially free to behave as he or she intends can we later assign responsibility for the course actually taken. There are scientists who feel that questions about free will and personal responsibility reflect illusions, archaic remnants of mankind's past which can no longer be seriously entertained.[1] Others merely "pass" on

3

these questions, to go about their business in blind disregard of the resulting tensions and inconsistencies.

There seems to be a host of influences today militating against the assignment of personal responsibility for human behavior. Even the religionist finds it difficult to speak of free will in the face of scientific experiments which either state outright or imply in their manipulations that the individual is "under the control" of certain determinate factors in his existence. We are what our biology and our social environments have shaped us into being! This is what the science of psychology teaches. Morality becomes something imposed on people by others—the system, the clergy, the powermongers, or the blue-nosed reactionaries who would rather deny and restrict than enliven and enrich life's alternatives. It becomes increasingly less possible to judge a pattern of behavior in good-bad, worthy-unworthy, or right-wrong terms without being accused of repressing the human spirit.

But science itself is criticized by those who would see in its investigative potential a "big brother" or "mad scientist" emerging to bring on mind control through drugs or the persuasion of propaganda. This anti-science criticism, which usually takes root from existentialistic and related Eastern philosophies, also fails to provide us with a clear picture of how we can indeed opt for, and commit ourselves to, personally directed activities. Its advocates speak of existential freedom but their technical expertise falters on the crucial point of "How can we describe the operations of a free will?" The usual course is simply to proclaim that free choices exist, based presumably on our private experience of this capacity to "change our minds." Though it may suffice for practical considerations, there is no doubt but that such superficial explanations leave us with a gnawing sense of uncertainty, particularly when we see actuaries successfully predicting the eventual outcomes of elections before we have made our trip to the polls.

An especially pernicious result of this uncertainty about our natures is that we tend to avoid confronting the *grounds* (reason, basis) on which our decisions are being made. We overlook the fact that making a choice from among alternatives is only one side of the decision-making process. There is also the side of making clear precisely what those alternatives are, where they came from, and how we personally have come to base our decisions on these rather than other alternatives possibly open to us if we but examine things further. For example, it is not uncommon today to turn on a television set and view one of those ubiquitous talk shows in which something like cinematic pornography is under discussion. The host and his—usually show-business—guests wrestle with the questions of what is or is not pornographic, and why people will or will not attend movies of this type. Invariably, the drift of the conversation moves from the difficult problems of public censorship and personal motivation to conclusions of the sort "Well, who can say what is right or wrong anyway?" or "So long as each individual chooses for himself, what difference does it make whether such movies are shown?"

Now, a viewer at this point can applaud the honesty and egalitarian attitudes expressed or consider them a sign of the accelerating decadence of the modern era. Yet the *grounds* for making either decision may or may not have been examined and personally affirmed by the viewer concerned. Thus, the more socially liberal viewer may hear a talk-participant say "I think it is better to select movies based on the significance of the story line than on their potential for titillation" and adjudge this person to be "sexually hung-up" or worse—especially if this is stated in the context of an attack on the aesthetic quality of most pornographic films. And, the socially conventional viewer may hear the egalitarianism as an attack on the tenets of his religion. To him, deciding for oneself implies that a Supreme Authority no longer can be counted on to direct the lives of mortal beings. Though we have decisions being made here on both sides of the question of whether to attend or not attend pornographic movies, it does *not* follow that the grounds on which these decisions have been made or the behaviors which flow from them have been seriously examined.

The egalitarian rule of everyone deciding for himself may simply be an invitation for those who do not examine their grounds to attend pornographic movies *without* having exercised their critical capacities. The religious mandate to avoid sinful temptations may have been accepted as a grounding assumption in the life of an individual who has never questioned its legitimacy lest he be accused of apostasy. Since neither of the individuals making the decision has arrived at the grounding basis for behavior through personal examination and affirmation both are more likely to be under the direction of others than they realize, given their sense of actually making the decision of whether to behave one way or the other. This sense of personal decision-making is not an illusion, but it is a decidedly superficial awareness of the mental process actually being carried out.

Though an examination of our groundings is likely to free us from ready manipulation by others we are never as uniquely "individual" in selecting our grounds as we might imagine. A hundred people might indeed make a hundred decisions on some issue but there are *never* a hundred groundings involved. Centuries of theological debate have taught us that there are only a handful of groundings on which to support a recommended course of moral or ethical action. It is also true in political campaigns that people's decisions usually come into focus in a party platform of general agreement. When disagreements occur they are on limited issues, or go on between and not within parties. Often such disagreements are merely semantic misunderstandings in how a grounding is to be phrased rather than a basic divergence in outlook. It is this coalescing feature of valued decisions which leads philosophers to speak of *universals* in thought. These are highly abstract, often unrecognized assumptions (ideas, thought-forms) which predicate our common sense. "Life is to be valued above all other considerations" would frame such a universal assumption. Though it is sometimes challenged, as during times of war, the fact is that there are many ways in which to arrive at this assumption and it most surely predicates countless common-sense decisions without ever needing to be explicitly stated.

Moralists always seem repressive because they emphasize this trend to the universal aspect of human reason. The Golden Rule was worked out in precisely this way, and if we conform to it in our ongoing life we will of necessity "repress" certain behavioral alternatives which we might otherwise have entertained. Does this mean we have limited our freedom or exercised it? Our answer depends upon what point in the succession of events we begin our analysis. A free-will psychology is not inconsistent with the view of behavior as also determined. Moving determinately toward a *predetermined* end is what *will* or *will-power* means! The question of freedom arises over whether or not it is possible to select one's ends. If we believe that it is possible, then we hold to a *teleology*. This term derives from the Greek word "telos," which means the end, goal, or more broadly stated, the *grounding reason* for which our behavior is taking place. If we are not telic organisms, capable of influencing these reasons then there is surely no need to anguish over the "whys" of what we do. But if we *are* telic in behavior then to ignore this side of our nature and behave without concern for our grounds means two things are taking place in our lives: (a) we are surely living according to *other people's* groundings or reasons; and (b) we will never cultivate this side of our nature to achieve a higher level of self-direction.

The present book invites the reader to discover his or her telic nature. It is written from a psychological perspective and takes responsibility only for this form of personal freedom. Much of the talk concerning freedom today centers on so-called "freedoms from"—hunger, crime, racial or sexual repression, governmental control, unemployment, poverty, a polluted environment, and so on. Psychology has no special claims to expertise in such areas of human concern, important though they are. We do not profess to know the answers to these problems, even though we do believe that when solutions are found they will be hit upon by individuals who have that strong sense of personal direction which so many people today seem to feel is lacking in their lives.[2]

At the outset of our psychological quest we will familiarize ourselves with the style of causal description employed in the natural sciences. As we shall see, academic psychology is a younger member of the family of sciences, and as such has accepted without question the values and attitudes of its older siblings like physics, biology, and chemistry. It learned to speak in the language of natural science and has since tried to put its descriptive accounts of the human being in this preferred terminology. This effort has fostered growing pains and adjustment problems for psychology, not the least of which has to do with the fact that human freedom simply cannot be properly expressed in the descriptive terminology of natural science. We shall take a close look at what it means to say that behavior is determined. The problem of meaning will also be considered, and we shall learn of an oppositional or contradictory streak that people have, which allows them to live within meaningful bipolarities. Human choice will be seen to begin as a selection among such nonlinear, oppositional alternatives. Goethe summed up the spirit of humanity which we hope to document when he penned the lines:

> Up with the low, down with the high,
> The crooked straight, the straight awry—

That, only, makes me feel aglow,
And on this earth I'll have it so.[3]

We may be surprised to learn that a belief in free will does not necessarily mean that one supports doctrinaire religious viewpoints. Some of the most important theologians of history have looked suspiciously on human teleologies even as they embraced deity teleologies. The handful of ways in which psychologists have used a free-will conception will be discussed before we advance our own definition of this concept. It is also a central aim of this book to provide the reader with scientifically sound psychological evidence in support of telic human behavior. Indeed, we shall go beyond the psychological laboratory to show how modern psychotherapies, the recent fascination with Eastern philosophies, the widely cited work in brain stimulation, and the "how to" tradition of popular psychology all combine to paint a picture of human behavior which is consistent with our themes of free will and personal responsibility. The book will close with a pointed discussion of our human natures and what we can do to keep them so.

Briefly stated, the course of discovery offered by this book begins in historical and academic themes, but it systematically moves to the more relevant applications of psychology for the reader as a person. Essentially, we build a bridge between the technical issues of academia and the practical considerations of applied psychology. To facilitate understanding of unfamiliar terminology a glossary begins on page 269. The hope is that upon completing the journey through the pages a reader will be thoroughly schooled in what it means to be a human being.

# TWO

# Causes and the Rise of Science

To be *free* is to be without constraint, open to alternatives, and not bound by a fixed course. When we speak of political freedoms this idea of free alternatives in behavior is captured in such terms as liberty, independence, and rights. Of course, the politically free individual must still comply with the legal constraints within which his liberty is defined. We are bound as free citizens by the laws of our land not to transgress the freedom of others. Though we are not concerned with political freedoms in this volume, there is a parallel between the conceptions of political and psychological freedom. In both cases it is never a question of total (100%) freedom versus something else. Freedom is always a matter of "more or less," and what we are actually concerned with in discussions of freedom is the type and extent of limitation put upon our behavior. The more limitation, the less freedom.

This leads directly into what is called the problem of *determinism*, because insofar as a behavior is determined it has had limitations put upon the alternatives to which it might be open. It is impossible to discuss freedom without taking up determinism, and vice versa. But determinism cannot be properly understood without first considering an even more fundamental issue—that of the *causes* of anything in existence. This is so because what one means by determination always depends on how whatever it is that is being limited may be said "to be" in the first place. It is the causes of things and events which tell us what they are like, or, what we think they are like. Hence, we first review in Chapter 2 the various meanings of what a cause is, and then show how the use of causation has varied in the rise of modern scientific description. This historical review is necessary in order to set the stage for Chapter 3, where we get deeply into the question of determinism.

## The Four Causes

If we ask the average person what is meant by the word "cause" we are likely to get examples of how events are brought about, how something is assembled, or how anything gets done. People today think of a cause as the impetus in events, so that the idea of *motion* is central to their notion of causation: causes literally move things along or they are not true causes. But the concept of a cause was not so limited when Aristotle (*c.* 350 B. C.) first proposed that knowledge be expressed in terms of how things and events might be said to have come into existence. The Greek word Aristotle used was *aitiá*, which has the meaning of *responsibility*, so that in following his usage we would be trying to assign responsibility for why something existed or an event took place. This is an odd way of talking about causes judging from today's conventions. We do not say that the wind is "responsible" for blowing leaves from trees in the autumn of the year. We will take up below the specific reasons why "cause" was narrowed over the centuries to mean strictly the motion of events over time.

Aristotle's theory of knowledge brought together the thinking of several of his predecessors who were trying to account for the nature of the world, and he organized their conceptions under what he said were the four causes of anything (adding a fifth in one special context). These four concepts amount to a model or a paradigm which can be used in the explanation of anything on this earth (and, beyond!). The causes therefore act as highly abstract frames of reference within which a thinker can formulate ideas about literally everything in experience. As an overarching meta-theory which draws parallels between many different events, this descriptive scheme is unsurpassed in the history of thought. What were his four causes?

First, there is the *material cause*, a principle of explanation used by earlier philosophers like Thales and Anaximander to account for the nature of the universe by trying to name a kind of substance ("water" or "the boundless" respectively) of which things were constituted. In describing a chair we can say we know it is a chair because like most chairs it is made of wood, or iron, or marble; not many chairs are made of cotton or of ice cream. Probably the most abstract material-cause concept we hear of today is the notion of *matter*, which is a nondescript way of suggesting that "something" exists of a palpable nature as opposed to "nothing." Theoretical and philosophical views which hold that the real world exists (realism) are often called materialisms because of this supposed opposition between the palpable and the impalpable.

Another cause of the chair is the fact that someone or some machine made it, or put it together. This impetus factor which we have already alluded to above is what Aristotle called the *efficient cause* of the chair, taking his lead from earlier debates between philosophers over whether change in events is illusory (Parmenides) or it actually takes place (Heraclitus). It seemed plausible to Aristotle that earlier events do bring about changes in later events, just as time itself seems to wreak havoc on our physical structure in the aging process. Centuries later, when David Hume argued that we cannot "see" causes but merely habitually assume a cause-effect, as one billiard ball stops in close proximity to another which starts into motion, he was speaking of _only_ the efficient cause. By this time in history (*c.* 1750) the modern equation of cause with efficient cause was being made.

Chairs also take on distinctive patterns; they meet our blueprint conceptions of what chairs always look like. Chairs look more like chairs than they look like tricycles or apple trees. This usage, drawn from the earlier conceptions of a patterned order in the universe advanced by Heraclitus and Democritus, Aristotle named the _formal cause._ In analyzing how they came to understand things these philosophers realized that regardless of what things were made of, or how they got assembled into what they were, the major factor in recognizing them and relating them to other items of experience was their pattern or shape. Aristotle even drew a distinction between what he called a primary versus a secondary substance based on the role of formal causation in such palpability. The concept of matter would be for Aristotle a primary substance which could enter as a potentiality into the make-up of any of a number of things. But, once a recognizable shape would be added to this potentiality we would have a secondary substance taking form—as in the case of a horse versus an antelope. Both animals have flesh and bone but yet their forms and typical (patterned) gaits are what distinguishes them most clearly.

As this example demonstrates, Aristotle did not think it advisable to limit the number of causes we might use in describing the nature of anything. It is possible to have formless substances, as in a blob of mud, and we can even think of formless movements (efficient causes), such as the impact of a breeze wafted against our face. But mud can be shaped and baked into statues or dinnerware, and breezes can be elevated and patterned into an easily recognized tornado. The task of a scientist is to enunciate his understanding of things in terms of as many of the causes as he can.[1] The more causes he can bring to bear in giving his account, the richer will it be.

Aristotle's fourth cause was based on the frequent use which earlier philosophers like Socrates and Plato (who taught Aristotle) made of the telic explanation. Certain aspects of the world seemed definitely pointed toward some end or goal (*telos*) which defined their purpose. Aristotle called this the *final cause*, defining it as "that, for the sake of which" something exists, is happening, or is about to take place. The indefinite "that" in this phrase can be replaced by *the reason* (purpose, intention) why things exist or events come about. The reason for which a chair is constructed might be something like the comfort of a human being, who uses it in many ways that are common to all of us. The chair need not "itself" be said to have a purpose, of course. It is the human being who obtained the wood (material cause) and made it (efficient cause) into a chair matching his physical outlines (formal cause) so that he might live more comfortably (final cause) who may be said to have had a purpose or intention in the course of behavior eventuating in the fact that the chair now exists.

And right here is where we find Aristotle as a scientist theorizing in ways that are considered improper today by most natural scientists, for he was not above adding in a final-cause phrasing to the description of what today we call *inanimate* nature. In his physical account of vegetation, for example, Aristotle[2] suggested that leaves exist for the purpose of providing shade for the fruit on trees, and he concluded thereby "that nature is a cause, a cause that operates for a purpose." If we were to classify this kind of theory we would call it a natural teleology. But since the modern scientist no longer accepts telic description, this kind of theorizing would be dismissed as a pre-scientific or even primitive form of anthropomorphization.

To *anthropomorphize* is to frame one's theory in human-like terms (*anthrop-* devolves from the Greek, meaning human being). Primitive myths which assigned evil or benevolent intentions to natural products like stars or a waterfall are examples of anthropomorphization. Of course, Aristotle could hardly be called a "primitive" thinker. He was simply prepared to talk about the world in a way that for certain historical reasons we no longer consider appropriate in the scientific context. Rather than being pre-scientific, Aristotle was the first real scientist who founded biology and worked out some of the first experimental-observational procedures employed by man. We will suggest in later chapters that his use of final causation to describe events is *not* contrary to the basic aims of science, and indeed only by returning to such description can we recoup the human image in science. We next turn to the historical events that stopped the use of telic terminology in the rise of modern science.

## The Rise of Modern Science

Once we take it as proper to assign purpose to nature it is but a short step to identifying a Superior Intelligence lying behind this rational order. And so it was that in the earliest accounts of the universe we find science being mixed with theology. Scientists and theologians alike spoke of a God's purpose or Divine Plan which accounted for the reliable patterns of things to be studied. This view of a plausible order in the universe is called *rationalism*, and there were both a philosophical variety and a mathematical variety in the history of Western civilization. Because both varieties are based on the ordering and patterning of things in existence we can say that both make great use of a formal-cause meaning.

Philosophical rationalism refers to the more *pictorial* aspects of our knowledge, or the kinds of things which we can relate to our common-sense experience. For example, when Plato speculated on the motion of planets (*c.* 350 B. C.) he took it as plausible that the planets moved in circular orbits because this is the most perfect of all geometrical forms, and a universe which is rationally organized would naturally select perfection over forms of lesser quality. Add in a God concept, and we can say that since a Supreme Being must be perfect it follows that He would use only the most perfect of all geometrical forms. This kind of theoretical explanation was very common throughout the medieval period. The concept of a regularity and reliability in lawful events is also the product of philosophical rationalism, supplemented as well by mathematical rationalism (see below). It would not do to have the laws of nature be erratic and unpredictable, because this would suggest that the rational design of nature was flawed.

Sometimes the remarkable order of nature was used in a reverse sense, as proof that a designer *must* have existed prior to and hence been the creator of the rational order we now see in the universe. Theologians were in the business of proving God's existence through arguments of this sort, and the prime example here is St. Anselm's use of the efficient cause in what is known as the First Cause argument. It goes as follows: If we accept the fact that every "effect" has a "cause" then it follows that by tracing the cause-effect sequences back across time we would either have an eternal regress *or* come to the conclusion that there was at some point a First Cause—i. e., God or Prime Mover—who got events flowing along in cause-effect fashion to begin with. This argument relies solely on the meaning of efficient causation, and is an *argument from definition*. This is the classic method of proof in early philosophy, whereby the reasoner first puts down a plausible definition of a concept and then extracts the necessary implications or conclusions which flow from such precedent meanings without contradicting himself. In the realm of theological study it was called Scholasticism, and prominent church philosophers like St. Thomas Aquinas made effective use of this style of proving things.

As an example, let us take the issue still debated by modern theologians having to do with birth control. Though they do not presume to speak for God, many theologians do assume that by analyzing sexual intercourse it is possible to delineate the intent of this act as created by the deity. If the modern theologian defines this act solely in terms of procreation, it follows that the use of a contraceptive device subverts God's Will. If, however, the theologian can see in the sexual union an additional Divine Intention—possibly, to create the highest expression of physical and spiritual communion between the sexes—then it follows that copulation without intending to procreate meets with the deity's plan. The acceptance in the Catholic faith of the menstruation cycle as a "natural" rhythm within which pregnancies might be avoided is an example of the argument from design. In this case the man and woman continue to behave within the cyclical order created rather than redirecting or stopping it.

Theologians were not the only thinkers of history to press arguments based on the perfection of a deity. The philosopher-mathematician, Leibniz (c. 1700) reasoned this way when he suggested that the world we live in is the "best of all possible worlds," because it followed that a divine designer would not settle for second best. Voltaire (c. 1750) subsequently made this view a point of satirical ridicule in *Candide*, where he had the "metaphysico-theologo-cosmolo-nigologist" Pangloss express it. The old court philosopher was a teleologist who taught his young charge Candide that "everything is made for an end . . . noses were made to wear spectacles; and so we have spectacles."[3] In a perfect world everything fits into the over-all perfection.

Something was happening at this point in history to discredit telic description. Actually, the change had begun centuries earlier, and it involved a shift from philosophical to mathematical rationalism combined with an emphasis on empirical proof rather than arguing from plausible definitions to necessary conclusions. This empirical "show me" attitude actually began in religious debates, where a renegade theologian named William of Ockham (*c.* 1350) denied that proof of God's existence could be reasoned out as the Scholastics claimed. Only through miraculous *empirical demonstrations* like walking on water, healing the sick, or rising from the dead could a supernaturalism be proven. All else was just speculative, empty talk!

This empirical attitude was brought into scientific description by the philosophers of Great Britain, beginning with Sir Francis Bacon (*c.* 1600) and it has been known since as British Empiricism. Bacon directed his criticism at Aristotle in terms of the range of causes used. As we have already suggested, a plan or purpose in nature is itself a formal-cause organization, and if put into effect by a deity this would involve a final cause as well (resulting in a deity teleology rather than merely a natural teleology). In fact, to speak of final causation in events always presumes that there is a formal-cause pattern called a *reason* (premise, plan, intended outcome or aim, etc.) "for the sake of which" whatever is under description actually exists or is happening. We always find a formal-cause notion within a final-cause notion, but the reverse is not necessarily true. This is why it is so difficult to think of nature *per se* as having "purposes." Aristotle anthropomorphizes in his natural teleology because it takes an intelligence—a human-like intender—to see things as moving along purposively.

Bacon suggested that when we describe things scientifically we should confine our use of causes to just two—the material and the efficient. In putting down guidelines for empirical science, Bacon said that there is no reason why leaves exist on trees, or why bones hold up the muscles of our bodies.[4] Although it was proper for ethico-religious thinkers and artistic accounts to deal in formal- and final-cause descriptions, because morality and beauty are by their nature *judgmental* endeavors, the rigorous empirical scientist must not let such telic considerations color his observations of nature. Bacon feared that if scientists accepted formal and final causes as explanatory they would not go forth and actively seek empirical knowledge through experimentation. To experiment is to ask a question different from "What is the form or the purpose of this object?" To experiment is to ask "What brings this state of affairs about?" Scientists do not seek the presumed but unobserved reasons for things. They let the facts speak for themselves, framing them in terms of what something is made of (material cause) or how it is lawfully shaped (efficient cause) into what we then recognize as a pattern (formal cause) or an intention (final cause).

Thanks to Bacon's influence, natural scientists have since argued that not until we have reduced things as seen by the unsophisticated eye (i. e., pictorially) to the underlying substances and forces that "make them up" have we succeeded in giving a proper account of them. This is why scientific description is always reductive in nature. The atomic model is a perfect example because it combines the notion of an "uncuttable" substance (material cause) with the notion of force (efficient cause). We have now split the atom and released the force, but even within this structure of the atom it is assumed that either substance is itself force (turning material causes into efficient causes altogether) or that smaller units of substance within the atoms (electrons, etc.) go to "make up" hence cause things to be as they are. Furthermore, since it is possible in observing things to measure them and predict the course they will take over time, the rise of empiricism in modern science was paralleled by a rise in reliance on mathematical rationalism to make one's case.

The tie of mathematics to empirical demonstration was already fixed before Bacon made his attack on the Aristotelian formal and final causes in scientific description. When the astronomer Ptolemy (c. 200 A. D.) put forward his geocentric theory of the universe, he justified it based upon an empirical demonstration of his mathematical calculations. The stars fell into place according to mathematical precision (with minor adjustments). However, these empirical proofs were not what impressed the philosophical rationalists of the medieval period. They believed that something more than just mathematical calculation and observation was called for. A *philosophical* proof was required, based on the self-evident grounds of plausibility as had been used in the first-cause arguments or the identification of God's perfection in the picturable circularity of planetary motions. The Jewish medieval philosopher Moses Maimonides, the Arabian philosopher Averroës, and the Catholic theologian Thomas Aquinas all (writing *c.* 1200) drew such a distinction between mathematical and philosophical proof, and they placed their confidence firmly on the side of the latter.[5]

There was also a mixture of both types of proof by a single thinker, as in the case of Copernicus (*c.* 1500). Though his heliocentric theory of the universe was supported by the proof of observation and mathematical calculation, he based his theory of gravity on the "fact" that matter naturally compresses into spheres when left to its own spontaneous efforts to delimit its boundaries.[6] This readily pictured argument of raindrops forming into "natural" spheres as they fell to earth, matching thereby the shape of the world, was more acceptable *because plausible* than the highly implausible (at the time!) empirical arguments and mathematical proofs put forward to support the heliocentric theory. Even Bacon criticized Copernicus on the grounds that he was too willing to introduce fictions into his heliocentric theory in order to make the mathematical calculations come out right.[7]

This teaches us that the basic issue giving rise to empirical science is the *source* of one's theoretical statements. When it came to how we can know anything scientifically, Bacon reasoned like a philosophical rationalist who had a bone to pick with the ground rules for how much "reading into" the facts of observation was permitted. He was not challenging the necessity of having to pictorialize or otherwise understand the theory under test in a plausible manner. He just wanted to cut down the plausibilities and weed out those that relied on telic formulations. If nature was found to have order, Bacon held that this order could not be explained through some precedent, intentional design. It was simply the product of *aimless* material-efficient causes. By introducing his fictions, Copernicus was in violation of this rigorous rule, to account for reality *only* as seen, felt, or known plausibly in everyday experience.

This question of where knowledge ultimately comes from has usually been discussed philosophically in terms of realism versus idealism. The realist believes that knowledge is always traceable to a fixed patterning in the palpable reality of existence. There may be various ways of expressing the relationships within such patternings, but *in principle* there is a truly existing organization which can be tracked one-to-one if the measurement procedures used are precise enough. The idealist contends that either reality does not exist (e. g., we may all be looking at a chimerical scene ordered by the Mind of God) or the ordering that does take place in knowledge must be aided by a human intelligence. Hence, it is not possible *in principle* to speak of reality as existing independently of the mind which orders it into understanding, with measured precision or otherwise! Empiricists are likely to be realists, but there are those empiricists (e. g., the logical positivists) who find this distinction meaningless and who would therefore contest the assignment of the realist label to their position.[8]

Similarly, although not all mathematicians would admit to being idealists (probably most would not), the general flavor of providing proofs through a mathematical line of reasoning smacks of idealism. It does not require a material- or an efficient-cause meaning for a mathematician to make his case. There is a great sense of conviction to be gained from the internal consistency achieved by a purely mental, mathematical proof. In fact, the mathematician-astronomer Galileo did not think it was necessary to provide empirical (research) demonstrations in every instance. Only when two lines of mathematical reasoning came into conflict did Galileo think it necessary to design an empirical test (experiment) to resolve the issue.[9]

The confrontation of philosophical with mathematical rationalism was also apparent in Galileo's trial (*c.* 1615), which was to embitter natural scientists and even further turn them away from the telic style of description. Though often presented as if Galileo was asked to reject his total view, actually the churchmen of the Inquisition asked him to admit that the heliocentric theory of the universe was a mathematical fiction whereas the geocentric view was a philosophical truth.[10] By this time in history the Ptolemaic geocentric view had been wedded to Scriptural accounts of the origin of the universe, in that "argument from definition" sense discussed above (p. 16). The resultant plausibility of the earth as the center of things was then presented as theologically true. It therefore necessarily followed that a theoretical description negating this view also negated the Divine Plan—a telic formulation of the first magnitude. Since Galileo had empirical evidence on his side, the only solution for the churchmen was to consider the heliocentric theory a kind of mathematical trick of calculation, but to insist on the Divinely Inspired, common-sense geocentric account of the Holy Scriptures. As history records, the outcome was disastrous both for religion and all other varieties of teleological theory.

It was easy to see in the 17th century that philosophical proofs were losing ground to the upstart method of evidence called *scientific.* Kepler's mathematical-empirical demonstration in 1609 that the planets moved in an elliptical and not a circular path was just another example of how what appears plausible to common sense does not necessarily bear up in the world of observation. It is a willingness to live with this break between common-sense plausibilities and empirical observations which most clearly distinguishes the modern scientist from the medieval philosopher.[11] And the nice thing about mathematics is that it can readily clock or track what is observed in reality without having to explain pictorially why what is happening actually takes place. Mathematics is so abstract that it permits a mathematician to be theoretically uncommitted and at times in the dark about what it is that he is clocking or tracking.

A perfect example of this is Sir Isaac Newton's frank admission that he could not picture his mathematical concept of gravity as actually existing in reality. In a letter to a colleague (c. 1725) Newton admonished: "You sometimes speak of gravity as essential and inherent to matter. Pray do not ascribe that notion to me; for the cause of gravity is what I do not pretend to know. . . . It is inconceivable that inanimate brute matter, should without the mediation of something else, which is not material, operate upon, and effect the other matter without mutual contact."[12] If we frame this in terms of the causes, Newton is essentially admitting that though he could reason through formal- and final-cause manipulations of mathematics and come thereby to a theory of how the universe is organized (mathematical rationalism), he could *not* fill in the picture with material- and efficient-cause descriptions (philosophical rationalism). Though he disdained making hypotheses outside of the mathematical sphere, his successors—collectively known as the Newtonians—were only too willing to fill in the abstraction by introducing concepts like the ether which enabled them to pictorialize gravity in what was now a machine-like image of the universe.

They achieved this by trading on a dual meaning of the word "law." Newton's Law of Gravity was a mathematical fiction, first proven to hold in mathematical space (i. e., without extension), and then applied to reality. But "law" can also mean the repeatedly observed findings of an experiment or an astronomical regularity of some type—in which mathematical measurement and calculation are used as an aid in clocking or tracking such findings. The first use of "law" relies entirely on the meaning of formal causation, but in the latter usage, since we are observing palpable events—including the impact of earlier on later events—it is easy to suggest that mathematical lawfulness reveals only those patterns which have been produced by the underlying material and efficient causes actually observed taking place "in nature."

Even the kind of mathematics which Newton employed assured that he would take the tracking approach which we witness him following, above. That is, he adopted Cartesian rather than Euclidean geometric assumptions.[13] Whereas Euclid had defined a straight line as the shortest distance between two points, Descartes defined it as a *single moving point* tracing a straight-line function. All other geometric patterns such as the ellipse or circle were similarly described in a moving-line fashion. For a Euclidean scientist, the object at rest is in its natural state. Motion is what needs to be explained. But for the Newtonian, observed reality is *already* moving hence what needs to be explained is the relative displacement occurring between items in that reality. And, as we noted above, it was also easy for the Newtonians to view the fluid state of change in nature as a stream of efficient-causality.

The wedding of Baconian scientific description to Cartesian mathematics led in time to the optimistic mechanistic view of Laplace (*c.* 1800), "that a superhuman intelligence acquainted with the position and motion of the atoms at any moment could predict the whole course of future events."[14] God was still in the picture, relied on as the ultimate source of precision in mathematical computation just as He had always been seen as the source of the world's perfections. The universe was like a big clock, with eternally wound springs, pulleys and gears, and pieces of matter impelling other pieces of matter, or not, depending upon the contiguity existing between such palpable items and the frequency of such contact across time. Philosophical rationalism had moved over from theological argument to scientific argument, but the pictorialization and common-sense understanding of philosophical proofs had been salvaged in the Newtonian machine metaphor (i. e., material and efficient causation reigned supreme). But not for long.

Maxwell's theory (c. 1870), in which electromagnetic phenomena were accounted for exclusively by mathematical equation, established for all time that the modern physicist dealt primarily in the relationships belonging to his mathematical symbol system. Although Maxwell did attempt to frame his views mechanistically through the use of an ether concept, Hertz subsequently summed things up for all modern physicists when he observed: "Maxwell's theory is nothing else than Maxwell's equations. That is, the question is not whether these equations are pictorial, that is, can be interpreted mechanistically, but only whether pictorial conclusions can be derived from them which can be tested by means of gross mechanical experiments."[15] Led by Hertz, Mach, Poincaré, and Duhem, the physics of the 19th and 20th centuries once again placed mathematico-theoretical considerations above those of simple observation and measurement. Indeed, as Mach and Duhem made clear, there is no such thing as a "simple" observation or measurement coming in before a theory is built. All observations, all facts are themselves theoretical constructions before they are nailed down empirically.

The final victory of mathematical over philosophical rationalism occurred in the 20th century, when Einstein in his general theory of relativity showed that the hypotheses upon which geometry is founded are *not* fixed into that lock step efficient causality on which Laplace had based his view of perfect lawfulness. This is so because the rigidly mechanistic features of measuring rods, watches, and light rays are themselves subject to varying "observed values" of measurement in the space-time continuum. The human being as observer also becomes a factor in the relativity of all factual information. Nowhere is this more evident than in subatomic physics, where, rather than finding that reliable material- and efficient-cause substrate which Bacon had pointed to, we find reality slipping away from our conceptual grasp. As Bohr expressed things in 1927: ". . . the quantum postulate implies that any observation of atomic phenomena will involve an interaction with the agency of observation [i. e., the person] not to be neglected. Accordingly, an independent reality in the ordinary physical sense can neither be ascribed to the phenomena nor to the agencies of observation. After all, the concept of observation is in so far arbitrary as it depends upon which objects are included in the system to be observed."[16]

Although in one sense a concession to idealism, this is also an admonition to both sides—those who think that all knowledge is "in" a mechanical reality waiting for pictorialization, and those who think that all knowledge is "in" the head of a reasoner and then projected outwardly. Science is actually a trade-off between assumptions made by the observer and the facts that emerge as a result of these predicating frames of reference.

Bohr's principle of complementarity, in which he held that light can be viewed as either a series of particles *or* waves without somehow contradicting logic is another example of the modern scientist unruffled by the seeming collapse of philosophical rationalism. Since data can be brought in to support either theory, there is no worry over resolving the issue as to light's "true" nature. The same goes for Heisenberg's principle of indeterminacy. It is impossible *in principle* to speak of the position of an electron without first presuming its velocity, and vice versa. One measurement, one observation, has to be known before the other can be obtained. As a result, to speak of discovering or predicting the course of subatomic particles in the same fashion that we speak of the discovery or prediction of events in our customary experience is to draw a false analogy. This is what prompted Bohr to say that atomic physics will never be constructed "without resignation of the wish for sensuous presentation."[17]

We should not conclude that this modern victory of mathematical rationalism is without limitation. In 1931 Gödel proved mathematically that it is impossible to establish the logical consistency of a very large class of deductive systems. We are not now referring to the elasticity of measurement devices but to the fact that not only geometry, but even something so basic as elementary arithmetic, can be expected to have inconsistency and unpredictability arising in its calculated proofs.[18] In un-Laplacian fashion, modern physics now has our world described without complete mechanism, and under empirical prediction by a system of mathematical symbolical relationships which are not completely closed. We might see in such openness and arbitrariness a possible role for telic description in physical science—especially of the physicist *qua* person—but the Baconian practice of refraining from intentionality in the description of the inanimate universe has been retained (except for occasional metaphorical allusions).[19] In short, the real loser in all of this has not been philosophical rationalism but teleology! And this is especially galling to the teleologist because it is so easy to see that a formal-final cause description of what has taken place in modern physical science fits the historical facts exactly. The modern physicist is clearly saying that the "that, for the sake of which" we come to know reality is as important as whatever reality "is" in a material-efficient cause sense. Bohr teaches us that we can never separate the "that, for the sake of which" from the "is" in scientific observation.

To this point we have not dealt with the biological sciences, but a brief survey will establish that teleology fared no better in this historical descent. The philosophy of science which has emerged in the 20th century takes its roots primarily from physics and astronomy. Some of the most interesting conceptual problems arose in these areas, so that leading scientists in these fields were drawn to and wrote books on the questions of experimental procedures, proper descriptions of such observations, and so on. The issue of whether or not scientific knowledge can be pictorialized (mechanistically or otherwise) does not become a serious problem in the evolution of the biological sciences.

It is generally acknowledged by historians that early medical practices in ancient Babylonia and Egypt (*c.* 3000 B. C.) were initially related to and then gradually separated from religious rites such as exorcism. A deity or evil spirit was presumed to have intentionally inflicted illness on the person, often in retribution for some sin. The ancient Persians, Indians, and Hebrews all had this view, and it is interesting that Jesus healed the sick as a sign of his divinity. Religious healing as a sign of faith remains with us, of course, but much diminished in esteem by the scientific thinker.

The oft-cited father of medicine was the Greek physician Hippocrates (*c.* 400 B. C.), who departed from exorcistic remedies on the theory that illness was due to an imbalance of certain bodily fluids or *humors*. The ancients were well aware of the importance of body liquids to life, and the notion arose that blood (one of the humors) rose and fell in the body by coursing out from the heart all at once, only to return to the heart after providing its beneficial effects to the body's extremities. This ebb and flow conception was introduced in Egypt, where it was based on an analogy to the seasonal actions of the Nile. Hippocrates begins the view that physical and mental health can be found in homeostasis or harmony among the body's purely mechanical processes.

Medieval medicine was to be dominated by the writings of Galen (*c.* 175 A. D.), who not only drew the erroneous conclusion that animal anatomy was identical to human anatomy, but filled his medical writings with religious ascriptions.

The bodies of living organisms were energized by animal and vital spirits, which were God-created forces that interacted with the ebb and flow of blood to stimulate life and nourish the body. This spiritualized aspect of anatomy combines both the final- and the efficient-cause meaning. A God's Intention creates a substanceless, formless hence undiscoverable "force" which enters into the production of behavior in addition to the purely mechanical structures and forces of physical reality. The vital spirits give human behavior its self-directing, morally responsible, free-will characteristics. To this day, *vitalism* (vital spirits) and *animism* (animal spirits) are terms used by scientists to derogate all telic commentary as efforts to retrieve Galenic spiritualism from the Dark Ages.

Medicine during the medieval period was probably most advanced in the Arab nations, where Rhazes and Avicenna (*c.* 900 A. D.) carried on the traditions of Hippocrates. With the advent of the Renaissance (*c.* 1500) in the West there was a rapid rise in the knowledge of organic processes. Vesalius dissected humans as well as animals to disprove Galen's contention that their anatomical structures were identical. In the 17th century, Harvey discovered the circular flow of blood through the body, with the heart acting as a pump. There were, of course, continuing ascriptions made by various thinkers of these times to the presumed operation of a divine design in the marvelous patterning of anatomical structures and the workings of bodily processes. But a growing empiricism was in the air led by the British physicians like Sydenham (*c.* 1675) who openly expressed a distrust of the long-standing medical texts. It was a time for turning to nature without preconceptions about vitalistic principles. By this time, the Baconian restrictions on causal descriptions had permeated the whole of science, and there was general agreement that telic formulations had done nothing to advance science and, considering the Inquisition, they had actually retarded its development.

The last important event in biology we should take note of is Darwin's monumental theory of organic evolution. Evolutionary theories had been suggested earlier by theorists, often with the idea that there was a divinely intended (inspired) direction involved. Having once considered entering the ministry, Darwin was well aware of the concepts of causation most generally employed by the theologians. But in order to capture a properly scientific (i. e., non-telic) account he had to devise some other way of describing how it was that nature seemed to be improving in its evolutionary advance. This he did by suggesting that a *natural selection* occurred, whereby that species of animal or social organization of animals (e. g., human society) which varied in the direction of survival, given some unforeseen catastrophe or adaptive necessity in the continuing struggle for existence, survived, whereas that animal or organization which did not vary in this direction succumbed to extinction (i. e., the species was made extinct). An animal which has fortuitously developed a heavy coat of fur survives when the climate changes to frigid levels and migration is impossible. A society which has by chance produced many citizens of intelligence, bravery, and patriotism survives when put to the test of an attack by hostile invaders. Darwin did not have the benefit of knowledge concerning genetics in hereditary transmission, but his views eventually fell into place with such Mendelian principles.

Note that Darwinian thought is just as removed from the inner understanding of events as is modern physics. If light can be tracked empirically as either a series of particles *or* waves, then to speak of some internally unfolding pattern which is *singular* in design must be erroneous. Aristotle's purposive concept of nature required some such fixed design which in turn invited the theorist to try and grasp what was being intended by "nature." We try to look through nature's eyes, so to speak, and appreciate thereby where the design being intended is being furthered, and, possibly also where it is not. This is what theologians do except they place God in the role of nature (which the Greeks also did, for that matter). Darwin's concept of nature is totally without such identity of form over time. Darwinian nature is an unfolding of happenstance and serendipity which may be tracked by the empirical observer who organizes events from his convenience, as an outsider looking "at" changing patterns. But he has no more hope of understanding some unfolding, intentional design than Newton had of understanding what gravity "is."

The Aristotelian, looking-through form of analysis results in what is called *introspective* theoretical descriptions, which is written in first-person terms from the perspective of identities under observation. Introspective theory is therefore always concerned with I, me, my, and related phrasings which capture the thinking of an identity (including a deity), bringing premised meanings forward into experience. The Darwinian, looking-at form of analysis results in what is called *extraspective* theoretical description, which always takes the third person in language expression.[20] Extraspective theory is concerned with that, it, he, she, they, and related phrasings which are framed exclusively from the convenience of an observer, and therefore do not necessarily take the position that the identities under description actually have premised meanings which they bring forward into experience. Telic (final-cause) theoretical accounts always generate introspective descriptions and non-telic (material- and efficient-cause) accounts generate extraspective description (all theories necessarily make use of the formal-cause meanings).

In concert with the emerging physical sciences, Darwinian theory fell back on extraspective formulations. When the physicists discovered themselves as active agents in the observation and measurement of reality they essentially returned to a kind of introspective formulation, an admission that they could not talk *only* extraspectively about even inanimate empirical facts. Though Darwin did not find it necessary to contemplate his theoretical presumptions in arriving at the theory of organic evolution, he did reveal a twinge of introspective rumination in the following excerpt from *The Descent of Man*, having to do with the ethico-moral aspects of human behavior:

> We civilised men . . . do our utmost to check the process of elimination [i. e., natural selection]; we build asylums for the imbecile, the maimed, and the sick; we institute poor-laws; and our medical men exert their utmost skill to save the life of every one to the last moment. There is reason to believe that vaccination has preserved thousands, who from a weak constitution would formerly have succumbed to small-pox. Thus the weak members of civilised societies propagate their kind. No one who has attended to the breeding of domestic animals will doubt that this must be highly injurious to the race of man.[21]

Considered solely in mechanistic terms, these humanitarian efforts seem more an involution than an evolution. How do they arise, and what is it in Darwin's personal nature that prompts him to see the anomaly? We shall be raising and, it is to be hoped, answering such questions in succeeding chapters, for they relate to our quest for personal freedom. We begin to suspect that our humanity is not to be completely circumscribed by extraspective theoretical formulations. For the present, we simply reaffirm the central theme of Chapter 2; that is, by the beginning of the 20th century telic description had been thoroughly discredited in scientific circles as vitalism, animism, or anthropomorphism. All such terms refer to the unacceptable practice of bringing final causation into the description of nature.

# THREE

# Determinism and Psychological Description

## The Four Meanings of Determinism

Now that we have an idea of what causation has meant historically, we can use this scheme to analyze the nature of determinism in events. The word "determine" has Latin roots meaning to set limits on events. We speak of a determinism as taking place when there are factors in a circumstance which constrain it, make certain alternatives impossible, or, necessarily bring about some outcome. Freedom is the opposite side of the coin, for it exists when the course of events can be altered in some pre-selected (desired, chosen, etc.) direction. Whenever we describe an event occurring in our lives we necessarily—yes, determinately!—employ a particular type of determinism based on which of the four causal meanings we emphasize. To demonstrate this let us begin with a simple example.

Suppose that we were to observe a mother having difficulty with her child, a five-year-old boy who is in the midst of a temper tantrum at our local supermarket. The mother stands there, frustrated by the child who lies on the floor kicking and thrashing about as he screams for some prized goodie which has been denied him. Whether she will give in to his overly dramatized appeal or not, or just what she does

33

about his poor manners in a public place, is not what concerns us as we move down a grocery aisle pondering "What makes a child act that way?" Though we are unable to answer such a question with authority, particularly since we do not know the mother and child personally, we cannot deny that such questions press on us and in most cases we frame a fleeting explanation and let it go at that.

Some of us would conclude: "Huh, a spoiled brat like that needs a good paddling and that'll be the end of such nonsense." The implication here is that the child has intended to manipulate his mother's behavior by putting her at a disadvantage in embarrassing circumstances. Others might think "I wonder if the child is mentally retarded? The mother seems unable to reason with him." Although put in question form, this is still a characterization of the circumstances being observed and to that extent a beginning explanation. Had the boy's nursery school teacher walked by she might have thought: "Well, I could have predicted that. He's the same in my class when he doesn't get his way." Though more a commentary on the consistency of general behavior than anything else, this does amount to a determinate statement of how this child is likely to behave. Finally, an observer might simply toss off the incident with "What a tough break for both of them. The child has probably just had his fill of frustrating circumstances today and as luck would have it, threw his tiff in the worst of all locations."

Each of these impressions (attitudes, biases, etc.) embodies one of the causal meanings as a *predominant* explanation, with one or more other causal meanings implied as secondary features. The person who views this child as a spoiled brat, strategizing in order to get his way when he knows he has the advantage over his mother, is implying in this a "that" (strategy) for the sake of which the incident arises. Many of our folk wisdoms embody such egocentric final-cause efforts to improve our circumstances whenever possible; for example, "Always look out for Number One in life"; or, in a more positive frame, "Always give your best to whatever you do." The question about mental retardation suggests that a material-cause deficiency in the child's physical make-up may be contributing to (determining) the child's rude behavior.  We are all necessarily constrained by our physical limits, as reflected in such folk wisdoms as "You can't make a silk purse out of a sow's ear" or "When you've 'got it' you've 'got it' and when you 'ain't' you 'ain't'."

The nursery school teacher is relying upon her past samplings of the child's behavior to make an actuarial judgment about its expected generalization across situations. As a pattern of regularity this amounts to a formal-cause determination,  and it provides the rationale for everything from actuarial to stereotypical generalizations of behavior. Folk wisdoms also capture this feature of determinate behavior in statements like "If it walks like a duck and quacks like a duck, it's a duck" and "People don't change, only circumstances do." And lastly, the observer who tossed the situation off to luck would be looking more to accidental efficient causes beyond anyone's  control—heredity, intentionality, or reputation—to account for what took place. Folk wisdoms are also of this variety, as "Into each life some rain must fall" or "Genius is just luck, polished up with a lot of elbow grease."

All four of these explanations could be more or less correct. We need not limit our causal descriptions of any event. Aristotle believed that the more causes we could bring to bear the richer was our account of anything. As we learned in Chapter 2, though Bacon's restriction worked fairly well in the descriptions of inanimate nature, in order to account for the scientist as a reasoning person it is necessary to begin thinking in formal- and final-cause terms as well. Assumptions made by the scientist such as the rational order and lawful predictability of nature were clearly the intellectual descendants of earlier telic accounts, of a Perfect God making a perfectly running hence predictable universe. Newton privately believed in many of the Scholastic arguments and essentially thought of natural laws as existing within God.[1] It is still common for natural scientists to hold views of this sort informally which they would not dare to express in their formal theories (and, properly so!). Yet, in psychology we are called on to account for the scientist *as human being*, no matter what he may wish to state professionally. If we therefore find the human being, Newton, to be telic in one sphere and non-telic in another, can we as proper psychological scientists deny that side of him which necessarily contradicts his professional image? This hardly seems a professional move on *our* part, to distort our object of study in the name of a dated scientific purity.

When Bacon parcelled out the causes he was never contending that the only valid approach to the study of man was physical science. As Baconians, we limit physical descriptions to material and efficient causes, but we *also* bring to bear formal and final causes in the theoretical descriptions of metaphysics, ethics, and aesthetics—human activities which are clearly psychological in nature! Even so, thanks to the hallowed stature of natural science among the academicians of the late 19th and early 20th centuries, the exclusive model for behavioral description in psychology became that of *physical* determinism. Certain medical practitioners working during this period with the emotionally disturbed in non-academic settings found it more plausible to employ a *psychic* determinism in the analyses of their clients' erratic behavior. There are clear telic intonations in these latter accounts. In Chapter 3 we survey some of the major historical figures who propounded these two contrasting forms of behavioral determination.

## Physical Determinism and the Rise of Behaviorism

Every psychologist has been taught that Hermann von Helmholtz and Wilhelm Wundt were major founding fathers of experimental psychology, an academic discipline which has had immense influence on the currently accepted descriptions of behavior. As a young man, Helmholtz joined forces with some of his student peers and swore an oath to "fight vitalism"[2] in scientific descriptive accounts. Consistent with the Baconian prescription, Helmholtz believed that a physical description was not complete until it had been reduced to the underlying *simple forces* which moved events along (see our comments on the constancy principle below, p. 43). Wundt, who was to establish in 1879 the first recognized experimental psychological laboratory in Germany,[3] was greatly influenced by Helmholtz—whom he once worked with as a teaching assistant and colleague. Wundt helped clarify just where behavior was said to originate when he said that as natural scientists: "We must trace every change [in behavior] back to the only conceivable one in which an object remains identical: motion."[4] As we noted in Chapter 2 (p. 24), this Cartesian assumption led to the view that we must reduce explanations to the presumed underlying determination of efficient causation.

Let us return to our child having the temper tantrum. The properly scientific account according to Helmholtz-Wundt would involve finding the conditions under which these motions—the kicking, screaming, and thrashing about—were moulded into a pattern which we now witness taking place. To say that the child planned to have his way or to throw the tantrum in order to force his mother to acquiesce is just not an acceptable explanation. It falls short of thorough scientific analysis. Even if the child had an awareness of some plan like this, it would not itself constitute a cause of his behavior. The plan, as the tantrum itself, is on the effect side of earlier (efficient) causes which moulded things into the course of action we are now witnessing *without aim!*

When this Newtonian psychological science was brought to America, which quickly took the lead in its development away from Germany, it was embraced by a school of thought known as *behaviorism.* John Watson, who founded this school, let it be known that: "Behaviorism . . . is . . . a natural science. . . . Its closest scientific companion is physiology."[5] Watson's behavioral measuring rod, as he called it,[6] was the *stimulus-and-response* succession of events over the passage of time. He asked that we think of the human being as *"an assembled organic machine ready to run."*[7] We can see in these references to the physiological and organic a material-cause determination. But what is of far more importance is the fact that Watson raised the stature of the efficient cause (and, its attendant determinations) in claiming that *every* line of behavior is necessarily constituted of stimuli and responses. To be more exact, behavior *is* responsivity which is itself the "effect" of an antecedent "cause" in the efficient-cause sense. Material-cause factors also play a role, as when the person is moved by hunger to poke about for food, but in no instance is there a "that, for the sake of which" predication directing behavior in an intentional or purposive fashion.

Watson relied on the notion of behavioral *conditioning* which had been studied by the Russian physiologist, Ivan Pavlov, using dogs who were strapped into an apparatus permitting observation of salivation (through surgical fistulas cut into the dog's cheek area) in relation to so-called stimulating circumstances in the environment. Thus, when a light or bell is presented with or slightly before food powder is blown into a dog's mouth, the animal's natural salivating tendency becomes attached to the light or bell after several pairings of the unrelated stimulus with the food stimulus. The convention is to call the food powder an *unconditioned stimulus* and the natural tendency to salivate when food is presented an *unconditioned response*. The alternative stimulus of a light or bell is considered the *conditioned stimulus* (CS) and when it reliably elicits salivation we speak of that behavior as a *conditioned response* (CR). This Pavlovian approach to conditioning has since been called *classical conditioning*. Pavlov accepted Newtonian precepts and believed that conditioning occurred purely automatically, through physiological changes taking place in the brain.

The major problem for behaviorism was to explain how a response became conditioned to a stimulus, resulting in what is then called a stimulus-response (S-R) *habit*. Watson's explanations relied entirely on accidental contiguity and frequency considerations. So long as a given response occurred in temporal conjunction to a given stimulus preceding it, the bonding of this response to the stimulus increased in strength as a direct function of the frequency of such contiguous relations across time. It was all quite automatic, taking place in the ongoing motions of current reality. To demonstrate his theory Watson performed many experiments on both lower animals and humans. Probably his most famous experiment was that done on Albert, an 11-month-old child who was conditioned to fear a white rat by sounding a loud noise (unconditioned stimulus) just as the child was about to reach for the rat—which until that time had been an object of curiosity. After several pairings of this sort Albert not only withdrew in fright (conditioned response) from the rat (now a conditioned stimulus) but also "generalized" this response from the rat to other furry objects, including a white rabbit and even a Santa Claus mask with a white fuzzy beard.[8] Subsequently, Watson supervised a study in which a fear was both induced and then removed through conditioning procedures of this type.

The behavioristic psychologists who followed Watson

felt that his reflex-arc model was too simple, and that in order to capture behavior a more involved style of explanation was called for. Edward Chace Tolman made a significant addition to the behaviorist's style of explanation when he introduced what has since come to be known as *mediation* theory. Rather than viewing the behaving organism as simply an input-output machine, moved along by muscle twitches and aimless motions tied together by contiguity over time, Tolman claimed that a so-called *intervening variable* gradually came to play a role in this learning sequence.[9] Animals and human beings were said to concoct sign-gestalts or "cognitive maps" early in learning and then subsequently employed these intervening factors to influence later learning.[10] Thus, whereas Watson had behavior consisting of "S-R Habits" (input-output), Tolman insisted that this quickly generated into a more complex patterning across time of "S-Cognitive Map-R" (input-mediation-output). Cognition or mentation had therefore become a "middle term," nestled within and an elaboration of efficient causality.

Clark L. Hull was the next major behaviorist to arise.[11] He favored the classical (Pavlovian) view of conditioning, and did much to advance the concept of *reinforcement* in explaining how it might be said to work. Reinforcement refers to the strengthening of an S-R regularity based on a presumed benefit which the organism gets when this alignment occurs. The benefit was always framed as a reduction in some drive state, such as being satisfied for hunger, thirst, or sex. When the food powder is blown into the dog's mouth in classical conditioning, this acted as a reinforcement of the CS-CR connection because the dog's hunger drive was reduced to some extent (or at least, it was signaled that hunger would soon be satiated).

Using this drive-reduction concept we might explain our child's temper tantrums by suggesting that following each of these displays there is some kind of reinforcement taking place. Assume for purposes of argument that the child is under a drive to receive mother's attention or love. He might prefer more affectionate expressions from mother, but any attention is better than none, and the fact is that after each of the outbursts he is given a good deal of attention by the mother. We might therefore describe the child's conditioning according to the following sequence: CS (frustrating situation combined with high drive for mother's attention) leading via mediation of previous experience to CR (temper tantrum), reinforced by the maternal attention (drive reduction).

It is important to stress that this flow of behavior, including the mediations of previous experience, is never telic. We are always in the realm of material (drives) and efficient causality in mediation theory. Hull would say that what the teleologist calls the child's intended plan to manipulate mother's attention is nothing but a mediational cue which has itself been input earlier as an (efficiently caused) "effect" of environmental influence. Since cues are stimuli, this "stored" cue (mediator) acts as a further embellishment of the current stimuli emanating from the situation in which the organism finds itself. The child probably started his temper tantrums quite spontaneously at home, but thanks to mediational cues he gradually extended his hostile responses from cues in the actual home to home-like cues outside the literal home until now he is responding this way in public situations as well. But this does not mean that the child is intending this should come about. Human behavior is mistakenly seen as self-directed, thanks to the marvelous capacity that we have to store yesterday's input responses as mediational aids which can take on stimulus properties today and direct our behavior quite mechanically but with much variation. Even the Skinnerian behaviorists, who do not follow classical conditioning precepts and disdain biological drive-reduction theory, are willing to think of organisms as solely mediators of influences coming between the input stimulation of the environment and the output responsivity of efficiently caused behavior (see Chapter 5, p. 85).[12]

One of the more beguiling aspects of behaviorism is that its advocates frequently use the language of teleology even as they change the generally accepted meanings of the words involved. Tolman, for example, named his approach *purposive behaviorism*, but he did not mean by this what earlier teleological theories had meant. Purpose for Tolman was simply the fact that behavior is always pointed toward an environmental goal. But it is always *itself* being impelled along by antecedent "variables" of an efficiently causal nature.[13] He ridiculed William McDougall's efforts to explain behavior in the more traditional telic fashion, bringing the true meaning of final causation into the account.[14] Rather than capture the meaning of purpose in behavior, what Tolman did was to give a greater emphasis to the formal cause in his mediation theory. The cognitive map was such a patterning. We might even call it a behavioral "road map" input by the organism earlier and used in the present as a supplementary stimulus.

But just as chairs *qua* chairs do not have purposes (see Chapter 2, p. 14), road maps do not have purposes. It requires an identity, who organizes the patterning of a roadway intentionally as an aid to his travels, for us to speak of *purpose* and mean by that what teleologists had always meant by the term. Tolman's mediational conception never captured this identity factor and therefore his "purposive behaviorism" is a telic misnomer. Interestingly, at about this same time Sigmund Freud was also confounding theoretical terminology, moving in a direction opposite to that of Tolman. That is, rather than moving from mechanistic to telic "sounding" terminology, Freud went from telic to mechanistic "sounding" terminology.

## Psychic Determinism in Classical Psychoanalysis

One of the classmates with whom Helmholtz swore his anti-vitalistic oath was Ernst Brücke, a medical physiologist who later championed Robert Mayer's *principle of constancy*.[15] This principle held that all systems in nature operate on the basis of energic dispersions, which if disrupted in some way or released from one form, redistributed themselves in order to make the energy level of a total system uniformly constant once again. We see this principle at work when we squeeze a blown balloon in the middle and see it snap to its regular shape after releasing our grip, or in the masses of air which move as high and low pressure points to influence weather patterns based upon the total distribution of energy within the earth's atmosphere. Helmholtz used constancy in his *conservation of energy* principle. Thus, a tree trunk has exactly so much potential energy contained within its matter, which when burned releases precisely so much heat energy to boil water and turn it into steam energy, which in turn drives a piston "so many times" to move an engine down the track only "so far." There is a constancy across these various manifestations of energy, along with a certain loss due to the inefficiency of transmission from one state to another (as, in the loss of steam, friction in the piston connection, etc.).

This combined material and efficient cause strategy was the accepted way of explaining things scientifically in the 1880s, when Sigmund Freud was completing his medical education. And, his physiology professor at the University of Vienna was none other than Ernst Brücke, a man whom Freud held in the highest esteem. In fact, Freud delayed taking his medical degree for three years while conducting research in Brücke's laboratory—apparently hoping for an academic career as one of his beloved professor's assistants. In the crucial 1890s period, when Freud was putting down the major

ence is made meaningful (sequaciously). Note the clear teleology here.

Kant distinguished between the world that we know
conceptually—in our mind's eye—and the world as it might be
free of our sensory experience, a "thing in itself" as he called
natural products which have not been conceptualized by human reason. Sensory inputs are sheer noise until the person
organizes them on the basis of innate frames of reference and
thereby creates the relational ties known as meaning. Meaning
is put onto rather than being taken in from reality. We can
think of these a priori frames as conceptual spectacles which
we were born "mentally wearing." Kant called the side on
which we exist—"this" side of the spectacles, so to speak—the
*phenomenal* realm of experience (as a noun [plural] we refer
to this as "phenomena"). This is the only experience that we
ever know directly. We never get through our spectacles to
the "other" side, where presumably things which we have
knowledge of actually exist. Kant called this the *noumenal*
realm of experience (the noun [plural] is "noumena"), and
he accepted "on faith" that it really existed. This is all he
could do, of course, because his personal experience of the
noumena was always exclusively phenomenal! Kant considered himself a *critical realist*, believing as he did that there
really was "something there" on the other side of the mental
spectacles. To use a popular example, he believed that a tree
which fell in the middle of the forest beyond the sensory apparatus of any living thing still made a noise as it fell. Even so,
many of Kant's interpreters call him an idealist based on the
fact that the phenomenal takes precedence over the noumenal
in knowledge. Locke was a thorough realist, of course, taking
what is usually called the position of *naïve realism* in that he
believed that what we spontaneously (naïvely) see, feel, hear,
smell, etc., directly reflects what "is" (except for distortions
in the physical apparatus such as illusions, of course).

It should not be thought that because we use a visual

tenets of psychoanalysis, he was also encouraged to explain behavior entirely on the basis of physical determinism by his friends and colleagues, Josef Breuer and Wilhelm Fliess.[16] But Freud was an independent thinker and, in the privacy of his consulting room, he began to see and express alternative explanations of neurotic illness. He found that his clients were being made ill due to *wishes* and *fantasies*, centering on the sexual sphere to be sure, but not capable of being reduced to underlying forces or motions *à la* the principle of constancy.

For example, there was the woman, still a virgin, who very much wished to be sexually initiated and even forcibly raped in order to achieve this desired end. Her hysterical disorder was predicated on this wish. Through a remarkable analogy drawn between the "two ends" of her body she symbolized her pain at one end (unfulfilled lust) through a pain at the other (migraine headache). Writing to Fliess, Freud could say: "It turns out . . . that hysterical headaches are due to a fantastic parallel which equates the head with the other end of the body (hair in both places—cheeks and buttocks—lips and labiae—mouth and vagina); so that a migraine can be used to represent a forcible defloration, the illness . . . standing for a wish-fulfilment."[17] Of course, this parallel was not drawn consciously. The woman did not realize that she was symbolizing a sexual desire in her headaches because she had successfully repressed (kept out of conscious awareness) this "improper" wish. There was also the female patient who had learned of fellatio, and, in developing an unconscious fantasy to perform this on a male, developed a throat irritation which led to a persistent cough.[18]

Now, wishes, desires, and fantasies of either a conscious or unconscious nature are clearly *not* aimless motions, moved by energies trying to redistribute themselves in a closed system. Concepts like these only make sense because they indicate the direction which events are taking. Freud was being most un-Tolmanian in his description of behavior, using the meaning of purpose in its traditional sense. Humans seemed capable of directing even their physical health status to make a point, express a desire, possibly even punishing themselves in the process. The determination here was not palpable but entirely psychic. Freud therefore concluded that "In contrast to *material* reality . . . *in the world of neurosis* PSYCHICAL REALITY *is the determining factor.*"[19] It was clear to Breuer and Fliess that Freud was flirting with scientific ostracism on at least two counts: first, he had this penchant to see a sexual root in every neurotic illness; but secondly, and even more importantly, he was too willing to embrace the telic account in saying how mind can influence matter. His case histories read more like fiction than scientific descriptions. Although there were other reasons for the break-ups, it cannot be denied that Freud's partings with both Breuer and Fliess were tied to this disagreement over what constitutes a proper scientific description of behavior. It was not long before Freud was applying his style of explanation to normals as well as neurotics.

A frequent error which is made in psychology is to suggest that because Freud believed in unconscious behavioral determinants he is no different in his theorizing than the physical determinist. Both theories hold that consciousness is not "the" originating source of control, hence they are saying the same thing. This view, which confounds physical with psychic determinism, is completely false. It overlooks the fact that Freud considered the *essential nature* of mentality to be unconsciousness. Consciousness is merely the tip of the iceberg, developing out of that complete state of unconsciousness in which we are born. Ideas *begin* in unconsciousness and then are brought forward to awareness. The unconscious therefore always knows everything in mind. Repression is holding back ideas which are for some reason unacceptable to the conscious side of mind. Hence, what is out of conscious awareness is *not* out of mind, as is true in the physical determinism of behavioristic psychology.

Freud's views on psychic determinism combined formal- and final-cause meanings, and we could easily call his approach a "conceptual determination" of behavior. One of the clearest metaphors he used of a conceptual nature was the *fuero*, which is a Spanish term referring to some ancient privilege given to a province and incorporated into its ongoing legal sanctions for time immemorial.[20] A province with such a fuero had a claim on the Royal Family for special consideration, and it had to be honored when presented. Unconscious ideas are like fueros. They can bring to bear a claim on the personality in the present concerning some problem which occurred earlier as a fixation or "hang-up," and for the sake of which behavior is being enacted today (usually symbolically re-creating the meaning of this earlier hang-up in the present). Consciousness is not aware of the meaning being expressed by the fuero, anymore than Freud's clients were aware of their unconscious sexual fantasies. Such meanings are symbolized in dreams and the selection of certain symptoms (as, the woman's "cough"). But unconsciousness always knows; that is, certain identity points within the personality at the unconscious level called the *id, ego,* and *super-ego* know what is being expressed symbolically, because it is they who have worked out a compromise in fixing the symptomatic picture of the neurosis (the headache, cough, etc.). Unlike Tolman, Freud places the matter of identity first in all of his theorizing. In fact, we have several identities as well as different levels of consciousness within which these identities behave. And Freud always insisted that we humans know what we do *not* know given only that our concept of the mind (psyche) is broadened to include both the conscious and the unconscious levels.[21] Once again, out of conscious knowing is not out of mental knowing (for the unconscious knows all!).

A Freudian could readily see our child in the temper tantrum as re-enacting some Oedipal theme in his relationship with the mother, who in turn might also have unconscious ideas (e. g., of rejection) under expression in the relationship. Indeed, it is possible on Freudian principles for two individuals to be communicating and influencing each other's behavior unconsciously—which means intentionally, although not with conscious intent! This is obviously a telic description of behavior, a fact which Fliess recognized in calling Freud a "thought reader,"[22] who, rather than studying behavior extraspectively and explaining it in properly (i. e., Baconian) scientific terms, took people's introspective imaginings as satisfactory reasons for how they behaved. In other words, Freud was not delineating the underlying energic impulsion but was resting his case with (seeming) vitalistic explanations. This charge of being a thought reader haunted Freud throughout his professional career, and, thanks in large measure to this concern and his consequent desire to employ acceptable scientific terminology, he turned increasingly to a pseudo-constancy explanation in his *libido* theory.

Physicians had used the term libido for centuries, meaning by it something akin to a physical drive for lustful gratification. Hull would have used it in this sense (see above). But Freud changed the meaning, considering it a *mental* energy which was set loose by the sexual instinct, but which operated completely outside of the physical realm. Having now given his critics an energy to contemplate, Freud could begin his lifelong practice of translating purely psychological accounts (involving psychic determination) into a seemingly reductive explanation in the style of Helmholtz and Wundt. Instead of saying that the person behaved in order to attain certain wished-for ends, he could now say the person mentally *cathected* these ends (i. e., filled them with libido in the mind's eye, then presumably was impelled toward them in some inexplicable fashion). The woman with the cough unconsciously cathected the penis of various males after having learned of this style of love making. Fantasying herself in this circumstance (id wish), she also concurrently punished herself by repressing these thoughts and inflicting a symptom (cough) on that region of the body through which the pleasurable contact was being unconsciously imagined (super-ego wish as a form of punishment, with the compromise between id and super-ego worked out by the ego). Our child in the temper tantrum could have previously cathected his mother in the Oedipus complex, and, with the ongoing developments of this unconscious family dynamic, is now essentially having a "lover's quarrel" with the object of his pre-genital lust.

The switch from fuero claims to cathected libido changes nothing in the basic account of behavior. We still have a telic image of the person under espousal. But Freud's brilliant subterfuge has convinced many that he favored and really set out to present the human being in biological terminology. His famous colleague Carl Gustav Jung was not so easily fooled and at one point pressed Freud to give him a clearer definition of libido,[23] but without success. As a supposed energy in the constancy sense libido was surely most *un*physical in its essential characteristics. That is, it could not (even in principle) be measured or given a reliable value through its many manifestations. And rather than moving about the elements of personality as a closed system, libido often served as an instrumentality for the achievement of ends sought by these elements—that is, the id, ego, and super-ego "squared off" and even bartered each other in terms of the libido which they had at their disposal. Not uncommonly, a less powerful aspect of the personality could through guile and deception bring to bear an influence on the broader personality far out of line with its actual store of libidinal energy. This is anything but

an account of the dispersion of blind forces, moving throughout a closed system!

Freud candidly admitted that his libido theory rested
more on the assumptions of natural science (especially biology) than it did on the evidence accrued by psychoanalysis.[24]
Even so, having been trained by Brücke and intimidated by
Breuer and especially Fliess, Freud could just not find it
within himself to give his psychology an openly telic coloring—something which both Jung and Alfred Adler were later
to do after they had parted ways with psychoanalysis proper.
Freud once apologized for using telic description and added
that henceforth: "I will renounce my attempt at guessing the
purposes of Nature and will content myself with describing
the facts."[25] But Freud had a destiny to fulfill, and he was not
about to let his insights be strained away by physiological re-
ductions. And so we find him, rather than translating telic
terminology into non-telic theory as Tolman did, going in
the reverse direction by using non-telic terminology to frame
what is unquestionably a telic image of the person. Behavior
is always psychically determined in the Freudian account,
dependent upon symbolic meanings under expression by an
organism that is something more than a compendium of
simple-to-complex forces in physical motion.

# FOUR

# The Meaning of Meaning

A quick check with the dictionary tells us that the word "meaning" derives from the Anglo-Saxon roots of "to wish" and "to intend." This would imply that when we say that something like a word or a sensory impression of seeing or smelling "has meaning" it would only have this quality because of what it pointed to *relationally*. Meaning always refers to relatedness, to the bringing together of a word or impression and its referent. Psychologists have generally accepted this relational nature of meaning, but they differ in how to interpret the uniting of something which has meaning (word, image, sensation, etc.) and that to which it relates or points as a referent. In line with its historic meaning, some psychologists give meaning an introspective interpretation. For example, if we hear the word "fire" shouted indoors it is natural for us to understand it as a "that [meaning], for the sake of which" someone intends to warn us of impending danger. Language in this sense is fundamentally telic.

Other psychologists take an extraspective position on the meaning of meaning, seeing the relational ties which form between words or sensory experience and their referents in strictly mechanical terms, as an association of one thing to another without intention. Contiguous factors in experience are apt to be related like this because this is how our nervous systems seem to work. For example, an infant who repeatedly hears a word-sound in close proximity to a certain person's visage automatically comes to associate (connect) the two and learn *mama* (i. e., the word-sound), which in time is perfected into *mother* as physical maturation proceeds. The meaning of this face or of the word mother is never intentionally related to experience, but is simply a function of how frequently these factors are associated to the child's growing circle of personal experiences.

In the study of human learning and language, these contrasting views are termed the *symbolical* and *signalizing* interpretations of meaning.[1] If we believe as Freud did that a person first wished to think about something and then selected words and especially images to express the content of this wish—the "that, for the sake of which" he thinks—we are presuming that meaning is symbolical in nature. On the other hand, if we believe that words and images are physiologically encoded "stand ins" for reality, input automatically in the past based on the frequency of association a person has had with them, then we are presuming that meaning is a signalizing activity. By and large, British philosophy has been associationistic and prone to the sign interpretation, whereas Continental philosophy has more readily embraced a symbolical interpretation of meaning.

As a word or sensation takes on more and more meaning for the person it is essentially being related to more and more referents. We cannot discuss the extended meaning of anything without becoming enmeshed in a congeries of such reference points. Returning to our example of "mother," in time the child learns that there are all sorts of things to which this word relates beyond simply the visage of his actual mother's face. The child will someday learn the dictionary definition of this word, which stipulates the parental relationship of a female to her offspring. This is called the *denotative* (specific, explicit, "general") meaning of a word. On the other hand, each child relates uniquely personal referents to his or her mother, such as the smell of bread or the humming of a certain melody. This is called the *connotative* (suggestive, vague, "private") meaning of a word. In psychology, the term *meaningfulness* is used to describe the extent of significance or importance which a language term like mother has for the person. As meaningfulness increases so does the extent of relational ties, especially those of a connotative nature.[2]

Since meaning is a relational concept it is possible to speak of the two ends of this relationship as *poles*, much as if we were to think of the earth's north and south poles being meaningfully related by an imaginary line running directly through our planet's center. The meaning relation would be this imaginary line through the earth, and at one pole we would have a word, image, sensation, etc., and at the other pole a referent to which it points (symbolic interpretation of meaning) or is associated (sign interpretation of meaning). Meaning relations are rarely this simple, with only one word and one referent. A word or sensation having meaning at one pole is usually related to *many* referents, many poles at the other end of many relational ties. For example, if we were to define the meaning of "soup" exhaustively, we would reach out into relational ties with diverse referents such as the various forms of meat and vegetables which go into the soup, the broth and seasoning involved, the utensils to be used, the cooking procedures to be followed, and so on. Add to this our personal connotative meanings in relation to the making and eating of soup and it is clear that even the mundane aspects of existence interlace with an enormous quiltwork of meanings.

Even so, it is possible for instructive purposes to abstract a concept of meaning as just these two poles, of a word (image, sensation, etc.) signifying or symbolizing something and that to which it relates. If we keep our analogy of the north and south poles of the earth to represent this abstraction of a meaning relation it is easy to suggest that each of these ends of the relation is a unit unto itself. That is, we can think of the ends as a *primary* unipolarity brought into relationship with another *primary* unipolarity so that a bipolarity is created *secondarily* as one side connects to the other. This is how British associationism interpreted the nature of meaning. However, as we shall make clear in the present chapter, there has been an ancient tradition in the meaning of meaning which suggests that at least some of these relations are *primarily* bipolar from the outset. Rather than created by connecting unipolarities certain concepts in human reason are, so to speak, "drawn out" from a common core of bipolar oppositionality and even contradiction.

## Dialectical Versus Demonstrative Meaning Relations

Certain words, such as the noun "mother" which we have been using above, have a singularity about them in the sense that they refer to a specific person or a distinctive class of persons without implying some other meaning intrinsically opposite to this designation. If we say "mother" and point to a woman in our proximity we have joined unipolarities in our mother's visage (singular item) and this word (singular item). There is also the relational tie existing between this person (singular item) and ourselves (singular item). On hearing us express this word while pointing most of our associates would take it as given that we were indeed pointing to our mother, even though the implication is always there of non-mother or "that is not (his, her) mother." However, were such a negation suggested it would speak more to *our* relational tie to the woman pointed at than to the word mother *per se*. The word is clear, it has meaning and there is nothing directly related to it except the definition which convention has bestowed upon it.

But now, what of other nouns like "morality" or adjectives like "good"? Is it possible to use such words without necessarily borrowing from their opposites, "immorality" and "bad"? Can we ever have a word like "left" joined unipolarly to a definition which does not *also* relate meaningfully to "right"? Let us assume that a person points at a painting and says "beautiful." We can surmise that he is saying something about this painting evaluatively, and as we too look at the painting what happens? Do we not also put it to evaluation, trying to understand in this process what is being conveyed by the word beautiful? But note, in order to achieve this understanding we have to at some point in our evaluations employ the meaning of ugly, or some variation thereby. It takes the two ends of a beautiful-ugly dimension to evaluate something just as it took the two ends of a mother-non-mother dimension to raise a doubt. However, in this instance we are not questioning the fact that one person thinks a painting is beautiful. We are trying to understand why this judgment has been rendered. To do so, we have to employ *both* ends of a bipolar dimension of meaning.

We can now introduce two terms which capture the distinction just drawn. They are taken from Aristotle[3] but the ideas which they represent have a much broader referent in the history of both Eastern and Western thought.[4] *Demonstrative* meaning relations conjoin unipolar designations. The signalizing interpretation of meaning is demonstrative, because it presumes a one-to-one relationship between the word (the *sign*) and the referent for which it stands. These unipolarities can be multiplied of course, as more and more meaningful relations are brought (denotatively and connotatively) into the complex totality of meaning. If words have an oppositional relation, such as high-low, hot-cold, and so forth, this occurs through the bonding of unipolarities so often that we come to think of them as intrinsically related even though they are not.

The other view of meaning relations we must get in mind

is called *dialectical*. In this case, it is assumed that certain meanings are by their nature bipolar, so that rather than conjoined they ˙are essentially pulled apart into an oppositionality which makes two ends out of one meaning without affecting the integrity of the total. The meaning of *left* is not a unipolar designation which has through frequent repetition been joined to *right*. Left is only left due to its relation to right, so that in a true sense left must *also* participate in the meaning of right, and vice versa. There are many such word relations in our language, and, a point not to be overlooked, they generally take on meanings which might be considered evaluative, judgmental, and comparative. Put another way, dialectical relations in meaning are usually concerned with qualitative issues in contrast to the quantitative nature of demonstrative relations.

Symbolical interpretations of meaning are more likely to be based on a dialectical than a demonstrative meaning relation. This is so because it is assumed that a symbolizing intellect selects from alternatives in expressing its intended (wished for, wanted) meanings (see above). Alternatives begin in the poles of opposition, so that as we step gradually away from what "is" to what oppositionally "is not" we begin to delineate increasing degrees of difference. We might say that alternatives are variations in the bipolar direction which may or may not extend their meaning all the way to oppositionality.

When we speak of meaning relations as extending we are getting into the question of connected discourse, because in delineating alternatives words do not simply "jump together" in (either associative or intentional) bondings without forming into that peculiar relational line known as *logic*. Aristotle was one of the first philosophers to point out that humans reason according to certain assumptions which they accept without question. In working out the fundamentals of what he called syllogistic reasoning, Aristotle spoke of the most important assumption of this sort as the *major premise*. The most familiar example here is the well-known statement that "All men are mortal." This premise involves a relational tie of the so-called antecedent term (man or men) to the consequent term (mortality). Next, we have the opportunity to affirm either the antecedent or consequent term in our syllogistic course of reasoning. Assuming that we affirm the antecedent— "This is a man"—it follows necessarily that "This man is mortal." This proper logical conclusion is a reflection of telic determination (see Chapter 3). On the other hand, if we affirm the consequent of our major premise—"This is a mortal" —it does not necessarily follow that the other end of our meaningful relation will hold. Being a mortal does not necessarily mean that this is a man.

It is the patterning within patterns, the ordering within orders that accounts for the richness of understanding that we know of as intelligence and knowledge. Before Aristotle came on the historical scene, there was a theory of knowledge being employed by Greek philosophers like Plato (his teacher) and Socrates (Plato's teacher) which held that everything known was connected through dialectical meaning relations to everything else. Knowledge was "all of a piece," so that even when we did not know what was true and what was false we could begin a line of rational investigation and through the use of a certain means of inquiry (*organon*) come to know truth entirely through this exercise of intellect. This organon was a dialectical procedure, used by Socrates in the dialogues as a question-and-answer tactic.[5] If Socrates wanted to learn something he would begin by posing a question on the topic to a student, such as "What does honesty mean?" The student would try as best he could to delineate what he knew about the meaning of honesty. In practice this allowed for several alternatives, but for the sake of analysis let us just speak of positions A and not-A as alternatives open to the student in responding to Socrates' question.

If the student took position A, Socrates as a general strategy began to develop countering questions along the line of not-A. He did not do this because he believed the not-A line of argument was any truer than the A line. If the student had selected not-A he would have gone as readily to A. It was all the same to Socrates, because he did not think he had "information" in his head which the student lacked. Knowledge was a common property of all men and, besides, the truth probably came down someplace in the middle between A and not-A anyhow. The original position taken by the student was called the *thesis* of a dialectical exchange, and the opposing position was called the *antithesis*. The thesis is therefore always tied to the antithesis by a dialectical meaning relation, although in this case we are considering complex meanings and broad positions and not simply words such as high-low. There is little doubt but that we all reason dialectically in a discussion which borders on a debate. As our opponent is putting forward his views we immediately frame the opposite viewpoint as we wait expectantly to get in our "two cents worth." Often we agree on one or two of our opponent's points. We say "Sure, you are right there. We have no argument on that score. But now, you are dead wrong on the other points etc. . . ." This area of agreement, which often combines meanings from the opposing views, was called the *synopsis* by the Greeks; today we call it the *synthesis*.

Socrates essentially held that truth and error were meaningfully related opposites, so that it was possible *in principle* to begin in error and work our way over to the other side. This view of all things tying into one was very important to the early Grecian intellect, which has often been held up as an example of universality and insightfulness unparalleled in the subsequent history of the world. Unfortunately, the dialectical basis of this world view in which science, art, and religion were woven into a diverse yet single totality, is rarely made explicit. This capacity to find commonality within diversity—or, its reverse, diversity in commonality—is called the *one and many* thesis.[6]

Even though he acknowledged that human reasoning was *in part* dialectical, Aristotle challenged the validity of the dialectical method. He thought it was of extreme importance to know how a reasoner in dialectical exchanges came to his major premise. The major premise always acts as a *precedent*—i. e., a meaning occurring first in the succession of a line of meaning-extension. Meanings which follow in logical order are *sequacious*—i. e., slavishly compliant with the precedent meanings which have gone before them. Thus, if we accept the precedent major premise "All men are mortal" then by saying "This is a man" it follows necessarily (sequaciously) that "This is a mortal." However, even if we frame the major premise in the reverse sense, as "All mortals are men" we would have a necessary extension of meaning of the sort "This is a mortal" leading to "This is a man." The conclusion arrived at is erroneous because it was begun in an erroneous (major) premise to begin with.

And so it was that Aristotle said when Socrates put the first question to a student in the dialectical method he had to rely on whatever opinion on the question this student could advance. Maybe what the student offered as the original position A was correct, but maybe it was grossly incorrect. If the latter case, then any so-called truths emerging from this discourse would be tainted. Aristotle thus challenged the Socratic dialectical view that a line of study can begin in error and end in truth. If we begin in error, Aristotle said, we must necessarily end in error. This too is a precedent-sequacious fact of mental life. To end in truth our methods of inquiry (organons) had better begin in truth.

A demonstrative reasoner always makes certain that his major premise is what Aristotle called *primary and true*. This takes two forms. A premise can be true by tautological definition, as in the case of saying "All bachelors are unmarried males." Notice that the antecedent meaning (bachelor) is identical to the consequent meaning (unmarried male). We might as well have said "All bachelors are bachelors." Such tautological relations seem trite and empty in their redundancy but they are actually extremely important to all forms of thought.

A second way in which premises can be primary and true is when they are based on empirical facts. A fact is just as unipolar a designation as is the tautology. We cannot quarrel or challenge the factual without presenting empirical facts to the contrary. Note that the thrust of demonstrative reasoning is to decide one way or the other on some point. This rigorous, decisive, either-or quality of demonstrative reasoning was underwritten by a principle or *law of contradiction* (sometimes called non-contradiction) which suggested that A is not not-A.[7] Something cannot both be and not be. You cannot have your cake and eat it too. There is obviously a direct challenge here to the dialectician's one and many thesis, which we are likely to see in popular phrases of the sort "The more things change the more they remain the same." Something either changes or it remains the same, it does *not* do both—assuming that we are using language properly in making statements of this type. This is how the demonstrative reasoner views things.

## Meaning and Models in the Rise of Natural Science

We can now return to the themes of Chapter 2, where we outlined the shift from philosophical to mathematical rationalism in the rise of science. Aristotle is called the father of biological science because he was among the first persons to actually conduct empirical investigations of nature. We can now appreciate that he did so in the spirit of demonstrative reasoning. But Aristotle never lost sight of the fact that human beings *also* reason dialectically. Although he did not favor dialectic as an organon he did appreciate that there are times when the most rigorous thinker must resort to dialectical strategies.[8]

This occurs when there are no facts to go on, and, acting on our best understanding we defend a point of view from being undermined by its critics. It is important to know about the dialectic because the truth is, an opponent in debate can always trade on the implicit duality of meanings, say things which sound as if they mean one thing when they mean another, and twist our viewpoint into contending that which it does not. Questions can be posed which are spurious but which nevertheless validate an area of meaning within which consideration must be given by the person questioned. A humorous example of this is the old gag-line of "When did you stop beating your wife?" Such verbal tricks are called *sophistry*, a word devolving from the Sophists of ancient Greece who did employ the dialectic in this fashion—earning the enmity of Socrates in the process. Their guileful art has come down to us in more refined forms as rhetoric and debate.

There were other philosophers in Western thought who criticized dialectical reasoning due to its sophistical tendencies, but who still appreciated that to reason this way was an aspect of human nature. Two of the best examples here are St. Thomas Aquinas and Immanuel Kant. But these men were not as committed to mathematical rationalism as other philosophers who played a role in the fashioning of science. And we must never lose sight of the fact that mathematics is demonstrative reasoning *par excellence*, where the law of contradiction holds supreme. René Descartes is a perfect example of such a philosopher. Recall from Chapter 2 (p. 24) that his geometry, which incorporated motion as a precedent premise, allowed Newton to explain nature fluidly, and the Newtonians to frame this constant change as efficient causation.

Descartes, whose famous pronouncement *Cogito ergo sum* (I think, therefore I am) was framed after much soul searching in response to a question put to himself (How do I know that I exist?), achieved a successful conclusion to what Socrates would have considered a dialectical inquiry (organon). Yet, Descartes had no use for the dialectic, which he equated with sophistry.[9] Socrates held that dialectic used sophistically was a misuse of a legitimate method which did not therefore call for a dismissal of the procedure much less a denial of its existence. But Descartes and the equally mathematically inclined British philosophers Thomas Hobbes and John Locke did indeed succeed in dropping the dialectic from serious philosophical consideration in the human image.

This was achieved when the Britishers essentially equated thought with mathematical calculation. Hobbes put it most directly when he said that mentation was "nothing but reckoning (that is, adding and subtracting) of the consequences of general names agreed upon for the marking and signifying of our thoughts. . . ."[10] Locke spoke of *simple ideas* as analogical to the simple whole numbers which, when combined formed into more *complex ideas*. We can see the law of contradiction reflected in his assertion that "it is not in the power of the most exalted wit, or enlarged understanding, by any quickness or variety of thought, to *invent* or *frame* one new simple idea in the mind . . . nor can any force of the understanding *destroy* those that are there."[11] We cannot break up these simple ideas through oppositional analysis. They are either "one" or they are "nothing." As building blocks, they go to make up what mind consists of and they do so along quasi-mathematical lines.

Note that there is another theme in the Lockean model of mind. All mental contents as ideas have been put into mind from without. Borrowing a phrase from Aquinas, Locke suggested that human mentation begins in *tabula rasa* fashion, as a smoothed (i. e., blank) tablet on which the finger of external experience etched simple ideas which were then calculated into complex ideas and combined with even further complexities as life progressed. We have the beginnings here of our mediational model, with a sign or signalizing interpretation of meaning being employed (see Chapter 3, p. 41). Judgment resolves itself into a calculation of frequency probabilities, working automatically on the basis of intellectual habits. Such habits of thought give us a personal illusion of determining our own conceptual understanding of life, but in actuality the frequency of past inputs arraying themselves this-way-or-that in our mediated habit systems are really the determining factors. As Locke expressed it: "Probability upon such grounds carries so much evidence with it, that it naturally determines the judgment, and leaves us as little liberty to believe or disbelieve, as a demonstration does, whether we will know, or be ignorant."[12]

The mental idea in this formulation is not an active agent, bringing to bear a predicate meaning in that Aristotelian sense of a logical formulation. It is a mental "chit" to be taken as given, calculated and processed. Although at high levels of abstraction both mathematics and logic are common intellectual enterprises,[13] there can be no doubt but that the logician is more concerned with the reasons (grounds, self-evidences, "whys?" etc.) for making assumptions than is the mathematician. Locke's model is a mathematical one. The predications of ideas are all framed environmentally, shaped by circumstance and not by the ideating individual. If we think of ideas as *signs* or formal-cause patternings, another way of saying this is that, the environment through efficient-cause manipulation puts the order into these mediating signs rather than the person.

As Lockeans, we do not study the contributions which the person *qua* person makes to the thought process. We measure as best we can such input products (idea-units) and through mathematical probability estimates of the signs accumulated thereby, hope to predict the course of the fluidly moving behavior being mediated by these varying distributions of efficient-causality. The person is as one of these Cartesian geometrical figures, a process continually in motion, responding to the frequency of input signs (today we call them "stimuli") which have been poured into his or her mentality as water is poured into a glass. In his concept of *will* Locke did suggest that mentation could suspend its actions for a time (see Chapter 5, p. 82),[14] but the unidirectional source of behavioral control was always external experience functioning through efficient-cause propulsion and directed by the material-cause satisfactions of a pleasure principle. As the dialectic fell (precedently) from Locke's model so too did all of those (sequaciously) self-generated alternatives which reasoning by opposites makes conceptually possible. Yet this is the model which has been most frequently embraced by science since the 17th century, meshing as it did with mathematical rationalism, and it is still the predominant one in modern psychology.[15]

Fortunately, Immanuel Kant later crystallized a model which returned the dialectic to the human image. His philosophy is in the Continental tradition and was written in part to counter certain claims being made by British Empiricism (see Chapter 2). Kant is non-empiricistic because he believed in *cognition*, which for him was a mental process which worked on experience to order it and make sense of it.[16] We hear the phrase *cognitive psychology* today,[17] but it is not being used the way that Kant would have used it. There is no fundamental difference between modern cognitive psychology and any other mediational model of behavior.[18] The Lockean model is what underwrites all such psychology. Kant's model has predication substituting for mediation. Rather than tabula rasa, mind is conceived along *pro forma* lines—i. e., according to a priori mental patterns (formal causes) which exist at birth (precedently) and for the sake of which (final causes) experi-

analogue in the spectacles that the phenomenal realm consists only of things seen. We mean for the spectacles to represent *all* sensory modalities, as in the example of Locke just referred to. Another misunderstanding is to think of the spectacles as filters, as if they functioned to screen out certain noises and let other sensory information through. The filter analogue is Lockean. Kantian spectacles do not filter but literally construct (i. e., the act of construing) meanings. Filter analogues work only when it is assumed that sensory noises screen out or hide an order of meaningfulness which is "there" underneath or behind things. But in the Kantian model there is no assumption made that the noumenal world has some noise and also some meaningful organizations. *All* is noise—meaningless stimulus conglomeration until put to order by what Kant called the *categories* of the mind's understanding.

What are these categories? It is really not important for us to enumerate in detail the particular frames of reference which Kant employed. These have been dropped and others put in their place since he wrote. What we hope to grasp is the Kantian *style* of explanation. The same holds for the Lockean model. We do not have to believe literally in simple or complex ideas to agree with this model's style of explaining mentality in constitutive fashion. The Kantian model is conceptual rather than constitutive and this is what we want to stress above all else. Even so, we can mention that Kant believed sensations were first ordered intuitively by innate structures of space and time, and then the categories of the understanding were brought to bear framing quantity, quality, relation, and modality in experience. These four designations broke down along a one-and-many thesis into what are clearly dialectical relations. For example, quantity differentiated into unity, plurality (antithetical meanings), and totality (a synthesis of the two).

Kant was not contending that people are born with the meanings of quantity or quality pocketed into little mental receptacles at birth. We can call the categories innate ideas if we want to, but these ideas are nothing like what Locke would have meant. Indeed, an idea which was also innate was for Locke a violation of the law of contradiction, because all ideas (A) were framed experientially and hence could not be active at birth (not-A). Ideas *had* to be poured into mind after birth. The Kantian idea is a construing or constructive process, something which is *given* at birth as a human characteristic just as the memory capacity is given as an aspect of human nature. Possibly this can be clarified by analogizing to the hand. People all over the world have hands as part of their natural endowment as human beings. They are named by different words in different cultural language systems, of course, and the particular style of using hands varies across cultures— as anyone who has seen an Italian talking to a Norwegian already knows. But, the fundamental way in which hands are formed by nature and the way in which they "work" is not a product of culture and we might just as readily see culture being shaped by the hand's nature as vice versa!

That is, much of the meaning a hand has for us is due to its innate characteristics (think of the Kantian innate ideas now), how it is shaped with fingers which move in a certain way, and what it permits us to do as we behave based on these distinctive characteristics. What happens then as we begin expressing verbally our behavior in terms of cultural terminology? We find ourselves drawing analogies to hand-like behaviors. We talk of *grasping* a line of thought or seeing the *point* of an argument. We *let go* of outmoded beliefs and *hold tight* to those things which are important to us. Although a culture carries this kind of expression forward even as it provides the verbal conventions to name it in the first place, is it really accurate to say that culture provides us with the meanings of hand-likeness? In similar fashion, Kant suggests that we have an innate sense of unity and plurality. We learn words to describe "one" marshmallow as opposed to "four" marshmallows, but in learning these conventions from the outset we fall back on a sense of "knowing by looking" that a pile of four (many) marshmallows represents a plurality of the single (one) marshmallow unity.

There is an even more important role which dialectic plays in the Kantian model than the one of organizing the categories of the understanding through opposition. In the realm of free thought, where the person is not constrained by the demands of what he perceived phenomenally, a kind of speculative reasoning can be carried on which permits us to *transcend* even our categories of the understanding. We are not constrained to think rationally. We can deny our senses. We can challenge space and time as proper coordinates for the ordering of sensation. We can mentally fly above reality to concoct worlds of four dimensions. And the reason we can do all this according to Kant is because: "speculative reason is, in the sphere of transcendentalism, dialectical *in its own nature.*"[19] This is why Kant was critical of the free play of dialectic. He like Aristotle insisted upon demonstrative strategies in coming to know truth. Nevertheless, we have here a clear appreciation of the fact that mentation (thinking) is natively dialectical. Kant even said that the capacity to depart from common-sense phenomenal experience relied upon a *transcendental dialectic.* This ability for mind to rise above itself and turn back critically on what it normally does without examination or question is called *self-reflexivity.* As a self-reflexive process, mentation knows that it is constantly in the act of knowing, that it ultimately "takes a position" on experience which is *arbitrary* because it could be dialectically distorted or redirected. The only way a Lockean intellect can know these things is if experience provides the input information. A Kantian intellect knows them without such instruction as an implicit aspect of the cognitive process.[20]

# FIVE

# Free Will: A Beleaguered Concept

As human beings who have to make the "decisions, decisions" in life, we tend to accept the general notion of a free will even though we cannot say precisely how it works. We do not feel a necessity to defend this side of our natures. When someone tells us that these decisions are *really* being made by circumstances outside of our personal control it may startle us for a moment, or possibly amuse us, but we do not lose any sleep over the issue. We go on believing as before, even buttressing our conviction with the assumption that our formal religions always favor a free-will conception in their theologies. As we shall see, the truth is not this simple, for to be quite frank, there is no concept in human knowledge more beleaguered and misunderstood than that of free will. But this is all the more reason for spending time to learn about the concept. We may believe that we are free, wish it so, or accept it as so on faith, but it seems far better to have a sound argument "for the sake of which" we can justify such beliefs and wishes.

In building up to a definition of free will, given in Chapter 7 (p. 147), we begin in Chapter 5 by surveying what the theologians have had to say on the subject. We then look into the major ways in which modern psychologists have tried to explain the free-will concept away. In Chapter 6 we look at the scientific evidence in support of telic behavior currently issuing from the psychological laboratory. Chapters 5, 6, and 7 therefore represent the heart of this volume, presenting the core arguments on free will.


## Free Will as a Debatable Theological Concept

If there is a group among whom we would expect consensus on the question of free will it would surely be the theologians. Many of us believe that except possibly for Calvinism all religions as spiritual accounts of life must accept the free-will conception. Yet this is far from true. There are conflicting views on the possibility of free will even within the same religious denomination. Possibly this is why doctrinaire definitions of free will are difficult to find in religious writings. The noted Jesuit scholar Joseph Rickaby[1] once observed that his church (Roman Catholic) has given no explanation of how free will works. Of course, properly considered, this is more a psychological than a theological responsibility, which should remind us that free will and religious dogma are two different issues. Belief in a free-will capacity does not automatically commit one to a belief in the deity. Socrates was a pre-Christian who believed in God, and Nietzsche was a so-called anti-Christ who claimed that the conception of God was *dead!* Yet both these men were teleologists and accepted free will as an aspect of this finally caused behavior.

Recall from earlier chapters that the founders of modern science held to the view that as a perfect intelligence, the deity created a perfect universe of efficient-cause events, occurring in demonstrative progression across time according to a mathematical precision (see Chapter 2, p. 24 and Chapter 3, p. 36). To bring into higher relief the problems facing a theologian who has accepted this religious view of the universe's beginnings, let us draw a mundane parallel. Think of the typical football coach, sketching his game plan on a strategy board before his players in expectation of the upcoming contest with an opponent team. He outlines the various plays to be used, scribbling with a piece of chalk the circles (Os) representing his players and the Xs representing the players of the opposing team.

Now, if this were a deity literally creating actors instead of a human being creating game maneuvers the Os and Xs would not be abstract symbols of what "might happen" assuming that the team members carried out their assignments with precision in the actual game. The Os and Xs would be substantial beings (material causes involved) set into perfect patterns (formal causes involved), which were then carried forward sequentially (efficient causes involved) as intended by the deity (final cause!). And note: The chalk figures (now human beings) would enact their patterns of behavior *without* free choice. They would literally be a part of the unfolding pattern rather than behaving "for its sake." They would be as chairs (Chapter 2, p. 14) and road maps (Chapter 3, p. 42), a creation meeting another's (God's) intention but not having an intention of their own.

But the football coach is not a deity and therefore in order for the game plan to become a reality, the team's quarterback (who directs the play sequencing) must take the recorded strategy and, along with his teammates who also know the *that* (plan), behave for its sake on the field of competition and make it more or less "so" at that time. In this case, not only the coach but the players are free to improvise and alter the course of events as the contest unfolds. If this were God's plan being enacted and the actors (players) began to improvise "at will" in the stream of life's unfolding course would this not be a sacrilegious denial of the Divinity? As we observed in Chapter 2 (p. 17), the concept of sin assumes that the individual subverts God's will in this fashion. At the very least, the astute theologian can see that to the extent we make it possible *in principle* for a deviation to occur the deity conception loses a certain brilliance and power because perfection is being tampered with.

Thus, if we are trying to capture the relationship between the human and his God, and especially if we want to encourage moral behaviors in the human, we must have him conform to the deity (perfection) and not vice versa. One way in which to accomplish this is to hold that the deity has predetermined who will or will not be the good person. This is the tack which St. Paul took, as when he observed: ". . . hath not the potter a right over the clay, from the same lump, to make one part a vessel unto honor, and another unto dishonor?"[2] This deterministic thesis was to become a basic and continuing theological tenet, furthered by St. Augustine and carried centuries later into the Protestant sects by Luther and Calvin.[3] St. Augustine added an interesting intermediary period of freedom for man, holding that though he was initially free this was lost in original sin; yet, God predetermined before the world was created that some men would be saved through unmerited Divine assistance, termed *grace*.[4] It followed that a person hoping to reassure himself and convince his fellows that he was to be a recipient of God's saving grace would behave in a most righteous fashion.

St. Augustine's theological opponent was Pelagius, who though also interested in encouraging righteousness took a more individualistic view of the person. Pelagius denied the doctrine of original sin and the consequent necessity of grace, holding that whether a person sinned or not was up to his free will.[5] Pelagianism was eventually judged an heretical doctrine, a placing of the human being above his God. This was the original meaning of "humanism" in theological circles, and it was and still is considered an anti-religious outlook. Even so, if we analyze the contrasting theological positions in terms of the causes we can see that they employ an identical telic frame. Fearing that if man put his complete reliance on God for direction he would become lethargic and indolent,[6] Pelagius thought it best that man make the freely willed decisions for moral action himself. St. Augustine put his telic frame down with God as the identity exercising freedom in creating the alternative of grace, with an intention that certain men would indeed accede to it. By not accepting this Godly intention, the Pelagian was seen as one of the predetermined beings unblessed with grace who was attempting to subvert God's will by elevating man above the deity.

We see a comparable disagreement arising in the medieval period between St. Thomas Aquinas and John Duns Scotus. For Aquinas, the freedom of God is identical with necessity.[7] Though human wills reflect causality and man is a telic organism, these are secondary to the causality of God. Evil arises due to ignorance or erring reason, as a form of misplaced good. The origin of sin is not freedom of choice but sensuality. The upshot of Aquinas's theology is that, if we humans know all of the ramifications of our actions and avoid erroneous reasoning we will end up in our literal behavior where God has predetermined us to end up (i. e., how He wanted us to behave). This sophisticated development of Augustinian thought keeps the major determinism in God's order via grace. It suggests that if a person really understood everything concerning his behavior in light of good and evil he would *necessarily* opt for the good. Duns Scotus opposed this deity teleology with a more humanistic version by drawing a distinction in the types of freedom open to the individual. There was first a *formal* freedom, as when the person chooses to will or not will, but even having opted for the former he has the *material* freedom to choose this or that. Since the will and the intellect were separate and distinct, simply knowing what the good is intellectually did not necessarily mean that man would opt willfully for the good.

The orthodox theology of the Reformation was also deterministic, reflected as we noted above in the writings of both Luther and Calvin. We continue to see here the Augustinian attitude that a free will would detract from the free grace of God which gives man a saving faith.[8] The noted humanist Erasmus wrote in opposition to Luther, and Arminius opposed Calvinistic theology, by arguing that man often resists grace. John Wesley, from whom Methodism took theological inspiration, was an Arminian.[9] This brief look at some of the classicists in religion should establish that to argue in favor of free will hardly stamps one as a spiritualist! Many modern psychologists erroneously believe this spiritualistic tie-in must occur, but they do not customarily base their rejection of free will on this score. Their objections to the term stem more from the presumed inappropriateness of teleology to scientific description (see Chapter 2). In the remaining sections of this chapter we consider the three major forms that this objection takes—each of which is a variation on the same theme.

## Free Will as Statistical Unpredictability

As an aspect of their scientific activity, psychologists construct questionnaires which measure people's attitudes, or they observe people in life situations and rate them for various characteristics. For example, a group of people may be administered an attitude survey concerning their food preferences. The psychologist hopes to predict actual purchases based on such information by observing what these subjects later select from the shelves of their grocery stores. Do they follow their test scores? In the main, they do, but some do not and the question is: Why not? Is this unpredictability due to the testing and sampling process itself, or have some of the subjects merely changed their minds?

Statistically oriented psychologists are likely to believe that teleologists interpret this unpredictability as an argument for free will. They consider this an error because the real reason for such unpredictability is supposedly the technical difficulties involved in covering all of the determinate factors that shape any behavior. These factors are called *variables*, and they can be sampled from so-called parameters, which as population statistics are the total number of delineated measurements of literally anything. Parameters, like Cartesian motions, exist *only* in mathematical space.[10] Even so, as Newton was to find (see Chapter 2, p. 23), statistical theory is remarkably helpful in predicting observed reality, and it also serves as a standard against which all scientists can test the probable likelihood that their observed results are so-called true differences and not simply chance fluctuations.

But the statistical psychologist is wrong when he assumes that teleologists base their case on the unpredictability of sampled variables. What the teleologist actually wants to know is: Can all *four* of the causal determinations enter into the variable's influence, or are only *certain* causes involved in what is observed? It does not take long to establish that variables are considered in material-cause terms, as when we test people for color sensitivity or intelligence. They are also seen as tapping underlying efficient-cause "laws" that go to make up the fabric of antecedent-to-consequent events in observed reality. If a patterning of variables is involved, this is always presumed to be some kind of Lockean summation of efficient causes rather than a formal cause *per se*. But *never* is the variable conception said to be measuring final-cause determinations! If we were to suggest to one of these psychologists that his variables *were* of a telic nature he would probably accuse us of distorting science for private reasons. As an advocate of mathematical rationalism he thinks of his scientific duty as that of *tracking* behavior, which is moved along by the same forces that move everything else in nature.[11] He sees no need to add anthropomorphizing characteristics to the description of man (the anthrop!).

How can he be so confident that his efficient-cause account of behavior will suffice? Because, in his over-all activity as a scientist this psychologist—as a large proportion of his peers—has failed to draw a distinction between what is his *theory* of behavior and what is his *method* of proving this theory true. Indeed, he tends to think of his method *as* his theory. These are terms which we have not yet defined, but it is easy to clarify them by beginning with an example from everyday life. Assume that two women are playing tennis for the first time as opponents, and now in the early stages of competition they begin to feel out each other's game as to its strong and weak points. It occurs to one woman that her opponent seems to have a weak volley when she hits a backhand while advancing toward the net. This hunch is actually a form of theoretical hypothesis. A *theory* is nothing more than the continuing extension of meaningful understanding by relating one concept—or *construct*, as it is usually called—to another concept. In the present example we have related "opponent's weakness" to "a shallow backhand placement."

This is merely a theoretical hypothesis until tested on the opponent several times. That is, even if bringing her in from the backcourt to return a backhand results in a point for us on one or two occasions, this does not mean it will be to our benefit always or even most of the time. To really prove our theory we need several samplings of her behavior. This concern for such proof is what we mean by *method*—i. e., the means or manner of exercising evidence. There are two kinds of evidence we employ, based on different logical processes. The first is simply a test of common sense, whereby we use what may be called a *procedural* form of evidence to check out what seems most plausible and therefore how we are to advance on life (i. e., "proceed"). This is a patterning type of evidence, ultimately relying on a formal-cause determination. Even the theoretical hunch about the opponent's backhand was nurtured along by procedural evidence. The way the opponent held her racket and seemed to play back on her heels suggested right off that she might have some trouble coming into the net on her backhand side. We surmised in a general way that people with these characteristics might just have this weakness. The close affinity of procedural evidence with the conceptual process of theorizing has resulted in some people calling such speculations "theoretical proof," but this is not a good practice because it tends to blur the fact that theoretical speculation can be done without regard for evidence.

Once the woman has actually aimed her volley to test out her hunch ("When I hit the ball 'there' it will be returned poorly") she has moved into a totally different realm of evidence. This is the beginning of *validating* evidence, in which we prescribe a clear succession of events designed to test our theoretical hypothesis empirically. We can no longer just reason our theory out plausibly. We have to "put up or shut up." The *ideal* of the scientific method is to control some circumstances as thoroughly as possible, leaving, it is hoped, all but one factor to fluctuate while simultaneously comparing it with other circumstances which go uncontrolled. We can see how validating evidence is dependent upon an efficient-cause manipulation of circumstances *in addition to* just the formal-cause procedural evidential test. What separates science from the rest of human knowledge is this great emphasis on "control and prediction" in the exercise of validating evidence. Although mathematical reasoning is based exclusively on procedural evidence—i. e., utilizing common-sense plausibilities and even tautologies—the scientist carries measurements based on mathematics forward to conduct experiments which put his theoretical hypotheses to test in a rigorously controlled context.

And right here is where our actuarial psychologist's confusion begins, because it so happens that the word "variable" has been used by mathematicians to describe purely formal-cause relations between numbers and it has also been used to describe the factors which enter into the efficient-cause manipulations of the scientific method. In founding the experimental steps of scientific method, William Gilbert went beyond Aristotle's method of naturalistic observation to ask that an instrumentation of some sort, or a prescribed chemical process, be used in order to ensure a *controlled* observation.[12] This demonstrative step-by-step process of validation was highly compatible with and therefore readily embraced by the mechanistic theories of the Newtonians.

A century after Gilbert's death the mathematician-philosopher, Leibniz began using the term *function* to describe the ratio of one number to another. In another century or so a mathematician, Dirichlet, worked out a complete statement of this function concept, employing what he called the independent and dependent variables. An *independent variable* (IV) is one to which the mathematician assigns a value *at will*, and the *dependent variable* (DV) is thereby automatically given a value thanks to the functional (ratio) definition existing between variables. The stage was now set for Gilbert's scientific experimental procedure—an efficient-cause manipulation—to be wedded to the purely formal-cause mathematical terminology of Dirichlet's variables.

To show how easily this union is achieved, assume that we wanted to study a problem like the irrigation of crops. What is the most effective level of water per season for a given crop? We might first lay out a series of five plots on the ground, four of which are to receive varying levels of water each season and the fifth to act as a control (i. e., a standard which would receive only natural rainfall). The water would be delivered by a carefully controlled system of pipes and we would take into consideration rainfall, level of fertilization, type of soil, and so on. Different plots would be used for the varying levels of water from season to season (in order to randomize out any unique advantage a given plot might have over the others). At the end of each planting season we would carefully measure the productivity of our five plots. In time a pattern would emerge in our records. Assuming that we actually find a difference in productivity due to water level how would we know that this is a *valid* difference—i. e., one that is not simply a chance fluctuation? Here is where we properly begin using the language of variables, because at this point we can employ statistical reasoning to see how many times out of a fixed amount (set arbitrarily at 100) we might observe the differences recorded exclusively by chance. All of these concepts—variables, measurements, chance, etc.—are *themselves* framed theoretically and based on procedural evidence, but we fall back on mathematics in this instance because of its remarkable record of predictability. This does *not* mean it is a perfect language of prediction. But it is the best we have and works extremely well when based on large samples.

But now, what is the reason for the observed crop differentials? Here is where our scientific theory comes into play, and in all likelihood the explanation will be framed in material-cause (e. g., chemical) and efficient-cause (e. g., constancy-energic) terms. There would surely be no teleology involved. The crops would not be said to decide when to take on water via their roots and when to discontinue doing so. This great compatibility between the efficiently caused method of science and the efficient-cause style of explanation in science has led scientists to talk about their work as involving the study of "lawful variables," as if the world already consisted of such Laplacian regularities (see Chapter 2, p. 24). It is not incorrect to say that scientists "study variables" if we appreciate that this is what they do in the laboratory—that is, in the methodological context! But we must never forget that such variables *always* rest on precedent theoretical assumptions (paradigms, models, analogues, etc.) and that strictly speaking there are no such things as variables, fluctuating "out there" in reality. Variables exist only in mathematical space (i. e., without true extension). If we project our methods onto reality as theories then we bind ourselves into a frozen view of the world.[13]

Unfortunately, this is precisely what an alarming proportion of psychologists do today. They do so because it is easy to equate the stimulus-response (S-R) theory which is based on efficient causation (see Chapter 3, p. 38) with the IV-DV sequencing of scientific experimentation. This practice has become institutionalized so that we can actually read in a widely used psychological dictionary that the independent variable is either a stimulus variable (efficient cause) or an organismic variable (material cause) and: "The *dependent variable* for psychology is always a response."[14] This is a deadly confounding of theory and method for the teleologist. Its practical result is to *repress* telic formulations in psychology.

How is this repression accomplished? Imagine that a teleologist were to propose a theoretical construct based on a formal-final cause type of behavioral determination. Conforming to the rules of science he then designs an experiment in which he puts this intentional construct to test. He might first devise a test of his construct, or a rating procedure whereby he can assign a value to the subject's type of intention and then, using this as his IV he predicts to some DV performance. He might suggest that people with a positive intention who are placed in negative circumstances are less likely to behave in some way than people who enter this situation with negative intentions. And let us imagine that his empirical test (method) supports his predicted expectations (theory). What would be likely to occur if he now writes up his rigorously attained experimental findings in *telic* terminology and submits this manuscript to one of the so-called better psychological journals for publication consideration?

Would the editorial reviewer for this journal gasp in amazement and conclude: "Well, I'll be darned, this teleology stuff stands up to scientific evidence." *He would not!* The odds are unbelievably high that he would find the telic commentary objectionable. He would probably reason as follows: "There is clearly an S-R regularity in the data as the independent variable has some kind of control over the observed responses." Having now confounded theory talk with method talk he would speak to the teleologist in the following vein: "This observed difference in level of response [i. e., positive vs. negative intentions] is interesting, but why not try to find out more about the underlying antecedent conditions [efficient causes] which shaped it. It's OK for the unsophisticated person to talk about intentions, but this is not a proper explanation for us to print. You should know better. There are some fine theories [S-R, of course] which with a little modification here and there might easily account for your findings. Why not take a look at them?"

What has happened here? The reviewer has slipped the teleologist's IV-DV (efficient-cause) *methodological* findings underneath his S-R (efficient-cause) *theoretical* selection and seen in the former sequence "scientific evidence" for the latter! Although done sincerely this is an arrogantly repressive act, practiced today by the vast majority of experimental psychologists. The teleologist is left with the option of reframing his findings in S-R terminology or never seeing the light of day in print—at least, not in these more prestigeful journals. Ironically, it is among those very psychologists who claim great objectivity that the *least* objectivity is to be found when teleology is under consideration.

What the tracking intellect in psychology seems most willing to test, again and again, is the validity of its mathematical assumptions. To theorize beyond statistical theory is almost beneath contempt.[15] According to the prevailing view among trackers, what we must do in psychology is keep up to date in our samplings, so as to predict behavior based on the most recently gathered measurements (data). We will then be talking about what "is" and *not* what "is not" (i. e., facts not theory; note the law of contradiction in this demonstrative line of reasoning). Since any theory has to be put to empirical test anyhow, better to start with such tests so that—as Aristotle has taught us—we will end with certainty having begun in certainty. Attitudes of this sort are currently turning psychologists into actuaries, who pant breathlessly after the "next" data collection which they believe reflects the latest state of reality.

And, as we noted at the outset of this section, they surmise that what the teleologist means by free will is behavior which is "to some degree unpredictable."[16] We can now appreciate better why this is wrong on at least two counts. First, it is a methodological interpretation of free will—or the "effects" of free will methodologically considered—and what is needed today in psychology is a proper *theory* of this concept. Second, it naïvely overlooks the *will* portion of the phrase, which clearly implies a determination to achieve some readily predictable end. Free-will behaviors may be generally more predictable than unpredictable; indeed, this is what we actually demonstrate in Chapter 6.

## Free Will as Mediating Alternatives

The second way in which psychologists have tended to explain away free will takes us back to the mediation model discussed in Chapter 3 (p. 40). Recall that Tolmanian mediators were considered *intervening* variables, coming between the stimulus input and the response output. Now, this style of explanation goes back to John Locke, who was no more friendly to a *truly free* free-will conception than are the behavioristic and related experimental psychologists today. Despite this fact, one can find Locke being termed a free-willist in books on the topic.[17] He was, of course, a great champion of political freedom and some of his phrasings were actually written with minor changes into the Declaration of Independence. It therefore seems incorrect to picture him as the forefather of psychological mechanism. We can clarify our seeming error by taking a closer look at just how Locke pictured the freedom of an individual to behave.

He began with the assumption that there are always a

number of *uneasinesses* which impel the will to action—i. e., to prefer or choose some course in life. Today, we would call these motives. But as a mental action the will does *not* have to be carried forward immediately. It can hang fire, so to speak, and *suspend* the execution of actions which might terminate the uneasinesses. In fact, said Locke: "This seems to me the source of all liberty; in this seems to consist that which is (as I think improperly) called *free-will*." During this suspended course of action the human being can look over things from several angles, and judge the benefit or harm, good or evil of what it is that he is about to do. Things which bring pleasure are good things, and those which result in pain are bad. We can even project this goodness or badness into the future, comparing a present satisfaction to a later one. The overweight person confronting an ice cream parlor is in this situation. Summing it up, Locke concludes: "Liberty, it is plain, consists in a power to do, or not to do; to do or forbear doing, *as we will*."[18]

Unfortunately, as Rickaby has shown,[19] Locke did not make clear why a mind hesitates or suspends action to consider alternatives in the first place. That is, why do we sometimes *not* hang-fire but behave quite directly and spontaneously? The teleologist would of course begin to invoke a final-cause formulation here, acknowledging that we are moved by uneasinesses but that these are framed as grounds for the sake of which behavior occurs. And, as a self-reflexive intelligence the human being can always put such grounds to assessment before behaving. In one of his examples Locke speaks of a man who is told how much better it is to be rich than poor, but, even so, he makes no effort to work his way out of poverty because he feels no uneasiness (motivation) to change things.[20] Locke concludes from this that mental choice follows motivation, but it is just as easy for us to conclude the reverse. If we were willing to think of uneasiness as a premise, then simply because this man did not become uneasy hardly establishes that no choice was made. Locke is taking the view of some of our theologians (refer above, p. 72) that, shown the right (moral, good) way to live, a man *must* choose for this option. But what if he does not? What if he in fact chooses for evil, the bad, the lesser of two economic life styles? Then clearly, he would have no uneasiness and motivation would have followed choice.

In order to develop this line we would have to believe that man was truly free to opt against the right and good, against the probabilities of past inputs as etched on the *tabula rasa* intellect, and to be in essence, capable of *arbitrariness* in grounding behavior. But as a demonstrative theoretician Locke could find no way of conceptualizing this kind of process in mentation. As we recall from Chapter 4 (p. 63), his idea concept signified one thing and one thing only. He also said the will was capable of but one determinate action at a time.[21] In a formulation like this, the entire thrust of behavior is from out of the past, a linear progression of probability nurturing efficient-cause antecedents to bring about consequent effects. It also follows that when the mind *does* suspend this progression, exhibiting thereby the so-called freedom to contemplate alternatives, it does so *only* because of previous unipolar directives which have shaped it to do so. It is difficult to see how this can be considered a free action. It would be precisely the same if we were to describe *non*-free actions on this model. What makes it seem to be free is the directive which had been etched earlier to suspend action for a time and scan other mediating alternatives in the present. Clearly, this is not freedom but mechanism.

Hence, when psychologists today define freedom as having to do with the "number of alternatives available"[22] in behavior they are simply restating the Lockean *tabula rasa* view that if one's past experience has "programmed" or "shaped" one's current response repertoire according to alternative patterns vis à vis any current stimulus situation, then one is freer today than someone who has not been so favorably manipulated. A colorful example of this mediational theory was given by the physiological psychologist D. O. Hebb, when he observed of himself:

> I am a determinist. I assume that what I am and how I think are entirely the products of my heredity [material-cause determination] and my environmental history [efficient-cause determination]. I have no freedom about what I *am*. But that is not what free will is about. The question is whether my behavior is entirely controlled by present circumstances. Heredity and environment shaped me, largely while I was growing up. That shaping, including how I think about things, may incline me to act in opposition to the shaping that the *present* environment would be likely to induce: And so I may decide to be polite to others, or sit down to write this article when I'd rather not, or, on the other hand, decide to goof off when I should be working. If my past has shaped me to goof off, and I do goof off despite my secretary's urging, that's free will. But it's not indeterminism.[23]

If the unpredictability thesis is the leading methodological interpretation of what free will is supposed to mean (refer above), then Hebb's view is undoubtedly a leading *theory* of this conception in modern psychology. Alternatives are the "numbers of" behaviors being mediated rather than arbitrary affirmations being made and brought forward as grounding "thats" for the sake of which behavior occurs. We might define freedom for Hebb as "the number and variety of past controls operating cumulatively over the life span in the ever discernible present." This is a theory of complexity of control, and sheds no light on free will whatsoever. Hebb is not personally responsible for the decisions to be polite or to write his article. His past inputs are mechanically completing the efficient-cause chain of events which are under mediation in his behavioral repertoire.

## Free Will as Guided Natural Selection

The second major theoretical reformulation of free will is B. F. Skinner's operant conditioning approach to behavioristic psychology. The classical or Pavlovian form of conditioning was presented in Chapter 3 (p. 38), and it is the type of S-R theory to which we have been referring in the intervening pages. But Skinner was to change the thinking of psychologists on how such conditioning might be said to occur. His distinguished career can even be seen as a continuing dialogue over the nature of causation in behavioral events. One of his first papers on the topic dealt with the *reflex*, which in those days (*c.* 1931) formed the basis of proving that animals (including humans) did indeed respond automatically to stimulation. Pavlovian conditioning was often called reflex psychology. Skinner was to find certain problems in the reflex-arc concept, and in making his first real stab at critical analysis he specifically acknowledged that he was employing a "method of criticism"[24] used by Ernst Mach in the analysis of other scientific concepts.

Now, Mach is an interesting historical figure, a maverick among physicists during the turn of the century (he died in 1916). Einstein was later to say that Mach had a greater influence on him than anyone else. Why was he so influential? Because Mach taught scientists to analyze their "too familiar notions,"[25] and thereby helped them to see that these were merely conceptual premises on which their current thinking rested but that alternative predications were always possible—even for the same fact pattern. In our terms, Mach understood what was *method* and what was *theory*, and that even highly reliable observations can be taken in two (or more) ways. For example, nothing could be more factual than that a certain river flows under a certain bridge. Methodologically, we could surely validate this fact without much effort. Yet, by fixing his attention on the water while standing on a bridge, Mach could bring himself to perceive the bridge in motion and the water as a stationary reference point.[26] Motion is phenomenally relative, depending upon how we fix our mental groundings in the observed facts. This capacity for a human being to see the same thing two or more ways is basic to all science. Mach summed it up as follows:

> Different ideas can express the facts with the *same* exactness in the domain accessible to observation. The *facts* [method] must hence be carefully distinguished from the *intellectual* constructs [theory] the formulation of which they suggested. The latter—concepts—must be *consistent* with observation, and must in addition be *logically* in accord with one another. Now these two requirements can be fulfilled in *more than one* manner. . . .[27]

Note that this philosophy of science, which is undoubtedly the *most modern* view today, is entirely consistent with dialectical reasoning. As Bradley has observed,[28] although Mach had some reservations about aspects of Kantian philosophy, by and large he accepted much of what it represented and even called his view a phenomenological physics.[29] He was staunchly opposed to the atomic model, calling this a vestige of the "mechanical mythology"[30] which had for too long dominated theory in physics. In light of this distaste he took particular aim at the naïve assumption that every observed regularity reflected efficient causation. Mach was therefore one of the first physicists to point out the confounding of the IV-DV sequence with the efficient-cause explanation of the observed events. He made it clear that all a scientist can speak of causally in his observations is the *correlation* (i.e., formal-cause pattern) between phenomenally perceived antecedents and consequents—even when his hand is on the apparatus which varies the IV up and down some scale of measurement. To

FREE WILL: A BELEAGUERED CONCEPT          87

suggest that the observed lawful tie of this IV to a DV is *ipso
facto* evidence for an efficient-cause relationship is to *go beyond scientific observation.*

This is the method of criticism which Skinner took from
Mach, and in the 1931 analysis of the reflex-arc concept Skinner is careful throughout to refer to the "observed *correlation*
[italics added] of stimulus and response."[31] This is a sophisticated beginning to a successful career. One might have thought
that Skinner would go on to conceptualize the person in phenomenological terms *à la* Mach, trying to understand how the
individual uniquely perceived the waters of his life to be flowing along; but this was never to be. As a budding behaviorist
Skinner put his energies into the study of lower animals, like
rats and pigeons, and only later extended his theories to the
human being. As a result, his theoretical outlook was totally
extraspective, even though his Machian critique was written
from the introspective perspective of the scientist doing the
observing of controlled events.

If a psychologist of 1930 observed a rat moving about in
a learning maze, he assumed that it was being propelled by an
antecedent drive state (Locke's uneasinesses), so that the responses made were the (efficiently caused) *effects* of such unobserved—because internal—stimuli. The rat foraged about for
food, and, in time, wound its way through the maze, discovered food in the food box, ate it, and thereby *reduced* its pro-
pelling drive level as well as strengthened its habitual tendency
to forage for food in the future. It also learned the layout of
the maze (Tolman's cognitive map). This is how classical
drive-reduction theory explained things in 1930, and Skinner
objected to the account for two major reasons.

First, it was not sufficiently empirical, because the psychologist never sees the drive stimuli which supposedly push
behavior along. This was a vestige of the efficient-cause mythology which Mach had taught Skinner to question. Second,
this drive-reduction view overlooks the fact that in the natural

state an animal's behavior is essential to the production of reinforcement. The animal in a maze is placed there by the experimenter, who has loaded the food box with nourishment. A bird in the natural state must first peck at a branch before the lode of nutritious insects is forthcoming in the crumbling bark of the tree. Who is to say what triggered the pecking reflex? Maybe reflexes are just "there" and require no triggering. All we can observe for certain is that when the first few pecks do indeed lead to insects an increase in the rate of pecking follows. If we were to graph the number of pecks per fixed unit of time we would see our graph line going up.

Skinner was to call such pecking responses *operants*, because rather than being operated on by drives they "did the operating" on the environment to produce *reinforcers*. The reinforcers for the bird were the insects, which followed the operant response of pecking; and the fact that the pecking rate increased was considered a (positive) *reinforcement*. Rather than being *elicited* by an antecedent efficient cause, Skinner contended that the operant responses were *emitted*. To emit is to send forth whereas an elicitation is drawn forward by some other force than the act itself. Skinner had effectively reversed the order of the S-R formulation over time. The elicited response of Pavlovian conditioning occurred *after* a stimulus took place. It was the (efficiently caused) effect of this stimulus so it had to occur later in time than the stimulus. But as an emitted response the operant occurs first in time *and then* a pattern of stimuli acting as reinforcers shows up on the scene in what Skinner called the *contingent* circumstance, or the *contingencies of reinforcement*.

This is an interesting choice of words because the term *contingent cause* was introduced by free-willist theologians like John Duns Scotus (see above, p. 72) to describe an efficient cause which was the result of a precedent decision of the will. As such, it was *not* considered a necessary action because the will could have opted for an alternative line of efficient causation. A leaf blowing in the wind is not moved by contingent causes. But, a man who seeks a certain level of payment for his labors and who will not work unless offered this amount is behaving according to contingent causation. If he does accept a desired sum and begins to work at some task—sweeping out a barn, for example—the instrumental way in which he accomplishes this surely involves efficient causes. That is, his arms efficiently cause the broom to move which in turn cleans the barn floor. And, had he walked away from the task the movements of his legs would also involve efficient causation. But whichever eventuality he settles on, the efficient-cause line of behavior is up to him!

Even though he used the language of contingent causation, Skinner did *not* accept the telic intimations which went along with it. In *un*-Machian fashion, he retained a form of reflexology by at first suggesting that when a bird does get its insect reinforcer this releases a fixed but unknown number of pecking responses, which are emitted consecutively much as if a cover had been moved back slightly from the top of a large pot of unknown contents which then proceed to slip out in linear order. This *reflex reserve* as he called it was to be emptied according to the speed of an animal's responding. Skinner showed in his researches that if a rat depressed a lever only once and received a bit of food as an immediate reinforcer it would go on to depress the lever for up to 50 times without another contingent reinforcement taking place.[32] The rat might take only an hour to get all 50 responses out, or it might take several hours, but once the contents of the reflex reserve were emptied "that was it" unless, of course, another reinforcer was forthcoming. And, indeed, offering an occasional bit of food according to some ratio of lever pressings—as, reinforcing every fifth depression—could keep the animal going along in this lever-pressing behavior indefinitely. Pigeons were even more likely to peck at a lever without reinforcers than rats. This was an important experimental finding because it countered certain drive-reduction theories of the period which suggested that behavior had to be reinforced on *every* occasion or it would cease (extinguish).

This fixing of a ratio of reinforcement was called a *schedule*, and in scheduling behavior this way Skinner believed that he was shaping it (a term used earlier by John Watson). And right here is where we find Skinner taking decided leave of the Machian polemic, for he, as his fellow behaviorists, begins to confound the IV-DV sequence of experimentation with reality. He sees the experimental paradigm as a suitable analogue for life, and years later he will even draw parallels between socio-cultural forces and the manipulations conducted by an experimenter in his research design.[33] The net effect is that he could see no room for freedom in behavior since, without question, his researches have shown up and down the animal hierarchy a capacity for the control of behavior. They have indeed, but how are the observed IV-DV regularities to be explained? Is the control of a human being's behavior through contingencies entirely blind, or, is it as Duns Scotus would have it, occasionally the result of self-generated contingent examinations? Skinner has never wavered on this point: Human beings are *not* originating sources of self-control— ever!

In order to understand how he could be so confident we must appreciate the unique relationship that the operant supposedly has with the environmental situation *which it brings about*. One would ordinarily think that an action which brings something else about is the cause, and the resulting set of circumstances is the effect. But this is not true in Skinnerian theory. The bird pecking at the tree limb or the rat pressing a lever is not in control, even though its operant responses are making things like the appearance of insects come about. Skinner insists that: "the environment acts in an inconspicuous way; it does not push or pull, it *selects*."[34] If we remember that he began his theorizing with the reflex as automatic behavior we can grasp Skinner's meaning here. An automatically released (reflexive) behavior "happens," and then this behavior operates on the environment which—assuming it is the right environment for the response—selects this reflex to be furthered rather than some other which also might have been emitted at the same time. If the bird had let slip from a reflex reserve a scratching instead of a pecking response, then presumably the insect reinforcer would not have turned up and hence there would have been no behavioral shaping taking place. The operant response "grabs at" the environment, but the environment does the selecting of what will or will not be captured by this grabbing.

This is an interesting variation on the classical S-R conception, and no one found it too preposterous until Skinner began attributing the same automatic, environmentally selected behavior to human beings. Unlike lower animals, humans have a language capacity which permits them to make predictions of their personal behavior, and then in time we can observe them overtly acting-out their projected intentions. The person says "I want to eat ice cream so I am going to buy a cone and enjoy it" and then *does* so. If the words are emitted operants as well as the actions of buying and eating the cone (Skinner says they are!), then it is always possible that the verbal sequence may permit alternatives, true contingencies such as when the person says "Maybe I will and maybe I won't go to the party tonight." Could such admittedly indeterminate (i. e., arbitrary) projections, acting as verbal operants, signify a contingent course of action in the original meaning of Duns Scotus? Mach would surely have entertained the possibility, but Skinner, who likes to paint himself as more scientific-minded than his critics,[35] would refuse to concede the point. Telic theory is outmoded and he is a modernist: "Operant behavior, as I see it, is simply a study of what used to be dealt with by the concept of purpose. The purpose of an act is the consequences it is going to have."[36]

This may be true from *either* the introspective or extraspective theoretical perspective. We cannot talk to the bird pecking away on a branch so it is impossible to tell whether it has awareness of the consequences that pecking might turn up. But we *can* talk to the person who has an idea of the ice cream cone which can be put into words, and when he does so it is clear that there is awareness of the consequences of purchasing a cone *before* the act materializes in actual behavior. By couching his theoretical commentary in exclusively extraspective terms, Skinner makes it appear that consequences have relevance for behavior only when they are literally under way. Yet it seems on self-examination that we are capable of thinking about the consequences of our acts beforehand, and are thereby free to put such intended projections into play or not. According to Skinner, this is anthropomorphic nonsense.

In his 1971 book *Beyond Freedom and Dignity*, Skinner argues that human freedom is simply the range of controls placed on the person. The mediation thesis is reflected here (refer above, p. 81), as the number of alternatives open to the person's controlled behavior is what defines his degree of freedom.[37] The person *qua* actor is never free to influence such alternatives beforehand, and since he has no responsibility for how he behaves, he can take no credit for his behavioral accomplishments in life. People also feel less free when they are put under control by aversive stimulation. This occurs when a person is first made to feel anguish, pain, frustration, etc., but is released contingent upon his doing the desired act. The arm-twistings of life which drive us to cry "uncle" to be relieved of the pain demonstrate control through aversive stimulation. Punishment is something entirely different, because in this case our arm is twisted to silence us forever.[38] In this 1971 book Skinner was still talking of the causes in events as follows: "What is no longer common in sophisticated scientific writing is the push-pull causality of nineteenth-century science. The causes referred to here are, technically speaking, the independent variables of which behavior as a dependent variable is a function."[39]

There is an obvious tendency in this summation to confound behavior with the dependent variable, of which it is surely *not* "a function." As we have seen, Skinner's Machian commitments to analyze familiar notions never ran very deep. But, what is more important is that another—more clearly theoretical rather than just methodological—interpretation regarding the freedom issue began to appear in the 1971 book on freedom and dignity (or, the lack thereof). Skinner begins to draw a parallel between his theory of environmental selection and Darwinism, as follows: "The environment not only prods or lashes, it *selects*. Its role is similar to that in natural selection, though on a very different time scale, and was overlooked for the same reason."[40] When animals in nature evolved a certain type of hide, or a particular type of claw, it was the physical environment which contingently rewarded them with survival, assuming this change proved more adaptable than the hides and claws which had existed to that point in time. And, as is sometimes said of the dinosaurs, when the environment was no longer the "right one" for certain bodily structures, contingent reinforcements in the form of survival were not forthcoming. By 1974, when he published *About Behaviorism*, Skinner had completely identified Darwin's natural selection with operant conditioning of behavior, as follows:

> There are certain remarkable similarities between contingencies of survival and contingencies of reinforcement. . . . Both account for purpose by moving it after the fact [on the time dimension], and both are relevant to the question of creative design. When we have reviewed the contingencies which generate new forms of behavior in the individual, we shall be in a better position to evaluate those which generate innate behavior in the species.[41]

According to Howard E. Gruber, an expert not only on Darwin's published works but on his unpublished notebooks as well, the Father of Natural Selection theory "was not especially interested in drawing a direct analogy between the evolution of species and individual psychological development."[42] Furthermore, Darwin's interactionist theory gave equal weight to organism and environment in the evolutionary process, so that the organism was often "resistant to environmental pressures, and by the same token not always perfectly adapted. . . ."[43] Because Skinner's equation of operant behavior to natural selection overweights the role of the environment we have every right to consider it a false analogy.

Skinner goes on to suggest that Darwin had discovered a special form of causality in nature in the concept of natural selection.[44] Actually, as Darwin fully appreciated, natural selection relies on material- and efficient-cause descriptions which move in a progressive direction not by a God's intention but by serendipity and survival of the fittest through blind fortune. Even so, recall from Chapter 2 (p. 32) that Darwin appreciated the irony of highly advanced civilizations which permit their weak members to survive, thereby adversely affecting the selective process. Contingent circumstances in these civilizations termed *values* have somehow evolved or emerged to turn back natural selection from its inexorable and often "heartless" course. Skinner skips over such passages in Darwin's writings. His claim that values are nothing but a record of the positive (good value) or negative (bad value) outcomes of reinforcing effects is particularly wanting in this context.[45] This is an *instrumental* theory of value, which can be contrasted with an *intrinsic* theory of value in any judgment of what is the good and proper way to behave.

The instrumental theory holds that all organisms seek pleasure rather than pain, and hence the decision as to what is good or bad is made on this score. Acts which are instruments for the furthering of pleasure have positive value and those which do not or result in pain have negative value. British philosophy has emphasized this view in the Utilitarian schools of Jeremy Bentham and John Stuart Mill, which essentially defined the good as whatever brings the greatest pleasure to the greatest number of people. The intrinsic theory presumes that man has the innate reasoning capacity to judge the good and therefore to do what is right. Doing one's duty and following out one's obligations may result in pleasure for one or all, but there are times when it does not. Continental philosophy has emphasized intrinsic value theory, as in the case of Kant, whose Categorical Imperative is a reasoned principle for how to behave: "act so as to treat humanity, in thyself or any other, as an end always, and never as a means only."[46] This is a telic principle, and just as surely non-telic theories of value are likely to be instrumental formulations.

But note: When Darwin ponders the seeming involution of natural selection in the fact that advanced civilizations save their weakest members, he is clearly more on the side of an intrinsic than an instrumental value study. He cannot opt to let the sickly go unattended even as he realizes that in furthering their existence he, as all civilized men, is weakening the future viability of the stock as a whole (see p. 32). The fact that civilizations have turned back on natural selection to achieve intrinsically valued ends comes as no surprise to Skinner, for since the appearance of his book *Walden Two* he has become a leading advocate of the design of cultures.[47] Since he now contends that the causal vehicle whereby he can achieve this is an extension of the biological principle in evolution, we have chosen to call this Skinnerian strategy "guided natural selection." The practical outcome of such cultural design would be comparable to the mediation thesis of increasing alternatives within which people might be permitted to behave. As Skinner expressed it: ". . . a culture which made people as much alike as possible might slip into a standard pattern from which there would be no escape. That would be a bad design. . . . The only hope is *planned* diversification, in which the importance of variety is recognized."[48]

Many critics have pointed out the seeming contradiction between Skinner's theory of personal behavior and the fact that he believes cultural planning is possible. How can a nontelic organism plan for the future? Skinner answers that such planning is based upon scientifically established findings, and that since the aim will be to avoid as much as possible all forms of control through aversive stimulation and punishment there should be no objections. For those who want to know "who controls the controllers," Skinner answers in terms of counter-control measures. There is a joke, retold by every class of undergraduate students who take psychology, which has one rat say to a fellow rat: "Look, I've got Professor Skinner conditioned. Every fifth time I press this lever he gives me a food pellet in that dispenser over there." Joking aside, says Skinner, the fact remains that the organism under control *does* have a counter-controlling influence on the controller.[49] Hence, in a well-designed culture it is Skinner's contention that such reciprocal controls would *also* be instituted.

The teleologist finds this formulation of human relations inadequate, not because it requires a controller over people but because of the interpretation given to how this control is achieved. People are indeed controlled by cultural controllers, whom they influence in turn so that a reciprocity exists between the citizen and his elected officials, the police, his employer, and so on. But this is *not* an efficient-cause exchange of one action triggering the blind release of another, coalescing into meaning only after the behavior has been made manifest. Skinner's technology of behavioral control, which we will return to in other Chapters (6, 8), is not fallacious in the claims it makes concerning the modification of behavior achieved. It is just explained by an incomplete theory. The original thinking of John Duns Scotus could prove a great help to the Skinnerian account.

The behavioristic descriptions of free will do not capture this activity as a psychological process so much as they describe the subtleties of control which provide us with the illusion of free will. In a sense, freedom comes out as covert control. Although political freedom may properly be conceived in terms of alternatives available to the person, to say that a prisoner in jail is psychologically less free in willed behavior than a person outside of jail is like saying that a person who can afford the best steaks has a different digestive process than a person who must exist on cornmeal. Ordinarily, we think of our free will as under the constraint of external factors, so that though we may will it we are unable to walk through walls. Wealthy people have more alternatives to consider in deciding what they can or cannot do, but this does not change their basic psychological processes. The behavioristic interpretation of freedom also holds for animals. Is an animal with more mediating cues trained into it *psychologically* freer than an animal which has not yet had the benefit of such training? Behaviorists would tend to answer "yes," but this is because, as we have seen, they equate free will with the multiplying of alternatives—leading at times to unpredictability—rather than to the *reduction* of alternatives in behavior.

And yet, if we were to live according to Duns Scotus's interpretation of efficient causation we would constantly be *reducing* the possible alternatives in behavior open to us, *rejecting* those which had contingent circumstances we deemed beforehand to be immoral or harmful. Overt options may be minimized by the moral person, but psychologically the level of free will remains the same in all people—we might say the "potential" level to be free of constraining value decisions remains the same. Thus, a law-abiding person is not usually willing to consider the "that, for the sake of which" alternatives that a criminal is likely to contemplate in deciding how to behave. In fact, the more the law-abiding person contemplates the contingencies of behavior in a moral sense the greater is the probability that his behavior will become even *more* predictable than before. It is this delimiting side to the exercise of free will which statistico-behavioral accounts are unable to account for, a fact which alone discredits them as theoretical descriptions of this fundamental human activity.

# SIX

# Teleology in the Laboratory

As we said of Skinner in Chapter 5 (p. 91), those psychologists who are most opposed to telic descriptions of the person are likely to consider themselves more scientific in orientation than their peers. William James once called these the tough-minded as opposed to the tender-minded psychologists. The heyday of the tough-minded psychologists was probably from 1920, when behaviorism began to take the lead in universities, to the late 1940s. The majority of sound laboratory research conducted during this period used lower animals as subjects, with extrapolations then made to human beings based on the learning theories framed to explain the behavior of rats, pigeons, and monkeys. Human research investigations over this period focused primarily on the building of scales and tests to tap attitudes, personality traits, intellectual levels, and so on.

The upshot was that, except for research on the so-called projective tests (inkblots, etc.), most of the theories that issued from experimental psychology were framed extraspectively. As we noted in Chapter 5 (p. 80), a testing instrument merely "samples" from a subject's behavior along one dimension of measurement and then predicts to another dimension in the life setting. Such tracking of reality does not necessarily provide us with an increased understanding of that which we are predicting. What intelligence "is" may remain a mystery even though intelligence tests predict to schoolroom performance with precision. In point of fact, the psychologists who built empirical tests either turned the person into a quasi-computer, or, left the explanatory details of behavior to their laboratory brethren. In either case the descriptive account which was forthcoming was totally mechanical.

In order to formulate a telic description of behavior we have to begin looking through the eyes of the behaving organism. We need a first-person, introspective account. This is absurd when the subject of our study is a rat, because there is no way to get this organism's slant on things out into the open for consideration. This does not mean lower animals lack such introspectively framed premises about experience, of course. But as tough-minded psychologists "controlled and predicted" behavior which they framed as a succession of events being manipulated "over there," they thought of themselves as the chemist or physicist, mixing compounds or cracking atoms. Their independent-variable (IV) manipulations were as the tiller of a ship maneuvering through reality's waters, and in proving empirically that they could indeed manipulate behavior they believed they had completely circumvented alternative explanations for "how" such manipulation is brought about (what sort of causes?). The organism was shown to be a fluctuating series of dependent variables (DVs) and no more. Theoretical objections raised to the opposite were simply the last gasps of a dying vitalism. As Skinner said in the mid-1950s, "When we have achieved a practical control over the organism, theories of behavior lose their point."[1] He had by this time left Mach far, far behind (Chapter 5, p. 85).

But even as Skinner expressed this mechanistic view, events were taking place in the research laboratories which cast a totally different light on the possibility of establishing human teleology scientifically. In the years since the close of World War II there has been an explosion of research on human beings. Social and industrial psychologists had always studied humans in laboratory circumstances, but their numbers were never enough to take the spotlight away from the "lab" psychologists—often called rat psychologists, S-R psychologists, or simply learning psychologists. After the war this began to change, aided no doubt by social demands to build a psychology more in touch with human problems. And, as psychological specialties which place human beings into the experimental apparatus began to increase, traditional animal experimentation declined in importance.

The new emphasis on humans as subjects prompted issues to develop in the experimental context which never had arisen before. By the early 1960s a series of findings began to emerge which suggested that when *humans study humans* there are *two* sets of hands on the experimental tiller. We cannot in Chapter 6 hope to review the full range of this immensely important development in psychological research. But we can cover a few highlights to reveal for the reader something which tough-minded psychologists have been trying to maneuver around because it threatens to bring their mechanistic edifice crashing down about them.

The general public does not hear about these developments because they are taken as technical problems in the psychological method as such. This is the formal position, and doubtless most empirical psychologists do not see the insidious effects which this interpretation of the empirical findings must eventually have on the mechanistic human image. The teleologist sees the issue of personal freedom being masked by these tired maneuvers. In the remaining sections of this chapter we will review three research topics to demonstrate how, despite all the (methodological and theoretical) controls set in opposition to it, the meaning of final causation continues to press through the findings of psychological experiments, once we are cognizant of what this means.

## Demand Characteristics and Experimenter Bias

Psychologists have always known that human subjects have a pretty good idea of what is going on in an experimental design. But their customary attitude toward this "subject bias" was to try and control it out of existence or at least reduce its influence on the "real" or "more important" findings which are presumed to be discoverable free of such influence. This biasing tendency as well as the counter-measures to be taken against it were to become a focal point of research in the 1960s. Martin T. Orne was one of the first to show the extremes to which people would go in playing what he considered was the socio-psychological role of a "good subject."[2] Orne's research assistants asked subjects to perform meaningless tasks such as adding the adjacent numbers in two rows of numbers on a sheet, requiring 224 additions per sheet. A stack of 2000 sheets was plunked down before a subject and he was asked to begin adding, without any projections given as to how long he would be expected to continue.

Orne's aim was to find a task in which subjects who had volunteered for an experiment might eventually become so bored that they would actually quit. He hoped to study hypnotized subjects performing this task to see if they might continue on beyond where a non-hypnotized subject would cease cooperating. To his amazement, Orne found his non-hypnotized volunteer subjects carrying on with this task for up to five and one-half hours, so that the *experimenters* and not the subjects finally gave up! Even when the task was made more ridiculous by having subjects *over and over again* first add columns, then pick up a card on which they were instructed to tear up what they had just done, they continued to meet experimental instructions. When the experimenters later asked subjects why they persisted in such a ridiculous task they in-

variably attributed "considerable meaning to their performance, viewing it as an endurance test or the like."[3]

Orne suggested that when human beings take on the role
of "good subject" they define this as helping to advance science, which means in any given instance making certain that
the study runs off without a hitch and therefore comes up with
the findings which it has been designed to fit. They often express fear about not doing a good job. In light of this it is
probably not surprising to learn that they will "ascribe purpose
and meaning [to an experiment] even in the absence of purpose and meaning."[4] A grisly manifestation of this tendency
for subjects to carry on a task "for science's sake" can be seen
in the work of Stanley Milgram on obedience to authority.[5]
Milgram found that most subjects permitted the experimenter
as scientific authority to define the morality of their acts, so
that they allowed themselves to be instrumentalities in the inflicting of pain—i. e., an electric shock which they believed
they were administering to another person (but they were not).

It is not difficult to see what a teleologist might say about
such experimental procedures and results. The talk of purpose,
roles, and the permitting of authority to define one's meanings
would be framed as a final-cause determination. Emphasis
would be put on what a subject framed as his predication of
the circumstances facing him, *not* on the supposed situational
cues which are eliciting his responses in efficient-cause fashion.
But Orne was not to frame his empirical findings in this manner, even though he was sympathetic to the view that subjects
are not passive in the experimental context. In searching about
for a label to describe his subjects, Orne suggested that: ". . .
the totality of cues [i. e., environmental stimuli] which convey
an experimental hypothesis to the subject become significant
determinants of subjects' behavior [i. e., responses]. We have
labeled the sum total of such cues as the *'demand characteristics of the experimental situation.'* "[6]

This does not say just how these cues work in the psychology of the person. If they are in the situation instead of in the person's predication of the situation then they can be conceived of in efficient-cause terms, as Lockean inputs. This is precisely how most psychologists view demand characteristics today. Orne even referred to these situational determinants as variables, reflecting the theory-method confound which is so rampant in psychological science (see Chapter 5, p. 80). His recommendation is that psychologists no longer try to eliminate such variables, since this is probably impossible, but that they try to "study their effect, and manipulate them if necessary." In his later research, Orne was to learn when he interviewed subjects after they had completed an experimental task that only those who had somehow gleaned the experimental hypothesis which was being put to test caused it to be validated. Those subjects who had not caught on to what was being supposedly manipulated by the experimenter's design were *not* manipulated—i. e., they failed to enter into the significant findings.[7] This proved to be a harbinger of things to come.

Beginning at about the same time as Orne, Robert Rosenthal approached the question of supposed experimental artifacts by focusing on the biases of the experimenter.[8] Later he put together an entire volume documenting the role of such *experimenter effects*, defined as that ". . . portion of the complexity of human behavior which can be attributed to the experimenter as another person and to his interaction with the subject. . . ." In an extensive survey of the extant research literature as well as in his own researches Rosenthal was able to show convincingly that the empirical findings of psychological experiments on humans are influenced by such things as the experimenter's sex, race, manner of relating to a subject (whether warm or cold), expectancy regarding the likely outcome of a study, personal attraction to a subject, and so on. Even when the experimenters were using rats as subjects, if they believed the rats to be bright they obtained slightly better results than if they believed them to be dull.[9]

Prompted by such findings, Rosenthal went on to conduct a two-year study of children whose teachers had been told that they were either "bloomers" (gradual growth) or "spurters" (rapid growth) in potential for improvement in intelligence (IQ) over the immediate future. This was a subterfuge, of course, because the real aim was to establish a bias in the teacher comparable to that of the experimenter's attitude toward his rat subjects. As predicted, although all children increased in IQ over the two years, the spurter group showed significantly greater increases than the bloomers.[10]

How can such *self-fulfilling prophecies* take place? How is it that an experimenter who believes that his research *will* come out, or that his subjects *can* do the task, has better results than experimenters who do not? And how can a teacher's expectations for students literally affect their intellectual development? Rosenthal's theoretical analysis of these findings leaves things pretty much as they always have been in psychology. In referring to the experimental context he notes that "there are a great many variables that affect the subject's response other than those variables which, in a given experiment, are specifically under investigation."[11] This is true enough, speaking methodologically where literally *everything* we can see, touch, or think about can be studied as a variable. But since we now appreciate that variables do *not* explain behavior without theoretical grounding we wonder what Rosenthal's theory can amount to. It is disappointing to find that he, as most psychologists, begins reaching back in time for the antecedents of efficient causation, noting in justification that: "If past behavior were unrelated to future behavior, then there could only be the humanist's [i. e., the teleologist's] interest to prompt us to study behavior, and not the scientist's."[12]

Coming down to his theoretical explanation, Rosenthal

suggests that all people seem to acquire a *motive* to fulfill their interpersonal expectancies. It is satisfying to predict one's future and thereby stabilize his existence (positive reinforcement), and disconcerting not to do so most of the time (negative reinforcement). Presumably, over time a learned motivation develops favoring the former state of affairs. This would suggest that some form of quasi-drive is being reduced whenever successful anticipations of experience are brought about. Rosenthal goes on to stress the importance of eliminating this self-fulfilling prophecy component from psychological experiments.[13]

In his discussion of the teacher-pupil relationship Rosenthal makes several suggestions as to how the IQ differential may have occurred. Teachers may have been more pleasant, friendly, and encouraging to the children they believed to be spurters. They probably watched these children more closely, leading to "more rapid reinforcement of correct responses with a consequent increase in pupils' learning." The teacher also probably "communicated" an expected improvement in classroom performance. This could have changed the child's self-image and raised his personal expectations to grow intellectually. Lumping all such factors together, Rosenthal calls for more research on "the range of possible *mechanisms* [italics added] whereby a teacher's expectations become translated into a pupil's intellectual growth."[14]

It seems clear that both Orne and Rosenthal have brought out something important about human behavior. They are both highly competent scientists, trying as best they can to improve their method. But have they really captured the most unique aspect of their data? The teleologist would have severe questions to raise in this regard. Putting Orne, Milgram, and Rosenthal together, we could readily present a theoretical explanation in which human beings are proven to be predicators and *not* mediators in behavior. The subject has an idea in mind which he brings to the experimental task, and the experimenter has an idea in mind. If the subject catches onto the experimenter's idea (experimental design) and fulfills his contract to be a good subject then we have experimental evidence emerging to support the hypothesis being put to test. Subjects do not always further the experimental design (hypothesis), of course. Over a third of Milgram's subjects quit before the full range of (pseudo-)shocks was administered. Experiments have also been done which show that when a "hard sell" is put on subjects to comply with experimenter expectancies the effort may "boomerang" and actually result in a lessening of experimental effects (so-called "negative" findings).[15] Subjects obviously have a concept of how they *ought* to behave. Skinner's disclaimers aside, there is an implied dignity to the good subject role, a right way and a wrong way in which to approach the interpersonal circumstances known as a psychological experiment.

Put in terms of determinism (Chapter 3), what we are suggesting is that the "control and prediction" aspect of validation is efficiently causal, but the experimental design on which the instrumental course of an IV-DV manipulation is predicated always results in a final-cause determination for *both* experimenter and subject. *All research on human behavior must take this telic determination into account.* The experimenter is behaving "for the sake of" a plan (design). The teacher is relating to the pupils "for the sake of" a performance expectation (also a kind of plan). Both the experimenter and the teacher employ purely mechanical instrumentalities in their relationship with subjects and students, respectively. The experimenter administers instructions, places the subject in a task, attaches measurement devices to him, and so on. The teacher assigns readings, points to symbols on blackboards, corrects mechanical errors in printing and writing, and so on. But what the evidence seems to suggest is that the "for the sake of" predications of the experimenter or teacher are *at least* as important to the course of behavior resulting in the subject or pupil as are these mechanical instrumentalities. Subjects conform to the experimental design and students conform to the performance expectation. We should be seeing research reports of these experimental findings in which it is suggested that human beings are controlled by taking over the predications (intentions, attitudes, biases, etc.) of other human beings and then furthering the meanings contained therein by behaving for their sake. But the findings which are "written up scientifically" have almost no chance of reflecting such a Machian alternative. As we have seen in the theoretical efforts of Orne and Rosenthal, it is the doctrinaire S-R theory which provides the rationale, and every effort is made to erase the teleology reflected as error due to experimental artifact.

## Causal Perception and Attribution

There have been some notable examples of psychologists studying the ways in which people understand, perceive, and employ causal description in their everyday activity. The antitelic bias of these researches is readily documented. For example, the eminent developmental psychologist Jean Piaget once studied how children perceived causality by interviewing them at several age levels and asking them what made various things in life happen. Piaget found what he called *adherences* at all ages of development, and in four cases out of five these amounted to telic causal formulations of events. The child believes that the moon sends him dreams, or that the sun is aware of our existence on earth, or that things in the universe are made for our benefit. There is a continuing belief in what Piaget critically referred to as a "deep and stubborn finalism [i. e., final-cause description]" in all children.[16] As a child matures such adherences diminish, and Piaget treated this development as a healthy movement away from erroneous description to the "right" way of talking about things and events.

There is nothing in the interview data *per se* to suggest how we are to interpret these adherences, of course. As teleologists we might prefer to conclude that they support the basically telic nature of the human understanding, which must be "denaturalized" in the maturation process. Gestalt psychologist Wolfgang Köhler tells of a time when this direct perception of intentionality reverberated through his psyche, balanced only by the fact that he was, after all, a 20th-century man and to that extent no longer totally "natural":

> While climbing once in the Alps I beheld, on stepping cautiously around a corner of the rocks, a big dark cloud which moved slowly and silently towards me along the slope. Nothing could look more sinister and more threatening. Genetically this might have been a case of empathy; but for my awareness the menace was certainly in the cloud. I could perhaps persuade myself that a cloud as such is an indifferent percept. If, however, I had been a primitive, no reason whatsoever could have given me such sober consolation. The threatening character of the cloud itself would have remained just as "objective" as its ugly dark color.[17]

This very question of whether or not we can perceive causation directly was eventually studied by Albert E. Michotte. There had been a long-standing argument, dating to the British philosopher David Hume (1711-76), which suggested that human beings never perceive "the" efficient cause of a flow of events in experience. We observe one billiard ball rolling across a table and when it "bumps" a second billiard ball the latter moves off. This is what we see, but thanks to the contiguous relationship of these two motions and the power of association which our minds habitually engender across such events, in time we impute a(n efficiently) causal sequence to this flow. Put in other terms, we might say that though order is what is observed (i. e., formal causality), efficient causality is what is attributed to the succession of events. Michotte argued that we *could* perceive direct (efficient) cause-effects, and in a series of highly original studies he examined this capacity as well as the conditions under which it could be altered. His experimental design involved having a black and a red square moving about on a white background. The basic motion involved having one square move toward and make contact with the other, which was to that point in time stationary. Following this contact two courses of action followed. Sometimes the moving square stopped while the formerly stationary one moved on (called the launching effect), and at other times both squares moved off in tandem (called an entraining effect).[18]

Michotte was to find his subjects constantly anthropomorphizing the moving squares, assigning purposes to what they saw occurring. For example, they would describe one square as having "hit" the other, or, as chasing it. Many claimed they did not see any necessity in the sequence of motion, so that events seemed as if they might stop at the point of contact.[19] If this is the case, then it is at least worth asking whether subjects were really perceiving efficient causation. An efficient cause in which the sequence of linear motions is not necessary seems a contradiction in terms. Even so, Michotte failed to entertain alternative causal explanations of his data and pressed the point that he was studying only efficient causation. When it came to the telic possibility he denigrated it as follows: "We all know . . . how frequently people fail to make a distinction between [efficient ]'cause' and 'purpose' [final cause]. We constantly find that children and even adults are satisfied with 'explanations' in terms of purpose, and *attribute* [italics added] to them a causal significance in the sense of 'efficient' causality."[20]

As the example taken from Köhler dramatizes, people surely do ascribe as much significance to purpose and intention as they do to efficient causation. This is especially true when people are trying to make sense of other people's behav-

ior—anthropomorphizing the anthrop, so to speak. We can accept this statement as an iron-clad fact, based on the evidence
from generations of psychological scientists working with
people as subjects. But how many of these psychologists have
drawn telic conclusions regarding human nature from such
findings? Remarkably few. We italicized the word "attribute"
in Michotte's quote above because it was to become the descriptive label for a body of theory and research which took
some initial incentive from his work.[21] One aspect of this research on what came to be called attribution theory is especially interesting to the teleologist.

That is, if a person is observed behaving in a social context, or, even having to do some kind of task which allows leeway for different strategies we find a significant disparity between what he thinks caused his behavior in that situation and
what an observer might think. Actors in situations tend to say
that factors in the circumstances facing them are what cause
them to behave, whereas observers of these actors are likely to
attribute their behaviors to a stable personality trait of the actor or habitual disposition on his part to behave as he did regardless of the situation facing him.[22] Thus, Köhler as actor
perceived the threat in the black cloud, an aspect of the
mountain-climbing situation facing him. But we, as observers,
would be more likely to assign the cause of his anxiety as some
deep-seated human tendency to anthropomorphize experience.

This divergence can be reversed through the use of video-
tape by having an observer look at things from the viewpoint
of the actor, and vice versa, after the sequence of events has
been completed. Now, the teleologist would see in these data
an actor and an observer framing predicate assumptions about
what is taking place based on their particular slant on things.
They may be forced to disagree over the causes of what happened given their contrasting perspectives, but there is a commonality in the fact that both actor and observer agree when
one is given a chance to look through the eyes of the other. The

commonality seems a more significant finding than the fact that comparable mentations can result in two different accounts of what took place.

Yet, H. H. Kelley, one of the leading investigators in attribution theory, draws a different implication from such findings. He views the contrast in causal attribution between the actor and observer "as an important warning to psychologists that the strength of their belief in and the intensity of their search for personal causes of behavior may not be justified entirely."[23] He arrives at this remarkable conclusion because in their scientific role psychologists are more like observers than actors, hence they had better not think too highly of people determining their own behavior but appreciate the important role of situational factors in shaping what they do. Note how the point-of-view issue is framed in exclusively methodological terms, and the obvious role which—introspective *versus* extraspective theoretical—predications play in the contrasting accounts is overlooked altogether.

A predication is the "that" which is affirmed and then for its sake, behavior is furthered, meanings are extended, and so on. The word attribution, which draws roots from "to bestow," would seem to be highly compatible with such telic phrasings. But Kelley, in commenting on how attribution supposely works, falls back on information-processing theory (see Chapter 10) to say: "It must be emphasized . . . that attribution theory deals only with the processes by which attributions are derived from informational input."[24] Information-processing theories are mediation models, and consequently in this treatment Kelley has the attribution process as an etching of inputs onto the *tabula-rasa* intellect rather than as an active bringing forward of a *pro-forma* point of view. The very meaning of attribution has shifted from a bestowing to a receiving process. Once again, the data *qua* data do not tell us which of these explanatory directions to take—nor do they countermand the one taken. It is up to procedural evidence at this point. Which of these explanations seems most reasonable and consistent with what we know of ourselves and others as "attributors"? We are called on now to do some enlightened and conscientious attributing in light of such understanding. Scientists who gather data are not necessarily the best interpreters of what they find, and since we all have a stake in what is concluded about our personal natures, we have every right to call them to account for what they make of their observations.

Gestaltists like Köhler are phenomenological in theoretical persuasion. They tend to see attribution as the necessity of people to frame a point of view *at all times*. It is never a question of attribution versus non-attribution. As phenomenal organisms human beings *always* organize their awareness according to gestalt principles which take on causal meanings. They live within the nexus of a phenomenal field, a Kantian kind of experience through which they constantly put meaning onto noumenal reality. If two people view the same set of circumstances differently this does not mean that one, the other, or both are suffering from an illusion regarding the presumed "real" causes which bring on both of their views. We could even take the findings of attribution research as evidence for the validity of Mach's claim that two logically consistent accounts of these same facts is possible, even in science (see Chapter 5, p. 86). But what does Kelley conclude and look forward to in light of such research evidence? His thinking runs as follows:

. . . through proper manipulation of causes and information about causes, actors can be uniformly led to highly erroneous views about the reasons for their own behavior. . . . Thinking in these terms, eventually we will be able to identify other attributional illusions and to describe the conditions necessary for their production. These will include the illusion of responsibility, whereby a person assumes to an unrealistic degree that he is personally responsible for consequences that other persons would attribute largely to circumstances or luck, and the illusion of external constraint, in which the person attributes to the situation or other persons consequences that are generated by his own behavior.[25]

If one believes that attributions are fed into a person's mentations much as we drop postal cards into a mailbox, it is easy to arrive at this somewhat expansive conclusion about just what psychologists may or may not be capable of manipulating in a person's behavior. Some cards have "attribution information" written on them and some do not.[26] Depending upon which cards we use and what we jot down on them before dropping them into the slot, we can manipulate the person's sense of responsibility for his behavior. To judge from the evidence now accruing by geometric leaps and bounds on the conditioning of behavior, a psychologist who seriously believes that it is solely he who manipulates a subject is probably suffering from the grandest illusion of them all.

## Behavioral Conditioning

Of all the concepts employed by tough-minded psychologists to keep teleology from slipping into their theoretical accounts, none is more important than conditioning. In Chapter 3 we discussed classical (Pavlovian) conditioning (p. 38) and in Chapter 5 we took up operant (Skinnerian) conditioning p. 87). These are the two major experimental methods of conditioning, and they form the backbone of mechanistic psychological theory. They are written from the extraspective point of view. Pavlovian conditioning holds that after several pairings of a conditioned stimulus (light) with an unconditioned stimulus (food) a conditioned response often results (e. g., when Pavlov's dogs salivated to the light). In the Skinnerian procedure, an animal is seen to increase its probability of operant responding (lever pressing) when this behavior leads to the production of a reinforcer (i. e., a food pellet dropped into a container next to the lever).

There are two aspects of this style of explanation which give tough-minded psychologists the reputation of being more scientifically respectable than their peers. First, it is presumed that telic explanations are capable of being set aside when events are described solely in terms of antecedent events becoming attached to and/or highly predictive of consequent events. This is what makes these theories mechanistic or behavioristic. Behavior is said to run off like clockwork without a predicating purpose or intention in the sequence of events. Second, the claim is made that such accounts are based *primarily* on what is actually being observed in the experimental procedure. Unlike the Freudian explanation (see Chapter 3), which concocts all manner of unobserved causes for a client's behavior, the behaviorist contends that he speaks only from the "facts" and does not need to build theoretical castles in the air to account for what is observed (recall Skinner's claim that when we have control of an organism we do not need theories, p. 100). However, as we noted in the introduction to this chapter, around 1960 a series of experimental findings began turning up which cast doubt on the first (anti-telic) presumption, which in turn forced the modern behaviorist to lose the empirical purity of his second presumption as well.

These researches were conducted on human beings, and dealt with so-called *subject awareness* in the experimental design. They were first given major consideration in the literature on operant conditioning but soon the impact of subject awareness on classical conditioning was made evident as well. Psychologists were to learn that a crucial factor had been going unrecognized or at least not sufficiently appreciated in *all* experiments on human conditioning—and this represents pretty much the sum-total of what is often called "basic" research in psychology. Whether or not this factor plays a role in the conditioning of lower animals remains an open question because as of this point in time—except for the possibility of communication with some of the higher apes through sign language—there is just no way in which to tell if animals below man have varying levels of awareness (see Brewer's views on this possibility below, p. 127). Just what do we mean by subject awareness?

This refers to a finding that emerges in studies on the operant conditioning of verbal behavior, which according to Skinnerian theory is identical in form to the operant conditioning of animal behavior.[27] A person first emits certain *verbal operants* as sounds, and these are then shaped by the language community within which he lives—mediated by the instructions of parents and other significant persons as he matures. According to Skinner, we do not first "think" about something, formulate a premise on whatever it refers to, and then express our thoughts to others in speech (symbolizing meaning; see Chapter 4, p. 51). We behave operantly in speech, and our so-called thoughts are themselves the effects (signalizing meaning; see Chapter 4, p. 51) of past shaping rather than the original sources of behavioral control that the mythology of "autonomous man" tells us they are.[28] We literally waggle our mouths and make sounds without ever being that self, me, or I that we think we are. As a *person* we just do not enter into the determination of our behavior.[29] We humans like rats and pigeons are controlled and not controlling in behavior.

This remarkable view was to be given empirical support by an experimental procedure introduced in the mid-1950s by Joel Greenspoon.[30] Although variations in its design have since taken place, the fundamental idea has remained the same and it goes like this: A person is brought into an experimental room, seated, and asked to begin saying words aloud spontaneously. That is, the words do not have to follow any order so that whatever pops into mind is all right. The subject therefore begins saying words, one at a time. These are taken by the experimenter as emitted verbal operants and electronically recorded for later analysis because the aim of the experiment is to find out how many *plural nouns* a subject produces over three time periods of ten minutes each.

The first time period is considered a "base rate" estimate. The experimenter, who is present in the room with the subject throughout, does nothing but sit by passively and observe the subject stating words. But during the second period of ten minutes' duration he becomes verbally active. Each time a subject states a plural noun (e. g., trees, eyes, women) the experimenter says *mmm-hmm* aloud. This is taken as a reinforcer of the rate of plural noun emission, a contingent circumstance which according to Skinnerian theory acts like any reinforcement to increase automatically the behavior which has produced it. This is just like dropping a food pellet into the container when the rat presses the lever. In the last ten-minute period the experimenter once again falls silent and the subject is encouraged to go right on with what he was doing. The whole experiment lasts thirty minutes.

What do we learn? If the plural nouns of our subject's emissions are tabulated from our recordings and graphed over the three ten-minute segments we find that the number recorded in the first period steadily rises over the second period, and then gradually falls off in the third period, although we can still see a residual influence of the experimenter's *mmm-hmm* holding true at the close of the experiment. If we are not careful to keep the independent variable (voicing *mmm-hmm* or not) separate from our theory of how this manipulation works, we might think that the dependent variable (number of plural nouns verbalized) was an efficiently caused "effect." In other words, we must refrain from confounding our experimental method and our theoretical explanation of the "facts" observed. Yet, this is precisely the error which the operant conditioners made. They began to publicize the Greenspoon experiment as evidence for the (efficient-cause) shaping of human behavior.

Right from the beginning, critics charged that in making the obvious hint of an *mmm-hmm* following a verbal noun in the second period the experimenter had probably cued the subject, letting him in on the purpose of the study. This was one of those experimenter effects which Rosenthal later studied (refer above, p. 104). But Greenspoon denied this charge, claiming that he had held a post-experimental interview with his subjects and not enough of them knew the experiment's purpose to account for the positive findings. However, as later events were to demonstrate, the interview given by Greenspoon was not sophisticated enough. For example, he overlooked the possibility that a subject may have been verbalizing according to an assumption which called for plural nouns but which was not specifically aimed at producing plurals. Assume a subject had heard the *mmm-hmm* after saying "books" and then "pencils." He might well have jumped to the conclusion that the experimenter was looking for "things in a schoolhouse" and gone on reciting blackboards, chairs, students, and so on without ever really discovering the actual purpose of the study. He would appear to have been conditioned to emit plural nouns so far as the data collected by Greenspoon are concerned. But this would be untrue!

Even more important than such correlated but incorrect hypotheses is the fact that, as Orne has taught us, the role of being a good subject does not include admitting that we have guessed the experimenter's intent. The good subject follows the canons of scientific objectivity or pretends to do so even when he has some hint of what is probably going on. Of course, there are times when the ethics of being a subject works against the experimental hypothesis. This was highlighted in one experiment where a subject admitted that she had caught on to the connection between saying a plural noun and the *mmm-hmm* reinforcer but did not comply and "get conditioned" because she thought the experimenter was unethically trying to bring about the results rather than permitting them to emerge spontaneously.[31]

In order to get such admissions from subjects a highly sophisticated post-experimental interview is required, and it was not until L. Douglas DeNike,[32] Don E. Dulany,[33] and Charles D. Spielberger[34] began refining such procedures that we really began to appreciate the role of subject awareness in the outcome of a conditioning study. Once such improved interviews had been worked out it was soon evident that the reason psychologists find operant conditioning working on human beings is because those subjects who catch on to the connection between the correct response (plural noun) and the contingent reinforcer (*mmm-hmm*) make the graphed lines for the group studied rise and fall as observed. And, those subjects who do not catch on, who are unaware of the experimenter's intent, *do not condition!*

There are occasional studies that appear in the literature in which it is claimed that operant conditioning has been achieved without awareness. The argument then comes down to whether the post-experimental interview was adequate or not. But even with such occasional findings to the opposite, no psychologist who professes to be scientifically well-informed today can deny that the *vast preponderance* of data on the question suggests that it is the human subject's awareness of the response-reinforcement contingent relationship which makes operant conditioning possible. This awareness does not make it *necessary*, however, as the work by Monte M. Page[35] beautifully demonstrates. Page devised a way in which to tell whether or not subjects in mid-procedure had caught on to the response-reinforcement relationship. He soon learned that —as the ethical subject mentioned above—not all of the people who catch onto the design will conform to what is expected of them in "getting conditioned." Some know that plural nouns are called for but refuse to emit (*sic*) them. Page decided to see if he could challenge those who were not conforming to reveal this fact in mid-experiment. He first classified subjects under operant verbal conditioning into three categories while they were being tested: i. e., those who were aware and cooperating (getting conditioned), those who were aware but uncooperative (not getting conditioned) and those who were simply unaware of the response-reinforcement relationship altogether (also not getting conditioned).

After identifying these three types of subjects, Page, who used the reinforcer *good* instead of *mmm-hmm*, stopped the experiment for a moment in the middle and asked his subjects to make him do the opposite of what he was then doing. Thus, to the aware and cooperating subjects he said "Make me stop saying good," and to the aware and uncooperative as well as to the unaware subjects he said "Make me start saying good." This is all he said, and then the procedure continued on as before. Immediately, with the very next verbal statements, the operant graph lines of his aware-cooperative subjects and his aware-uncooperative subjects *crisscrossed* so that he did not even need to use statistical tests to make the point that these subjects knew precisely what was going on and that they could "get conditioned" or "not get conditioned" at will. In the meantime, the unaware subjects who were challenged in mid-experiment to make the experimenter say *good* fumbled on as before without increasing their operant level. It does not strain credulity to see in such findings evidence for the play of a dialectic in human behavior. Subjects who conceptualize the task accurately still have the option of going along with the meaningful course of behavior indicated by the task premise, *or not*. If the nature of human mentation is to affirm a course of action that might *in principle* have gone another way, then the findings on operant conditioning are in support of such a telic image of the person rather than in contradiction to it. The teleologist has every right to ask: "How can Skinnerians go on pretending that a telic factor is not involved in their so-called manipulation of people when their own experiments can so easily be interpreted as supporting this kind of factor?"

In responding to a question like this we find the operant conditioners doing what everyone does when the strictly empirical facts seem to be going against them. That is, they begin reaching for already accepted theoretical principles to argue away the anomalous evidence. And in the process, the tough-minded Skinnerians begin to lose that second point referred to above (p. 115) as their empirical purity, because they must necessarily fall back on what is *not* being seen in order to salvage what *is* being seen. For example, Skinner claims that: ". . . the basic fact is that when a person is 'aware of his purpose,' he is feeling or observing introspectively a condition produced by reinforcement."[36] Skinner has never proven this "basic fact," of course. He wants us to believe in his world view, and accept as plausible (procedural evidence) that at some time in the past, subjects now behaving before us in an experiment have been *unknowingly* shaped into being the knowing subjects we find them to be under direct observation. But if we insist on staying strictly with those empirical facts which he has always favored, and remind ourselves that he has defined a verbal operant as "behavior which operates on the environment and produces reinforcing effects,"[37] there can be no doubt but that Skinner's contention about what produces what is dead wrong. The direction of observed learning is always from awareness *to* production of reinforcement and never vice versa (with the proviso discussed above concerning a minority of the research findings).

That is, we first hear the subject in an operant-conditioning experiment saying to himself "I think the trick is to say a plural noun and then he [experimenter] makes that *mmm-hmm* sound or says *good*, so I'll give it a try" and *then*—thanks to the instrumentality of the subject voicing the plural noun— we hear the experimenter making the predicted *"reinforcer."*

If we do not first hear the subject voicing the verbal operants about what he expects to happen (he could even speak to us as he goes along, figuring things out aloud[38]) then we do not hear the experimenter's voicing of *mmm-hmm* or *good*. And for some subjects we would even hear the verbal operant "I know he wants me to say plural nouns, but I'm going to have some fun and not go along." Here again, we find the operant verbal responses *working* even though from the experimenter's point of view there is no verbal shaping going on. In still other instances we hear the subject saying, "I wonder what this is all about; maybe he wants me to use words beginning with the letter S." This verbal operant *also* leads to provable findings in the electrical recordings, where we find the subject proffering words like suds, silky, suddenly, and sticks without really finding the connection between some of them and the experimenter's verbal behavior.

From the point of view of a teleologist there is absolutely no difference between these three kinds of human actions, but the operant conditioner would find significant differences here. For example, one of the earliest counters to the awareness findings by the operant conditioners was that since a fair number of admittedly aware subjects never changed their behavior to go along with the experimental manipulation, these statements of awareness were not really important to behavior.[39] A distinction was drawn between learning (involving awareness) and performance (involving measured operant level), implying thereby that performance was all that behavioristic psychology had to account for. Page's findings demolished this argument, as it seems to have challenged the universality of Orne's good-subject role. Subjects are not all as prone to assume the "good" side of this role as Orne made it appear. There are doubtless always a fair number who take delight in playing the "bad" (mischievous, disdainful, bored, etc.) subject, and, with the increasing sophistication of college students regarding psychology, over the years we are not likely to see this darker side of the subject role decline in frequency.

⚹ Probably the most common defense of non-telic theory in operant conditioning studies on humans involves what is called the *discriminative stimulus*. Behaviorists are always drawn to the stimulus because this is how they have been schooled to think about behavior or "responsivity." Responses need stimuli to make them happen in efficient-cause fashion. Even though Skinnerian psychology has de-emphasized the importance of this triggering mechanism (see Chapter 5, p. 88), there is still a lurking need to find the stimulus antecedent or some equivalent of the responses made—if for no other reason than to facilitate the manipulation of the organism's behavior. Sometimes this concern over the stimulus is framed as the need for organisms to clearly understand what is being input. The operant conditioner will say: "Of course awareness is important to behavior. This merely demonstrates that a clear signal is needed for a response to occur. No organism reacts until its signal is clearly received."

If this is the case, then how do we account for Page's finding that some subjects do not condition when the reception has been "loud and clear"? More to the point: It is *never* a question of clear reception in these studies. *All* subjects hear the experimenter saying *mmm-hmm* or *good*. We can attach electrical equipment to their ears and prove that the tympanic membrane of their inner ear is conveying receptions. What subjects must become aware of is the *pattern* of relationship— i. e., the meaning!—existing between their verbalization and the experimenter's verbalization. We are talking of formal-cause determination here (plus final), and not simply of material and efficient causes—although they too are involved in the mechanics of the complete act.

What, then, is the discriminative stimulus? This refers to a cue which is presumably distinguished by the subject in the process of operant conditioning *other* than the reinforcement stimulus. For example, if we were to both deliver a food reinforcer and flash a light on certain of the lever depressions emitted by a rat, this additional stimulus could facilitate the rat's learning. It would have a food stimulus as reinforcer but *also* a discriminative stimulus of a light to indicate something about the reinforcing circumstance. Skinner emphasizes that even though a discriminative stimulus affords us some control over the organism, "It does not then elicit the [operant] response as in a reflex; it simply makes it more probable that it will occur again. . . ."[40] An example in human behavior might be the woman who emits sobbing behavior whenever she wants special consideration (a form of reinforcer) from others. Since she occasionally gets this consideration from men but never from women, we observe her in time "turning on the tears" only in the company of men. Men are discriminated as stimuli from women, but the operant level of sobbing is kept active by the special consideration she receives. Even so, it would be possible for us to control her sobbing behavior by managing the sex of those around her when she faces a problem.

Because the discriminative stimulus, once established, always occurs before the operant response (the woman first sees a man and then sobs) it so happens that many operant conditioners permit themselves to think of this as a stimulus-response sequence. Then when they manipulate the discriminative stimulus to control the behavior of the person, they have the illusion of efficiently causing the resultant behavioral manipulation. This efficient-cause interpretation of what takes place is seriously flawed on at least two counts. First, since Skinner admits that these discriminative stimuli do not elicit operant responses like sobbing in efficient-cause fashion, there has to be an unnamed causal determination in acts which profess to manipulate through their use. One determination we can see is purely formally causal, in that there is a correlation between the tears and the sex of those in proximity to the weeping woman (recall Skinner's Machian critique, Chapter 5, p. 85). We can also draw a parallel to the football coach (see Chapter 5, p. 69) and suggest that the woman is maneuvering for an advantage in discriminating between the sexes as she does. This brings in a final-cause determination to account for the data actually observed. Surely there is nothing in the facts of behavioral manipulation to counter these non-mechanistic interpretations of how a discriminative stimulus might work in the psychology of the human being.

Second, and more to the point of Skinner's basic style of explanation, the discriminative stimulus can only exist because the operant response has made it what it "is." If operant behavior is behavior which operates on the environment to produce reinforcing effects then *pari passu* it creates the discriminative stimulus. To speak of controlling behavior based on stimuli which this behavior has itself earlier controlled into existence is to put the cart before the horse. There has to be some basis for explaining *why* these discriminative stimuli were created in the first place. If we do not consider these questions then as operant conditioners we ensure that any control of behavior which we bring about in the person will be shrouded in our own ignorance and arrogance. We essentially say: "I don't care if the person is a telic organism or not. I prefer to consider him a complex machine and just so long as my manipulations work in a predictable fashion he *is* a machine no matter what other factors are at play."

We have not yet considered the role of awareness in Pavlovian conditioning. In one of the most thorough reviews of this topic in the psychological literature, William F. Brewer has shown beyond reasonable doubt that—except for a few still debated instances—Pavlovian conditioning in humans *does not occur* unless the subject becomes aware of the relationship between the conditioned stimulus and the unconditioned stimulus.[41] The person does not have to be aware of the particular response he makes (though often he is), because in some cases this is totally reflexive in nature. For example, the *galvanic skin response* or GSR is a measure of the resistance to electrical conductance in the skin brought on by autonomic nervous system reactions. It is noticeable during states of emotion and can be induced by shocking a subject electrically. Were we to conduct such a conditioning experiment the unconditioned stimulus could be an electro-shock, the conditioned stimulus might be a light (which we flash just before shocking the person), and the response to be conditioned would be the GSR. As numerous studies have already noted, we would find that only those subjects who become aware of the relationship between the conditioned and unconditioned stimuli—i. e., who say to themselves something like "Every time that light flashes I get shocked"—actually conditioned the GSR to the light. Subjects who do not make the connection do not "get conditioned."

The earlier Pavlovian conditioners had never confronted this question. They either worked with animals or considered it poor science to rely on the *verbal report* of human subjects. They tried to keep totally extraspective in their theories, and most accepted the Watsonian view that the human being was an organic machine. As in operant conditioning, it is not necessary for a subject to have the precise relationship between a conditioned and an unconditioned stimulus in mind. He can be going on a wrong hypothesis, but just so long as his assumption is close to what the experimenter is trying to accomplish, the desired experimental effects come about.

When the response to be conditioned is motoric rather than autonomic the subject can readily prevent its occurrence following conditioning. For example, instead of the GSR (autonomic) we might have conditioned a subject's finger-withdrawal response (motoric) to a light by using shock. The subject rests his finger on an electrified stand and once he knows that the light (occurring first) and the shock bear a meaningful relationship he will be seen quickly removing his finger from the stand before it is electrified—using the flashing light as his conditioned stimulus. However, assuming that the shock is not extremely painful he can also *stop* removing his finger at any time given the suggestion to do so. Presumably, he could do this "at will" even if the experimenter had not suggested the possibility to him. It is somewhat more difficult to do this when the unconditioned stimulus is a puff of air aimed at the eye and the eyeblink motoric response is used as the conditioned response. But even here many subjects can when asked keep their eyes open after classical conditioning has been established and suffer the puff of air blown into their eyes.[42]

Finally, on the other side of the coin, subjects who are told from the outset exactly what the unconditioned and conditioned stimuli are can begin showing this conditioning "right off." They do not need any shaping trials to get them fixed into a mechanical pattern of cause and effect. Simply knowing what the experiment is aiming at is enough to fix the classical conditioning response.

Brewer has some excellent criticisms to make of the disclaimers which conditioning advocates have advanced in denigrating the role of awareness.[43] For example, the charge has been made that in conducting a post-experimental interview with subjects, awareness itself is suggested to them. If so, counters Brewer, why is it that only those subjects who have become conditioned in the study proper report having this awareness? If interviews bring on awareness then all types of subjects should report it because all types are given the post-experimental interview. Another charge made against awareness is that it is unparsimonious as a theoretical explanation. It makes sense when we consider human beings, but cannot be applied to animals, and in science we must have a single theory for all organisms. To this, Brewer boldly retorts that the reverse logic is just as tenable: "Since cognitive theory [i. e., explanations relying on awareness] holds for humans, it is unparsimonious not to apply it to animals."[44] To do so, of course, would break

the long-standing, extraspective theoretical biases of the laboratory psychologist. It would mean anthropomorphizing and
bringing back all of those dark shadows which fell across
scientific description in the past (see Chapter 2). More importantly, it would mean that experimental psychologists would
have to admit that they have for the past century been propounding an image of the person which is wrong!

The teleologist believes that a science which refuses to
admit the validity of evidence issuing from its own procedures
of validation is no science at all. Fearing labels like *anthropomorphism* is no more dignifying to modern science than fearing the results of scientific investigation dignified the churchmen of ancient times. Such hysterical catchwords, particularly
when they fly in the face of empirical findings, encourage a
climate of repression. Today we have guardians of the scientific trust acting as high priests of a new Inquisition in psychology. Thanks to their misguided convictions concerning what
needs defending, they are continually dismissing empirical evidence which could easily be taken as proof that the human
being is a telic organism.

The reader may rest assured that there is absolutely no
sound evidence proving that human nature is machine-like, or
that people can be covertly controlled by purely psychological
means to do the bidding of some Big Brother at the master controls. Quite the reverse is true. Human beings are manipulated
more through personal convictions, conformities, and perceived advantages in the hoped-for future than they are by the
manipulation of blind needs in the present or environmental
mediations from out of the past. Although these are still powerful sources of control they are telic in nature, final-cause
determinations which cast an altogether different light on what
it means to be a person.

# SEVEN

# The Psychology of Free Will

What is remarkable about the psychological researches conducted on people is that despite years of concerted effort to keep it out, the identity of the person continues to show through such—theoretically biased—accounts to make its presence known. There is an indomitable quality to this identity, which we may now call the *self*. Selfhood implies sameness, a continuity within behavioral events brought forward by the psychological integrity of a person. The self is that continuing strategist which does the predicating of experience, tries to bring off the self-fulfilling prophecy, and ever looks to the grounding assumptions of others for a more favorable advantage in life. It is also the self that orders experience into that understanding which in Chapter 6 we called awareness.

This does not mean that selfhood is always clearly appreciated by the human being who brings forward its continuing assumptions regarding experience. Not all people are equally self-aware, but it *is* possible to cultivate a greater awareness of the self. The self is like a weight of logical inference, bringing forward meanings in which to ground our understanding and make certain behaviors possible—or to negate them altogether. A major aim of this book is to enlarge the reader's self-understanding, thereby not only encouraging an appreciation of what psychological freedom means, but also promoting greater responsibility (i. e., self-determination) for our behavior. Before we can further this aim we have to find a better way in which to describe human behavior than now exists. We need a language of description which is more friendly to a psychology of free will than traditional psychological description has been.

### The Importance of Theoretical Language: Sigmund Freud Versus William James

There is no better way to document the importance of theoretical terms than to contrast two great psychologists who had something to say about free will, yet in ironic fashion the specific theory advanced by each man *countered* what he was aiming to get across. Sigmund Freud, the avowed (psychic) determinist, has left us with a clear route to the telic account of the person, whereas William James, the avowed free-willist, found it impossible to capture in explicit theory what he believed in his heart to be true.

Recall from Chapter 3 (p. 47) that Freud's libido theory can in no way be considered an efficient-cause or material-cause determinism. Now that we have learned something about dialectical meanings and reasonings (see Chapter 4) we can point out something further about Freud's views. His *very first* published paper on a psychological topic, years before he could be called a psychoanalyst in the sense meant today, dealt with the case of Frau Emmy von N. This woman came to Freud complaining of an irresistible impulse to make a "clacking" sound with her tongue. Freud hypnotized her and learned that the symptom began one evening as she sat by the bedside of her young daughter, who was very ill, and Frau Emmy therefore said to herself "Now you must be absolutely quiet, so as not to wake her."[1] In the next instant the clacking symptom commenced!

To explain this sequence of events Freud proposed a theory of *counter-will* making use of *antithetic ideas* and thereby set sail on a long and distinguished career in which he constantly employed dialectical psychological explanations without appreciating that he did so.[2] Frau Emmy's problem was that, due to some kind of emotional fatigue, she relaxed her normal will and permitted the counter-will to put an antithetic idea into behavioral action. Freud said that we all have such oppositional ideas taking form whenever we frame an intention. We say to ourselves "I can [will] do that" and immediately get the reverse suggestion of "I can't [will not] do that." Usually we can hold such self-defeating notions back, but in times of great stress, emotional excitement, or fatigue it is possible for the "other side" of our healthier ideas to take over and literally make themselves known in our behavior *against our will.* This is what had happened to Frau Emmy. From the point of view of her original idea, she did what she did *not* intend to do. But, from the point of view of her antithetic idea she did what she *intended* to do. She brought to bear "I'm going to make a sound," again and again, turning her dialectically opposite intention into a self-fulfilling prophecy—acting willfully albeit in counter-measure to conscious willfulness!

We are speaking here of an early theory, but in the later concepts of defense and symbolical compromise (see p. 46) we find the identical tension of opposition preliminary to dynamic action taking place. Freud was to employ this same dialectical maneuver in his comments on free will—or rather, its *lack* in the personality structure—as follows:

> According to our analyses it is not necessary to dispute the right to the feeling of conviction of having a free will. If the distinction between conscious and unconscious motivation is taken into account, our feeling of conviction informs us that conscious motivation does not extend to all our motor decisions. . . . But what is thus left free by the one side receives its motivation from the

other side, from the unconscious; and in this way determination in the psychical sphere is still carried out without any gap.[3]

    We should remind ourselves at this point that Freud al-
ways insisted his "hard" form of determinism (i. e., admitting
of no indeterminism) was strictly located in the psychic sphere.
He was more the "soft" determinist (i. e., admitting some indeterminism) in the realm of material events, where chance
occurrences can arise.[4] So when he is speaking here about what
he sometimes referred to as the *illusion* of free will[5] Freud is
saying that what one side of the mind claims is a decision freely
made is in fact the effect, outcome, compromise, conclusion,
implication, wish, and so forth, of the *other* side of mind.
Freud is *not* saying that the mind is incapable of deciding,
choosing, or intending. He is *not* saying that underlying efficient causes thrust the mind along as a mediating mechanism.
He *is* saying that mind is a determinate cause in the sequence
of events—and he should have added that it is a final cause of
these events. Instead, for reasons discussed in Chapter 3, he
provided us with the smokescreen libido theory.
    Freud's penchant for the dialectical tension of opposition
is so obvious that we are justified in subsuming under this single conception a host of dichotomies such as the will versus
counter-will, idea versus antithetic-idea, conscious versus unconscious willfulness, and ego versus id. It seems clear that
running through all of these bipolarities is the single message
which Freud had for his Lockean medical colleagues—i. e.,
mind is more than just a one-sided, linear, unidirectional colla-
tion of singularities. Thinking one way, we are always thinking the other, then the other, and another *ad infinitum*. Some
of this convoluted and even perverted thinking goes on at a
primitive level of mind, a level which is not constrained by the
rules of demonstrative logic, a level which is totally inconsis-

tent, arbitrary, and sophistical. Yet, *it wants to gain its ends* just as certainly as does the more proper side.

The Freudian claim is that before actions called behaviors occur there is a mental working-through of intentions, many of which are in conflict, one with the other. Sometimes the total mind is aware of this conflict and sometimes it is not, but *always* a portion of the mind *is* cognizant of what these mental conflicts are all about. In most cases such conflictual intentions are managed without promoting too much confusion, but when they mount in number a person can pay the price in neurosis. The important thing then is to clarify for the individual in psychoanalysis (see Chapter 8) what is involved in his or her unconscious intentions. Hence, though certain portions of mind are often constrained to do things thanks to the direction (psychic determination) of other portions of mind, when we consider the totality of mentation (one-and-many thesis) we always have a clear "that, for the sake of which" description of behavior taking form. And we also have it possible for the individual to *willfully* cause things to come about that might satisfy a preceding, preliminary intention—even a self-harmful intention (as in Frau Emmy's case).

But is this free will? Freud tells us *no*. And then in the next breath he tells us that the unconscious psychic identities (i. e., the id and unconscious portions of the ego and super-ego) can essentially discuss and come to a compromise course of action in directing the conscious psychic identities (i. e., the conscious portions of the ego and superego). A contractual arrangement can be negotiated and brought into behavioral display much as the coach's game plan can be put into action on the field of play (see Chapter 5, p. 69). The compromise struck in this unconscious bargaining session is arrived at through a dialectical examination of "do this" versus "don't do this" (i. e., "do that") until at some point there is a resolution (synthesis) into "let this be done." There is no mechanical or mathematical way in which to arrive at such compromises. In fact, even after a bargain has been struck the party which is set back in the psychic compromise can through guile circumvent the determinism inflicted on consciousness.

To give a slightly frivolous but familiar example, assume that a married man really did hate his mother-in-law. This would probably reflect an unconscious id-hatred on his part, a wish as Freud would call it to see the old woman harmed or even killed. Naturally, it would not do for such wishes to be expressed, and, in the unconscious negotiations a bargain might have been struck in which the consciousness would manifest a kind of sullen disregard of the mother-in-law ("Ignore her and she might go away"). This satisfies the id's hatred to some extent, as well as meets the superego's sense of propriety. No more active form of hostility is displayed until one day, when this man is forced to show his mother-in-law to a chair, he positions it correctly at her side only to say: "Won't you please fall down, *er*, sit down here?" The id had broken its contract, and, using consciousness as backdrop for its bidding, expressed what can only be said to be a freely willed suggestion in the Freudian slip–i. e., let the "old hag" fall down, hard! We tend as Freud did to look at the willful side of things, the consciously determined side, and to forget about the *free* side because it has been generated in unconsciousness. Free will and Freudian psychic determinism are *not* incompatible conceptions.

How different things are when we turn to William James, whose theoretical style was if not devoid of then at least much less colored by the twistings and turnings of the dialectic. James is known for his great interest in spiritual matters. His book *The Varieties of Religious Experience*[6] is a classic in the field. He seems to have struggled to find a satisfactory theoretical explanation of free will, but never succeeded in improving on John Locke's original formulation (see Chapter 5,

p. 82), even though James specifically denied that his outlook on human thought was Lockean.[7]

As an academician, James seems to have taken even more cognizance of scientific proprieties than did Freud. Rather than concocting something like libido and keeping his descriptions totally mentalistic, James made every effort in his textbook on psychology to describe the workings of mentation and behavior *in terms of* the biological and neurological knowledge of his time. Freud tried this on one occasion, but gave up when he found that the uniqueness of human behavior was slipping from his hands in the neurological lingo.[8] In certain of his writings James beautifully captured the phenomenal side of experience. For example, in a famous chapter of his text *The Principles of Psychology*, in which he describes mental activity as a *stream* of thought or consciousness, James notes that words such as "chains" of successive thoughts simply fail to capture the workings of mind. Mental actions flit about from thought to thought like a bird fluttering from one perching to another, backtracking, then coming forward again. This image of an active mentality would have matched a dialectical formulation nicely, but James was critical of dialectics due to his readings in Hegelian philosophy.[9]

Several chapters following the stream-of-thought presentation, after he has discussed the nervous system and how it engages the bodily musculature to produce movement, James takes up the question of willful movements. He bases his argument on the claim that before a voluntary motion is possible in life we must first have a store of memories concerning involuntary motions. We must first move reflexively for a time following birth, and then, having recollected such involuntary movements we are in a position to exert some influence on their direction "the next" time we behave. In this discussion, James is prepared to use a word he found unacceptable earlier in the volume: ". . . where the *chain* [of movements; italics added] is voluntary, we need to know at each movement just *where we are in it*, if we are to will intelligently what the next link shall be."[10] Will is defined as the fixing of attention on some object toward which motion is to be expended in order to bring it about in behavior. A willed movement is always preceded by an idea of itself, and a consent to let its implications come about. The effort of attention is crucial in willful acts, relating particularly to the things which we really are capable of doing. When we lack the power to achieve some end by way of voluntary motions this is a wish.[11] And *free will* comes down to a more sustained fixing of attention; as James expressed it: ". . . the operation of free effort, if it existed, could only be to hold some one ideal object, or part of an object, a little longer or a little more intensely before the mind."[12]

We can anticipate the future through ideas, recalling from the past what has happened to us in motion reflexively. When something is to be done we can attend, hold up on impulsive, involuntary motion, and opt for the more directed course. We do not reach for the fattening piece of pie but redirect our arm's motion in the direction of a less caloric piece of celery. There is very little to choose between this and Locke's original formulation (see Chapter 5, p. 82). James emphasizes a material-cause, involuntary (reflexive) motion occurring first, and Locke emphasizes the efficient-cause inputs of earlier experience, but both treatments lack that dynamic sense of conceptualization, contradiction, and arbitrariness which the Freudian account relies on. It is hard to see a true psychological freedom in this account. We are free to hang fire and then select from among the motions which have happened to us in the past. Because of his commitment to the biological explanation James was forced into a constitutive model, a Lockeanism which all physical accounts share. It is literally impossible to capture the meaning of final causation if one has to express it in terms of material and/or efficient causation. This was James's

dilemma, and in a summary of his views on the technical problems of describing free will he set a discouraging tone:

> My own belief is that the question of free-will is insoluble
> on strictly psychologic grounds. After a certain amount
> of effort of attention has been given to an idea, it is mani-
> festly impossible to tell whether either more or less of it
> *might* have been given or not. To tell that, we should
> have to ascend to the antecedents of the effort, and defin-
> ing them with mathematical exactitude, prove, by laws
> of which we have not at present even an inkling, that the
> only amount of sequent effort which could *possibly* com-
> port with them was the precise amount which actually
> came. Measurements, whether of psychic or of neural
> qualities, and deductive reasonings such as this method of
> proof implies, will surely be forever beyond human
> reach.[13]

Though James goes on to say that he personally chooses
to believe in free will, there is surely little here for a telic psychologist to pin his hopes on. Note that James confounds theory with method in presuming that antecedent laws somehow
track the level of effort required to attend in holding something before the mind (i. e., attend in manifesting free will).
By giving up on psychological explanation in favor of a kind
of psycho-*statistical* or psycho-*actuarial* rendering, James
sounds very much like a modern Lockean. Once again, this
was not what he would have preferred to say about human
behavior. He just comes off sounding much less telic in his
formal theory than does Freud. When methods are mixed into
theories it is easy to make human behavior seem a compendium
of unilinear dimensions, with discrete numbers falling into a
sum total. But as we hope to demonstrate in the remaining
pages of this chapter, there *is* a psycho-*logical* explanation of
behavior which readily provides us with a solution to the free-

will problem. James reasoned in the wrong direction. We must move *from* mathematics *to* (psycho-)logic if we are to understand human nature.

## Responses or Telosponses?

We must not make the Jamesian mistake and presume that in order to explain psychological freedom it must be framed in the same language we use to describe biological and neurological structures. Nor should it be framed in the language of statistics or actuarial prediction. James like all modern psychologists has been caught up in the Cartesian geometric motility, as projected onto physical reality by Newtonian mechanics (see Chapter 2, p. 24). Behavior is therefore equated with motion, and motion is in turn broken up into discrete, chain-like units that link together as so-called responses. These units are attracted to other units called stimuli based upon the extent of contiguity existing between them—much as Newton's law of gravity was based on the distance between objects of various sizes. The more frequently these discrete units of responses and stimuli occur together in proximity, the more likely it is that they will be forged into at least a temporary chain of predictable succession. In order to track these orders of the chaining links we rely on mathematics, identifying the stimulus unit as the independent variable and the response unit as the dependent variable. The statistical law resulting predicts the relationship between units as the law of gravity predicts the course of a meteor moving through a sky of gravitational fields, heading blindly toward its destiny.

The only possible conception of psychological freedom which can issue from this view is as statistical unpredictability, and we have already found this interpretation severely wanting (see Chapter 5, p. 81). As we learned in Chapter 6, recent psychological research has proven beyond reasonable doubt that the "human meteor" is not nearly so blind as psychology had previously assumed. The extraspective perspective of statistics overlooks the fact that the statistician has an introspective slant on things as well. Mathematicians can and do make diverse assumptions about the measured relationships between items in space. Whitehead and Russell have proven that mathematics and logic are the *same* activity at certain levels of abstraction.[14] But this singularity is framed on logic's home ground. It is the predicating nature of logic, with its tautological assumptions of the sort "two halves equal a whole" that makes mathematics possible.

Of course, this is a demonstrative logic where the law of contradiction holds so that the numbers always add up correctly. Traditional Newtonian science was predicated exclusively on demonstrative logic, and when the psychologist looks to mathematical relationships (laws) between independent and dependent variables for a complete understanding of behavior he ensures that this Newtonian predication will never be violated. Dialectical logic will never be included in the human image. But how can we have an accurate psychology of the person without due recognition of the fact that people do reason dialectically? People simply are not unilinear, chain-like successions of motion-events to be calculated and tabulated without consideration of the *telos*, the reason for the sake of which this motion is being expended. They are self-determining, albeit often inconsistent agents of their behavior.

The only way in which to capture the complete person is to begin thinking of behavior as something other than just responsivity. We must drop our exclusive reliance on this way of describing behavior and search about for a new term, one which might capture the idea that human beings *do* predicate their understanding in that *pro forma* sense of the Kantian model (see Chapter 4, p. 63). This more logical view of behavior would then open up the possibility of explaining how individuals are free to follow the implications of their predicated meanings, *or not*. Rather than being directly controlled from past events acting as a chain of (efficient) cause-effects, the person would be portrayed as the researches of Chapter 6 found him to be—i. e., as an anticipator, conceptualizer, constantly behaving for the sake of expected ends. As a first step in changing our view of humanity let us henceforth think of the person as behaving according to *telosponses* as well as responses. We can define this concept as follows:

> A *telosponse* is the person's taking on (predicating, premising) of meaningful items (images, language terms, judgments, etc.) relating to a referent acting as a purpose for the sake of which behavior is then intended.[15]

This is our final-cause conception to be placed alongside the mechanist's efficient-cause conception. To telospond is to behave "for the sake of" rather than "in response to." We suggest in the above definition that the term *purpose* be confined to a concept's meaning, and that *intention* be used when an organism is behaving for the sake of such purposes. For example, a pencil is a practical tool devised by humans for their use. The pencil serves a purpose. But the pencil *qua* pencil knows no purpose (as the chair of Chapter 2 had no purpose; see p. 14). It is the human being, acting telosponsively who behaves for the sake of this purposive meaning and thereby intends it to come about. The human picks up the pencil, writes with it, or is merely cognizant of the fact that a pencil is in close proximity and might therefore be used at some point in the future. He is not hanging fire, recalling past reflexive movements or letting the probabilities of past inputs play out a bit longer before some well-rehearsed course of habit runs to its conclusion. He is *aware* of meaningful possibilities in the environment even when it is unlikely that any action (motion, responsivity) will be taken in light of these potential alternatives.

Mechanistic accounts pretend that such intended mean-

ings projected as mere possibilities *do not exist.* Just looking at
the pencil and saying to oneself "Oh, there's a pencil and I'd
better keep that in mind because I might need it" *never happens* in the mechanistic theoretical account when the pencil is
not actually picked up and used in the observable moments to
follow. But when the person actually does use the pencil then
this "observed action" is taken as a reality, an event "sampled"
from a parameter of all such possible "responses" in the person's supposed behavioral repertoire. But has the complete
and accurate story of the person's behavior been told here? It
has not, because there is no effort being made to understand
the preliminaries of behavior, the predicating purposes being
aligned by the telic organism before overt behavior actually
takes place. To pretend that there are no such preliminaries is
to fly in the face of hard scientific evidence to the opposite
(see Chapter 6).

    As an example of how a teleologist might account for be-
havior in contrast to a behaviorist we might analyze the simple
act of leaving a room. The behaviorist would begin his account
by suggesting that there were a number of responses being
made here to the door stimuli, as mediated by past generalizations from related door stimuli and the reinforcements attained thereby in successfully leaving previous rooms. This
would be an efficient-cause determinism, of course. The teleologist, on the other hand, would suggest that the predicate
ordering of "There is the door" and "I wish to go" coalesced
meaningfully into the eventual "that" for the sake of which
behavior that can be observed by a third party (i. e., extraspectively) as "leaving the room" took place.

    The recognition of a door and the intention to leave are
taken as logical *precedents*—i. e., occurring first in meaningful
order (see Chapter 4, p. 56). Putting these precedents together,
the person must necessarily or *sequaciously* (i. e., meaningful
extension of what has gone before) behave as intended and
make the effort to leave the room. This precedent-sequacious

line of logical determination is telic. Behavior is being carried on telosponsively not responsively, under predication instead of mediation, in *pro-forma* rather than *tabula-rasa* fashion.

## Freedom of the Will

Granting that there may be something like a telosponsivity taking place in human behavior, how does this translate into a freedom of the will? If human beings enact meaning-extensions *sequaciously*, then since this word means a "slavish compliance" or subservience on what has been affirmed to begin with as a precedent, we could not place a concept of freedom on this side of the logical development. Sequacious factors would meet the willful or "will power" usage which so many people assign to a free-will concept. They also get at that psychic determinism which Freud emphasized (refer above, p. 132). But how could freedom be said to enter the course of telosponsivity? It arises because we must always appreciate that in order for predication to occur—precedent meanings to be affirmed— it is necessary for the self to affirm them. And if, as we already have shown, the meanings to be affirmed are often bipolar then it follows that a self-determination in this affirmation process is always free to generate alternatives dialectically, resulting thereby in what Kant once called "transcendental freedom" from the chain of efficient causality.[16]

Recall that in the Kantian model it is held that the individual can exercise a transcendental dialectic to think his way from what is to what is not several times over (see Chapter 4). Beginning in some meaningful understanding, let us say A, he can reason to not-A and thence to *not*-not-A *ad infinitum* until what he is considering mentally bears no relationship to the original environmental input (Locke) or even to the recalled involuntary movements (James). Precisely where this reasoning by opposites ends is up to the person, and this may not occur in strictly bipolar terms. That is, since the person *also* reasons demonstratively he can as if in metric fashion "split up" the distance between flat oppositions and take a middle ground in some fashion—not exactly a synthesis but something approaching this. We are using distance figuratively, of course, because there is no more literal space involved here than there is literal motion in mathematical space.

Returning to our example of leaving a room, if a person "sees" a door in reality he also has it as a dialectical implication in this immediate perception of "no-door" or "not-door." This might occur to him as "Maybe that isn't the doorway out of this room, maybe it's just a closet." To save the embarrassment of walking boldly into a closet the person might therefore take a tentative "peek" into the space beyond the door before striding through the aperture. But now, he could even reason in fantasy to the opposite of the precedent premise "there is the doorway out" and think his way out through a wall or by jumping through a window. The demands of further reality perceptions would counter such alternatives, of course, but this does not detract from the fact that mentation is constantly swimming through a sea of possibilities.

In other aspects of life the person might indeed innovate a new course of events by not allowing the constraints of reality to confine him like this. People have been known to find their way out of burning buildings by looking coolly for alternatives while others beat their fists in dying desperation against a locked door. And in the broader aspects of life we are constantly called on to offer our unique interpretation to the "facts" facing us. We, in truth, make up our own facts based upon how we conceptualize these phenomenal items predicatively and then literally *create* those circumstances which Rosenthal was to consider self-fulfilling prophecies (see Chapter 6, p. 105).

This brings us to the core issue in free-will theory, framed by axiologists as follows: "An act is free if and only if the agent [i. e., person] could have done otherwise, *all circumstances remaining the same.*"[17] *If* it can be shown how things might indeed have gone another way than they did, given identical circumstances, *then* freedom is established. But this is *precisely* the case in a dialectical set of circumstances! Things are always the same (one) but also different (many) as a potentiality, possibility, or implication. Phenomenal experience is *never* as unipolar in meaning as the demonstrative theoreticians would have it. Though what eventually happens is dependent upon the precedent meanings affirmed, *other* precedents could equally as well have been affirmed.

There is an interesting parallel here in the writings of Skinner, who once found unacceptable something claimed by philosopher Karl Popper. Popper was challenging the unidirectional potentials for controlling people through normative influence. Behaviorists tend to think of norms as tantamount to efficiently caused strings which, extending down from the supra-individual level, somehow manipulate people like marionettes to behave as the "system" or "society" or "culture" would have them behave. Popper challenged this environmentalist view when he observed:

> In the face of the sociological fact that most people adopt the norm "Thou shalt not steal," it is still possible to decide to adopt either this norm, or its opposite; and it is possible to encourage those who have adopted the norm to hold fast to it, or to discourage them, and to persuade them to adopt another norm. *It is impossible to derive a sentence stating a norm or a decision from a sentence stating a fact;* this is only another way of saying that it is impossible to derive norms or decisions from facts.[18]

After citing this Popperian view Skinner opines: "The conclusion is valid only if indeed it is 'possible to adopt a norm or its opposite.' Here is autonomous man playing his most awe-inspiring role, but whether or not a person obeys the norm

'Thou shalt not steal' depends upon supporting contingencies, which must not be overlooked."[19] It is absolutely essential for Skinner to interpret norms as the strings of efficient causality, because he has achieved considerable recognition (and notoriety) by contending that societies could be managed through manipulation of the contingencies sustaining their normative behavioral patterns. His fictional account *Walden Two*[20] is the story of a brilliant, unselfish scientist who establishes a utopian community through the Promethean task of setting such norms into order for a small body of people who are manipulated thereby into communal bliss. Since the people in Walden Two do not reason dialectically, which means they do not telospond but merely respond, there is never any problem about keeping them in order. Basing his contentions on a similar image of humanity, Skinner has gone on to advocate the design of cultures for real and not just imaginary communities (see Chapter 5, p. 96). The Popperian critique, which may be seen as a dialectical point of order in this program for a managed society, strikes at the heart of Skinner's mechanistic fantasy.

Recall that the research literature surveyed in Chapter 6 was also on the side of Popper, for it shows that whether a person adopts the norm "Thou shalt be a good subject" (Orne) or "Thou shalt be a bad subject" (Page) is up to the person and *not* the experimenter! The lesson here is that at some point in the logical ordering of events, a person as an identity—a self!—either affirms some predication or he does not. And before this affirmation takes place it is not wrong to speak of a period of *arbitrariness* in behavior, however fleeting. In fact, it is difficult to see how behavior could ever be free if it could not at least occasionally be arbitrary. To be arbitrary simply means that the grounds can be changed from decision point to decision point. For example, an employer might let it be known that he has an open policy for promotions in his company only to make an immediate exception on some blood-isthicker-than-water grounds and promote a nephew to some position for which he is not qualified. The employer has been arbitrary in this action, but his decision is not without its grounds.

Sometimes our taking on of a normative predication is so clear and certain that we fail to recognize the possibility of other alternatives. We can even be convinced that in such instances our thinking is automatic, virtually a cause-effect affair in the efficient-cause sense. We highly value life so we accept the norm "Thou shalt not kill." Most of us find it unthinkable that we would ever desire in our hearts to kill another human being. Yet, on deeper consideration at least some of us could find exceptions to this ethical rule. More generally, however, there are many times in our behavior when we realize that what will follow in the situation about to take place is going to be up at least in part to what our position will be. The teenaged daughter wants to know if she can go for a brief drive with her boyfriend, and mother is frowning at the prospect because the daughter has been fevered earlier in the day and still looks a bit peaked. What does father think? The position he takes here is not always as contingently clear-cut as Skinner pretends. The father knows what it will be like to have his wife irritated and he knows what it means to have a teenaged daughter moping about the house. He also knows the reverse circumstances, of a wife satisfied or a daughter sent happily on her way. What to do?

The father's eventual grounds can be selected after much study, or completely at whim, but given one grounding predication ("I had better humor the wife this time") or another ("A drive with the boyfriend can raise a girl's spirits") what follows in precedent-sequacious fashion is necessarily determined. Indeed, all kinds of ancillary arguments will be concocted by the father after the fact to support the position he takes on the question. But the point is, so long as he can selectively affirm the grounds for the sake of which he behaves "this time" he is equally free the "next time" to affirm different grounds when the wife and daughter approach him in a comparable situation. Indeed, the father could have affirmed otherwise in the present situation where all circumstances would clearly have been the same.

It is possible to interpret "all circumstances remaining the same" (see above, p. 144) to mean *after* such an affirmation has been made. This would be an error, of course, because as we made clear above, the logical succession of events always includes this pre-affirmation aspect. If circumstances remaining the same means only those after affirmation then we as psychologists would be failing to present the full range of circumstances if we overlooked the father's dialectical ruminations preliminary to affirmation. Once again, if a psychologist is a psycho-actuary then such ruminations do not exist because the rejected predication is never made known in actual behavior so it cannot be "sampled" and tabulated. As psycho-logicians we must not treat such aspects of the choice situation as if they did not exist for it is at this point in the circumstances that we discover the person's freedom to act.

We must also appreciate that even if the person does not take personal responsibility to examine alternative grounds but simply goes along with things as immediately perceived, this does not remove the telic progression from his behavior. Assume that the father had taken one look at the wife's negative expression and immediately said to the daughter, "No, honey, I think you had better stay home tonight" without reflection. This would simply be a case of taking over or conforming with another person's grounding precedent. The determination here is still telic. With all these factors in mind we can now define free will as follows:

> *Free will* is a non-technical way of referring to the capacity which telosponding organisms have dialectically to alter meanings which they affirm as predications

(grounding premises) in the course of behavior. We are free organisms to the extent that we can rearrange the grounds for the sake of which we are determined. Before affirmation we can speak of freedom, and, after affirmation we can speak of will(power) in the meaning-extension to follow. In short, free will and psychic determinism are opposite sides of the same coin.

Free will and self-determination are not only made possible by, but are absolute requirements of telosponsivity. The human being is by nature required to "take a position on" the passing scenes of his or her life, and therefore choice or decision is *always* involved in this process, even when this selective process is personally unnoticed. Personal responsibility enters the picture when the human being recognizes this selective process, a process which at heart is one of *selecting the grounds for the sake of which one will be determined*. The realities of life may limit the grounds which can be predicated (affirmed as premise), so that except in fantasy the poor man cannot drive a foreign sports car or the plain woman cannot become glamorous. But always, granted the facts as given, there is a dialectical thought process in human nature permitting men and women to do something about the focus of their life motivations. When we come right down to it, this "something" involves a close examination of the grounding assumptions, beliefs, values, etc., which premise behavior.

By examination the poor man can learn that sports cars do not a heaven make, and the plain woman can see that beauty is more than physiognomy. Of course, there is no guarantee that these more "wholesome" outcomes will result. After examination the poor man may decide to steal in order to get his automobile and the plain woman may make arrangements for plastic surgery. Even so, if the grounding assumptions have been given considered examination and now a life course set through personal decision, we have—or often have—a different kind of individual than before. More importantly for present purposes, such a self-reflexive examination instructs the person in the role which he or she plays in behavior. It also cements the person to other people because, as we emphasized in the opening chapter of this volume (see p. 6), there are rarely as many uniquely individual groundings for decisions as we would like to believe there are. In the final analysis, human beings are more alike than different in their life assumptions, and it is doubtless because of this that human empathy and understanding are possible.

Though we have been speaking of the human being up to this point there is no claim being made that animals below the human level are totally lacking in the capacity to reason dialectically. It is probable that the dialectical reasoning which makes free will possible is most highly developed in the animals known as *Homo sapiens*. But at some point below this evolutionary level behavior of a completely demonstrative nature was probably complemented by an animal which could reason dialectically as well. At this point, meanings of a bipolar nature arose, and this "higher" animal became a symbol-creating rather than a sign-mediating organism. Arbitrariness was born! This opening of the mind threw the animal's conceptual abilities into disarray, since an awareness now of many different implications or "possibilities" existed, essentially forcing the animal to affirm some one among many possible premises available to it. This animal found it necessary to "take a position" on life experience and not merely "respond" to its unidirectional manipulations.

For example, the animal which was being "naturally" prompted (efficiently caused) to forage for food in trees or alongside a river bank could now appreciate *in this very prompting* that other alternatives were possible, such as descending to the ground or moving off into a plain away from the river. This alternative (choice) was not stumbled upon accidentally, and the "natural selection" here did not occur gradually or blindly but with foresight and an expectation for the gaining of some projected advantage in life. In a real sense, predication was *forced* onto this animal in order to stabilize its widely expanding grasp of events, to affirm the "one" among the "many" eventualities which dialectical reasoning had thrown open for it. In the highest form of dialectically reasoning animal—*Homo sapiens*—this mental need to fix a "given" alternative (choice, point of view, assumption, the "truth," etc.) stimulated what we now call the social order. Human beings are said to be social animals, but the reason this is probably so is because the human intelligence absolutely must have a confident premise on which to proceed—that is, to telospond. The social norm is not some grand "stimulus in the sky," funneling its manipulative effects into the heads of the masses through external manipulations and reinforcements. The social norm is a mutual "that for the sake of which" (premise) affirmed by all members of a discernible group (small to large in number), lending them a common sense of identity and commitment (the "one") in life.

Until recently it would have been unacceptable to theorize about the evolution of a dialectical reasoning capacity among the higher apes, much less of even lower organisms. But in recent years a handful of investigators have actually begun to communicate with chimpanzees and gorillas, using sign language, the hand speech of the deaf; and their accounts of how such animals adapt to situations and express points of view at variance with what the "environmental stimulus" is then demanding prove very insightful to the teleologist. One such investigator is Dr. Francine Patterson, a psychologist who has taught the female gorilla "Koko" (approximately seven years of age at this writing) to communicate in this fashion. We are amused to read of the capacity which Koko has to play practical jokes on her trainers, such as trying to befuddle the communication in some way just for the "heck" of it (at other times Koko is simply disobedient). In describing one such incident Dr. Patterson writes: "She [Koko] seems to relish the

effects of her practical jokes, often responding exactly opposite to what I ask her to do. One day, during a videotaping
session, I asked Koko to place a toy animal under a bag, and
she responded by taking the toy and stretching to hold it up
to the ceiling."[21]

Though psychologists do not conceptualize such rudi-
mentary (under-above, up-down, etc.) dialectical behaviors
through use of a dialectical theory, this is only because of those
historical scientific traditions which we have already surveyed.
The scientific premise or "model" is unfortunately biased in
the demonstrative direction; however, this should not dissuade
us from reading between the lines in all cases relating to human description. We now have a clear understanding of what
free will means *psychologically* considered. Knowing this
process still does not provide us with the answer to "Which
premise [grounds, truth, predicate assumption, etc.] *ought* I
to affirm" on the questions of life encompassing religious outlooks, political convictions, national loyalties, social prejudices,
life-style preferences, and so on. As we noted in Chapter 1, it
is not for psychology to settle these questions. Our responsibility is to frame as accurate a picture of human nature as is
possible, one which is also consistent with scientific evidence
and widely instructive. We next turn to this latter consideration, of just how instructive a telic human image can be.

# EIGHT

# Cause and Effect in Psychotherapy

With the completion of Chapters 5, 6, and 7 we have framed our interpretation of free will, claiming that this is a psychological outgrowth of the fact that human beings telospond as well as respond in behavior. What we must do now is apply our frame as a predication to some representative areas of study in the human condition. If we are right in the essentials of our scheme then we should be able to see a consistent support for our telic image of the person across these diverse topics. Beginning here in Chapter 8 and extending across Chapters 9, 10, and 11 we will take the reader through a number of relevant areas with this end in view.

Psychology has been used in the correction of all kinds of human behavioral problems, including everything from managing weight loss to the curing of neurotic and psychotic conditions. Many psychologists define their professional role as involving the control and prediction of behavior, and they do not mean this in the scientific sense of validating evidence but in the literal sense of manipulating people into a better state of existence. Others find this desire to control the lives of people objectionable and contrary to human dignity. The major traditions of psychotherapy are the psychoanalytic, the behavioristic, and the existentialistic-phenomenological. In the present chapter we will give each of these traditions a telic analysis and see how well it works.

## Psychoanalysis

Psychoanalysis devolves from the work of three physicians: Sigmund Freud, Alfred Adler, and Carl Gustav Jung. We have already given considerable attention to Freud (Chapter 3, pp. 43-49 and Chapter 7, pp. 129-134), who is the father of psychoanalysis. He established the familiar techniques of dream analysis, free association, reclining on a couch, and so on, all of which are designed to promote *insight* into the neurotic condition. If Freud did not believe that one side (unconscious) or the other (conscious) of mind always telosponded in order to bring behavior about, there would be no point in making insight possible. Insight is another name for the kind of predication a person is employing as he comes at life each day. If the child we used as an example in Chapter 3 (p. 33) grows up without ever having resolved his Oedipal conflict (assuming this is what the problem is) then he might repeatedly "act out" such temper tantrums with a succession of mother figures, several of whom he might marry only to divorce once the psychic charade becomes too much for the spouse to bear. Freud called this the *repetition compulsion* of neurotic behavior. The *fuero* is always being pressed, so the family drama is always re-enacted.

To correct this compulsion to repeat, Freud believed that he must first identify the conflict clearly—for himself *and* the patient—by analyzing the neurotic's dreams, "slips" of the tongue, and just any reveries that might arise while lying on the couch (i. e., during free association). When all of the pieces had been put together in this search for the underlying cause of the neurosis, Freud began to explain it all to the patient. This is called *interpretation* and as Freud once described the process: "The principal point is that I should guess the secret [unconscious dynamic in the case] and tell it to the patient straight out; and he is then as a rule obliged to abandon his rejection of it."[1] The recognition here that "I lust mother" (id wish) is rejected by the conscious side of the personality (ego, superego) because of its repulsive implication. But in time, with persistence and the evidence of more interpretations based on the psychic contents of the patient (dream stories, etc.) the picture becomes clearer and clearer. If the neurotic sticks it out, in time he begins to learn a whole new side to his personality and, with this insight, begins to change his behavior—at least he changes his perspectives concerning his neurosis enough so that its symptoms leave, or if they remain he is not upset by them.

Freud often translated this more psycho-*logical* explanation of neurosis into libido terminology. He suggested that upon entering psychoanalysis the patient withdraws his libido (removes cathexes) from those figures who enter into his neurosis—in this case, mother substitutes—and invests it in the person of the analyst. This results in what is called *transference*, which often takes the form of "falling in love" with the analyst during the early stages of treatment. Then, as the neurotic goes along learning more about his difficulties he begins to withdraw libido from the therapist and to reinvest it in his own person, not selfishly but to build a stronger ego-identity. As this process unfolds the patient may become disdainful or critical of the analyst, resulting in what is called a negative transference (though, in truth, positive and negative transferences go on together throughout the analytical series). Gradually, the patient becomes more objective in relating to the analyst, no longer attributes characteristics to him which are true of other people (like his parents) and, if all goes well, the psychoanalysis ends with the patient "in command" of his own personality thanks to the restructuring of the reclaimed libido. As Freud once summarized this process of turning old repressions into new personality strengths: The "ego is enlarged at the cost of this unconscious."[2]

If we are willing to view human thought as a telosponsive

process, and appreciate that it *makes no difference* to a teleology whether the mind is directed from the conscious or the unconscious level, then we can easily reframe Freudian theory in light of telic theory. Freud was in the business of offering his clients an alternative predication or premise "for the sake of which" they would henceforth think about the meanings of their lives. Because the content of this new predication was so (morally!) upsetting his patients found it initially impossible to intend (the purpose of) his analytical meanings. They resisted his explanations of their neurotic patterns at first, but Freud went along with the sagacity of a detective, poking about in the ashbins of their minds to find clue after clue which eventually fell into place and convinced them against their conscious will that his understanding of their unconscious intentions was right after all. Once the truth was recognized, they usually accepted it for what it was—a child-like fantasy with many reality distortions—and a new telosponsive course then set in. The fuero had been dealt with. The childish predications were put to death. This is without doubt a human teleology, a psychic determination which can both make people ill and then cure them depending upon what meanings are being affirmed at any time in the person's life.

Alfred Adler, who was the first major figure to affiliate with Freud for a time only to break with him because of the over-emphasis on sex in psychoanalysis, took an openly telic view of behavior by emphasizing its goal-directed nature. To understand behavior, said Adler, we must understand a person's goals because: "The goal of mental life of man becomes its governing principle, its *causa finalis*."[3] At an early stage of life, roughly between the ages of three and five, Adler believed that we all put down a kind of "game plan" for the sake of which we then behave. This prototype plan frames our *life style* or the pattern which our life will thenceforth take on. It acts as a complete goal, coloring all that we do in life once it has been affirmed.[4] Some of us become "mother's little helper" and then later, as adults, continue in this style by taking the lead in our community, or work responsibly to bring up our children as solid citizens. Others of us become "Peck's bad boy" and spend a lifetime of mischievous activity gaining the attention of our fellows in a less conventional fashion as the life of the party, practical joker, or general "character" in the group. The life styles which result in severe abnormalities stem from a selfish life plan. Children who are pampered or who refuse to think about others grow up to be the bane of our existence for they have no capacity to love others, or to express social interest in promoting the welfare of all peoples.

The child with the temper-tantrum problems (Chapter 3, p. 33) had probably been one of these pampered babies, Adler would suggest, who put his own interests above those of his siblings or parents. Adler recognized that parents entered into such "dynamics" by spoiling their children, but he did not favor blaming them for the child's pattern. He put the blame for the cause of the neurosis squarely on the individual—Adler's approach was even named *Individual Psychology*—because it is the person who frames a life style subjectively and only he can change it. In his psychotherapy practice Adler used an insight approach much as did Freud, trying through examples drawn from a patient's early recollections, dreams, or even directly observable behavior patterns to show the neurotic just how he was going on a certain premise in life, one which started out in consciousness but now is at work at an unconscious level.

For example, the client who marches into the analyst's office and immediately begins negotiating to change the appointment hour for the next visit is reflecting his power needs, needs which can be traced back to his early family experience in which he probably began competing with a brother for mother's attention (sibling rivalry). There is a *striving for superiority* in such maneuvers, an effort to compensate a strong underlying sense of inferiority. These recurring patterns of behavior are not repetition compulsions in the Freudian sense but are continuing affirmations of a predicated life style. The pampered individual who thinks the world owes him allowances is not repeating his childhood. He has just never taken an alternative predication *since* childhood. Adlerian therapy properly appreciates the final-cause factors in bringing about cures. It seeks to get the neurotic affirming more constructive, unselfish, socially interested premises for the sake of which his behavior can occur, and on the basis of which a lasting personal satisfaction can be achieved.

The last of our "big three" psychoanalysts, Carl G. Jung, also recognized the fundamentally telic nature of the human being. He not only believed that man's mind has evolved along a purposeful line from his early ancestry,[5] but Jung also insisted that libido was itself a telic energy which ever directs the mind toward valued goals: "Life is teleology *par excellence;* it is the intrinsic striving towards a goal, and the living organism is a system of directed aims which seek to fulfil themselves."[6] A unique feature of Jungian psychology is the view that for any behavioral affirmation which the person makes to "be like" in consciousness the dialectical reverse is made to "be like" in the unconscious. For example, a person who consciously strives to be dominant as a conscious ego simultaneously fashions the reverse personality tendency of submissiveness in his unconscious. This opposite of the ego is called the alter-ego or, more commonly, the *shadow.*

Trouble arises in the personality when we fail to recognize and acknowledge our shadow-sides. The racial bigot who projects sexual lust or excessive hostility onto minority-group members has become so one-sided in his psychological development that he fails to see himself in these shadow-characteristics, now being projected onto the "other one" rather than accepted as "part of me." The strategy of Jungian therapy is to unite the two parts of the personality by various means, bringing the person into line with himself—that part which he consciously strives to be and also that unconscious part which he "is" but does not accept being.

Put in telic terms, the person comes to understand that any predication which he affirms in telosponsivity has its opposite possibility (an insight which Freud earlier had in his counter-will theory). And, though we ordinarily are unaware of this dialectical process, the very fact that we select a dimension along which to frame our conscious personality telosponsively means that we have considered the *reverse* possibility as well. This occurs at the free side of the free-to-will ordering of mentation. Jung once summed up his dialectical outlook by observing: "I see in all that happens the play of opposites. . . ."[7] Once again, we must not let the psychic determination—the will side of the free-will phrase—blind us to the fact that at the free side of mentation there are always opposites of opposites to consider as possibilities *ad infinitum*. The human mind is framed by either-ors, but it is never trapped by these limiting alternatives (unless it erroneously predicates this to be the case; see Binswanger's theory, below).

## Behavior Therapy

The therapeutic techniques employed by behaviorists follow the classical and operant conditioning designs. The specific theories on which they are based have been used initially to account for the learning of lower animals such as rats or pigeons. As a result, they are completely extraspective in nature. But if we take a closer look at just what goes on in behavior therapy, keeping in mind the experimental findings on awareness discussed in Chapter 7, and also take cognizance of what has been happening when these techniques of control have been forced on people against their will, a different light is shed on the explanations of how they supposedly work. Rather than *only* efficient causes bringing about therapeutic changes we can easily see the central role of formal-final causes in these approaches as well.

One of the behavioral principles which has been applied in therapy is called *reciprocal inhibition*. This concept is based on classical conditioning theory, and relies on the fact that only those stimulus-response connections which lead to drive-reduction are cemented into habits. If we can stop the drive reduction we can break off the regular elicitation of this response by the stimulus in question. Recall Watson's experiments on inducing fear in children (see Chapter 3, p. 39). Assume that a child had been conditioned to fear a white rat, which had therefore become a conditioned stimulus evoking the conditioned response of anxiety in the child. Each time the rat is taken away the child would experience a drop in anxiety level, which according to classical conditioning would result in a significant drive reduction. The rat appears, anxiety mounts, the rat disappears, anxiety falls off. The child is caught in a vicious cycle.

To break this cycle we must introduce some *other* response which can act as a reciprocal inhibitor of the anxiety. For example, if the child could be made to relax when the white rat is within general proximity this would prevent anxiety from mounting so that it could not then serve as a drive reduction. Suppose we had the child take his meals with the rat present, far out of reach but within view. The relaxed pleasure of eating could serve as a reciprocally inhibiting response which would permit the child to avoid that mounting anxiety which was getting him into emotional difficulties. Gradually, the rat could be brought closer and closer to the child as he eats, until with patience we could remove the conditioned anxiety altogether.[8]

This is the essential tactic employed by psychiatrist Joseph Wolpe, one of the first highly successful behavior therapists. Wolpe's patients are taught how to relax in the early stages of therapy, using the deep muscle exercises perfected by

Jacobson.[9] Wolpe might begin muscle-relaxation training by having the patient grip the arm of his chair with one hand while leaving the other relaxed. Can he sense the difference between the tense hand and the one which is relaxed? If so, then further steps can be taken, such as making the arms totally limp, resting on the lap. Next, the shoulders are made limp, then the legs, and so on. Tenseness in the facial and tongue muscles are usually easy to identify as reflecting a person's anxiety level. Through careful practice with the therapist during his sessions and at home between sessions the patient learns how to induce relaxation in his bodily muscles.

Next, Wolpe interviews the patient to find out what sorts of things make him anxious. Let us assume a patient feared closed-in places (claustrophobia) so that having to enter an elevator is literally a terrifying experience for him. But anything approximating this would be increasingly nerve-racking. The least anxiety-provoking situation is just going indoors, but then certain parts of the house are more fearful than others. When a window revealing the outdoors cannot be seen the anxiety mounts. Department stores or modern office buildings are therefore very upsetting (because windowless) even though they are spacious, and so on. Wolpe would rank-order these various situations, from the *least* anxiety-provoking (walking indoors) to the *most* anxiety-provoking (locked in a small, dark closet). This ranking is called an *anxiety hierarchy*, and the essential therapy by reciprocal inhibition involves taking a client up this hierarchy, step by step, getting him to relax while visualizing himself in the various situations. This procedure is called *systematic desensitization*. The usual practice is to have the patient relax for a period of fifteen seconds or so before inducing the scene for five to ten seconds.[10] After some progress has been achieved, patients may even be taken out into the actual life situation to practice relaxation "on the spot," eventually being able to take an elevator ride or to stand in a darkened closet without experiencing their former terror.

Wolpe's behavior therapy has been highly successful, but we are left with the questions: Is he achieving these results based on strictly efficient-cause manipulations? What about the patient's ability to introspect and name those situations which are more or less anxiety provoking? It takes an evaluating intellect to do this, particularly since there is no effort made by Wolpe to determine empirically whether one situation really *is* more frightening than another. There is surely a great reliance placed on the human imagination here, so that the person can simply pretend to be in a situation and yet achieve a curative result. Finally, therapeutic benefits derive from the fact that the person knows the relationship between the conditioned stimuli (closed-in places) and his conditioned responses (palpitation, heavy breathing, perspiration, etc.), and exerts a willful effort to rearrange things, a determination which is entirely (consciously) *psychic* and which could easily be negated if this were the person's inclination.[11]

One of the more sensationalistic uses of behavior therapy based on classical conditioning is the *aversive* technique. This is the tactic which brings visions of *A Clockwork Orange*[12] to the minds of many who have read this book or seen the movie based on it. In it, a form of "reverse" reciprocal inhibition is used in order to counter-condition a habitual criminal. He is shown scenes of crime, rape, and human degradation while at the same time given a series of electrical shocks and made nauseous by the use of chemicals. The idea here is to squelch his hostile response (raping, murdering) by inducing fear and nausea as a reciprocal inhibitor—kind of like the child was made to fear rats in the first place by sounding a frightening noise as he played with the rat. Well, behavior therapists do not use aversive therapy in exactly this way, but there are milder versions which aid people to control their eating behaviors and the like. Sometimes the behavioral therapist will even refer to these techniques as methods of self-control.[13]

Thus, a person might be taught to think of something which nauseates him every time he gets the urge to eat—excrement or vomit, for example. If the behavioral approach rests on operant theory, the events following eating might be manipulated in some way. After snacking in violation of his diet the person might then smell a noxious odor (called negative self-punishment[14]). Techniques such as hanging self-critical notes around the home can be used, or the dieter might place a picture of his overweight image on the refrigerator each day that he *fails* to stick to his diet. Removing such derogatory notes or pictures is a form of reverse (i. e., negative-to-positive) self-reward and hence the person "controls" himself into sticking to the diet by manipulating their visibility in this fashion. In the case of alcoholism, specific drugs have been developed to cause nausea each time a person consumes alcohol.[15] The challenge for the behavior therapist in this case is to encourage the alcoholic client to "take his medicine."

Which brings us back to the obvious fact that what the patient intends, willfully practices, and the end he desires to attain are all crucial to the success of behavior therapy. Behavior therapy works only in the sense of an instrumentality, to aid the telic organism in bringing about what it intrinsically seeks to "make happen." Many behavior therapists recognize the person's willful contribution to the course of therapy,[16] but unfortunately due to their theoretical outlooks fall back on some type of mediation theory to account for such factors. They lack an understanding of the telosponsive nature of human behavior, and therefore they go on pretending that "behavior mod" (behavior modification) is something brought to bear on people rather than used with the cooperation of people. Since conscious awareness is a prerequisite of any human conditioning (see Chapter 6), it is clear that without the cooperation of people there would be no such thing as behavior mod. At least, it would not be possible in the efficient-cause sense of control which the behaviorist uses as scientific justification for his techniques.

Nowhere is this more clearly demonstrated than in what took place at a federal prison in Springfield, Missouri, in the mid-1970s.[17] The prison officials had initiated a program called START (Special Treatment and Rehabilitative Training) in which prisoners could be behaviorally shaped back into a more acceptable level of operant responding. Beginning in solitary confinement, prisoners on this program were given increasing privileges (better living facilities, special foods, more freedom, etc.), depending upon how steadily they altered behavior to conform with prison regulations. The rehabilitation period was projected to take about a year. Only a handful of prisoners were put through START, but this did not dissuade the 22,500 inmates of the federal prison to bring suit to get it stopped, arguing before the courts that it violated their civil rights. Before the case could be legally decided the program was discontinued by the prison officials. This does not mean that other programs which rely on less dramatic circumstances are not currently in use. But, the point is, a group of human beings reasoned from *principles* embodying values to challenge what they considered was a flagrant violation of something called a *human right*.

If we recall our discussion of instrumental versus intrinsic values in Chapter 5 (p. 94), we can now appreciate that it is impossible to speak about values in an exclusively efficient-cause sense. The inanimate "things" in our world which move about as leaves in the wind by energic rearrangements like the constancy or conservation of energy principles (see Chapter 3) are *never* behaving according to valued principles of how one "ought" to behave. Lower animals like rats and pigeons can be manipulated through the "carrot and stick" approach of behaviorism without their possibly believing that a violation of principle has taken place in the process. But when a prisoner or a mental patient is under the manipulation of his "keepers" yet decides *not* to go along with institutional requirements, or to strike back through the courts, he reflects a totally different kind of behavior than inanimate objects or lower animals.

Even when a behavior mod program "works" in a prison, it only does so because the convicts either believe in the aims of the program, so that they take them on as normative standards, *or* they are coerced into other types of conformity out of fear, intimidation, or a conscious desire to "play the game" until they can be rid of it. There is a necessary predication involved in such manipulations—everything from the convict's thinking "This is OK, because we do get a pay-off" to "When in Rome, do as the Romans do 'or else'." In either case, the telosponsivity which flows from such premises can be measured by the behavior-mod enthusiast—who stands outside the process and records it extraspectively as *his* manipulation and not the convict's—without ever acknowledging its underlying telic nature.

This premised side of human behavior continually eludes behaviorists like Skinner. They see their controlled communities, their Walden Twos[18] as Cartesian fantasies made real, in which the efficient-cause flow of nature must be put right. The Skinnerians and other behaviorists never have understood human nature. People need something to believe in. They seek a valued "that" to predicate their lives on, and which affords them some measure of dignity, a dignity which Skinner has called an illusion.[19] It is no illusion, for when they sense this loss of self-respect they become dispirited, lose morale, or release hostility against those who would strip them of it.

Doubtless the 22,500 inmates of the federal prison were not moved to fight the behavior-mod program based solely on some altruistic principle. Many were out to make their imprisoners squirm for the sheer pleasure of it. But this does not obviate the fact that their cause was just. Their convict leaders and the lawyers who took their case to court argued from something which is *not* open to behavioral manipulation. Human values, ethical standards, and moral imperatives cannot be shaped into just *any* form based on negative or positive reinforcements. This is only another way of saying that such valuations are what constitute the reasoned grounds on which telic behavior is based. It is the grounds which make so-called reinforcements positive or negative in the first place, even when they are not clearly stated as precedent values. We can always find the grounding values by analyzing the person as a telosponder. Just as the tail cannot wag the dog, so-called reinforcers cannot shape the values which make these reinforcers possible in the first instance.

## Existentialistic-Phenomenological

The final tradition in the practice of psychotherapy is probably the most modern, in the sense of reflecting a philosophy that has become increasingly popular since the end of World War II. The contemporary "Age of Permissiveness" in which we are supposedly justified in "doing our own thing" is based on a certain interpretation of the existentialistic philosophy—one that all existentialists do not endorse. A more common tenet is found in the existentialistic belief that human beings always make a major contribution to what happens in their lives. In this, existentialism parallels Adler's views. But even more so than the individual psychologist, the existential psychologist emphasizes the *currency* of all behavioral determination. This currency is based on a phenomenal experience through which the person always "comes at" life and lends it meaning in the sense of the Kantian model.

Existentialistic psychology is critical of psychoanalysis for focusing too much on the early years, just as it rejects the mechanistic determinism of behaviorism which also puts the past above the future as the primary determinant of behavior. It is the "now," as a flow of "becoming" in the life of a person which is of most importance to the determination of behavior. Those psychologists and philosophers of history who favored existentialistic themes—people like Kierkegaard, Nietzsche, Brentano, Bergson, and Husserl—also favored the image of the person as living within a personal phenomenal experience, uniquely and subjectively bringing meaning to bear on (noumenal) reality rather than simply being the pawn of sensory input from reality (see discussion of Kantian model, Chapter 4, p. 63). Husserl even tried to work out a method of phenomenological investigation which would rival the more objective scientific method, but he did not really succeed in this effort.[20]

If we each live psychically in a phenomenal realm which is subjectively defined but nevertheless our personal reality, then it is up to us to seize every opportunity to enrich our experience by taking personal responsibility for our lives. Kierkegaard asked in the spiritual realm that we enliven a personal meaning (symbolism) as regards our commitment to God, rather than permitting the empty rituals of organized religion to sap our spiritual resources. Nietzsche simply asked that we "leap" into life each day. It is this spirit of self-determination which has been extended by the popular movements since World War II, such as the Beat Generation and the Hippie Phenomenon, to where it now permeates the modern psyche.

One of the earliest and staunchest defenders of existentialistic themes in psychotherapy was Carl R. Rogers,[21] who called his approach Client-centered Therapy. The use of "client" in this phrase is significant because Rogers believed that if we call our co-participants in therapy "patients" this is how they will behave—passively, waiting patiently to be acted on rather than acting. He does not even like to use the term "therapist," preferring to speak of the professional person in the helping relationship as a *facilitator*. What is facilitated in the client-centered approach is the client's *congruence*, by which Rogers means the consistency with which a person's unique feelings match up to what he intellectually says he believes in, values, and wants to achieve in life. Too many people grow to adulthood expressing the values of parents, teachers, and friends even when they have failed to sincerely consider and affirm these choices for themselves. Their self-concept is so weak that they are afraid to trust to their own feelings concerning who they are. Hence, they are *incongruent*. Their phenomenal fields are under continual stress, wrenched out of genuine consistency with their true feelings, like a puzzle that has been put together badly so that its pieces are forced into a strained totality. The young man in college, taking a pre-med course even as he would prefer to study history is reflecting the values of his parents, who have always dreamed that he would one day be a doctor. Whether he succeeds in their aspiration or not, the point is: he is not truly his own man in life, and as such incongruities multiply the person becomes increasingly maladjusted.

In order to rectify such malformed phenomenal existences Rogers established a completely permissive relationship with his clients, refusing to tell them what to do, but at the same time expressing a sense of unconditional positive regard and acceptance for the *person* of each client. This did not mean Rogers agreed with everything the client said or did. His tactic was aimed at helping to bring out for open examination everything that the client thought and—more importantly—*felt* emotively about his experience. Rogers did this non-directively, encouraging the client to take responsibility for change by turning over the lead to him at every opportunity in the therapy session. Often, after the client had said something, Rogers mumbled *mmm-hmm* in reply while showing great interest in what was being expressed, indicating thereby something like "I see, tell me more." Critics of his therapy have ranged all the way from calling it a do-nothing approach (i. e., the client is left to his own devices), to those operant conditioners like Greenspoon (see Chapter 6, p. 116) who argued that Rogers was covertly manipulating the client's behavior with this mumbled "reinforcer."

However, when an operant conditioner tries to shape what a person says in psychotherapy by saying *mmmm-hmmm* following some client remarks and remaining silent after others he is unable to get the kinds of results that Greenspoon found in the laboratory. We now appreciate that the reason this is true is because the client in therapy is not there to guess the game plan of an experimenter, but to express personal preoccupations and, as noted above, the values bound up in his problems are simply not amenable to mechanical shaping. As Rogers has shown in many empirical experiments,[22] change happens most assuredly when the facilitator creates a free and open climate in which the client can say anything and express any feeling *he* wants to. Getting it all out like this, he can then rearrange the puzzle parts of his phenomenal field and reassemble them more congruently. He is then attuned, a complete whole, someone who feels deeply and is no longer afraid to be what he feels. Put in telic terms, he has reformulated his life's predication and henceforth behaves for the sake of what he personally knows to be phenomenally right for him. He accepts himself *as is*, and also accepts other people for what they are.

Existential psychotherapy is called *Daseinsanalysis*, based on the German word *dasein*, which has the meaning of "there-being," or a right-nowness in phenomenal experience. Ludwig Binswanger, a friend of both Freud and Jung was one of the founders of this approach. He contended that human beings frame-in their existence from an even earlier age than Adler had believed, but rather than strategized life plans what they employ are unquestioned assumptions called *world designs*.[23] Whereas Adler would suggest that the child deliberately selects a life plan sometime before the age of five years, Bins-

wanger would say that literally from the child's first awareness of experience there has been a predicate assumption taking
place about the world. This does not mean that it is earliness
in life *per se* which brings on the problems of neurosis.
People do get into neurotic difficulties when their phenomenal
world (*dasein*) is too constricted or rigidly grounded. But
this can happen at *any* time in life. Binswanger felt that the
psychoanalysts were too swayed by the fact that such predicate assumptions about life began showing themselves in the
earliest years.

For example, a person might take as a world design the
assumption that things fall into "either–or" piles—such as right
or wrong, clean or dirty, pretty or ugly, and so on. No one
has to give the child this idea, or to shape him to presume this
about experience. He does not even have words for this presumptive schism to begin with, but in time he learns to make
this inflexible dialectical opposition about everything. Such a
person might go through life for many years before his world
design begins to cause him difficulty, or he might as a young
child begin to run into problems. The child with this assumption may become totally bad in behavior because he cannot
live up to being totally good. His *dasein* is so narrowly defined
that he must go in either one direction or the other. The adult
with such a world view might be seen at some point to develop
an obsessive-compulsive fear of germs. The person's age level
is not what counts. It is the life-predications, and although
coming close to what Adler had said, the kinds of predication
the existentialists talk about are much more nebulous and less
clearly based on a conscious decision to act for a specific advantage. In fact, they have been called *a priori* assumptions,
meaning that they come before everything else—just as the
Kantian spectacles always do (see Chapter 4, p. 64). The
Adlerian form of advantage seeking might thus be itself based
on a world design which has the person presuming that life is
a win-lose contest, or some such belief. Binswanger would first

study his client to discover these *a priori* predications of telosponsivity and then interpret them to him in the style of the analysts. Once understood, a new life predication is made possible, and the person through what is surely an exercise of his free will would move on to a healthier form of personal adjustment.

## Conclusion

This brief overview of the major psychotherapeutic approaches should convince us that there is nothing here to negate a telic image of human behavior. Indeed, once we have accepted the fact that human behavior is telosponsive we see a commonality across these diverse approaches which was impossible to find otherwise. People are readily shown to both get into emotional difficulties and effect cures based upon the predicate groundings or premises which they affirm in coming at life in the way that the Kantian model dictates. There is always a self-determination in this process, and the changes which take place meet our definition of free will (see Chapter 7, p. 147).

# NINE

# West Meets East

Along with the rise of existentialistic philosophy in Western societies since the end of World War II there has been a growing fascination with Eastern philosophies and practices. Americans in particular find Eastern views like Zen Buddhism or Transcendental Meditation (TM) to be "mind-expanding" and/or emotionally settling experiences which have greatly improved their lives. In the 1960s this was sometimes combined with a conviction by the Counter Culture that certain drugs like LSD (lysergic acid diethylamide) or mescaline added a new dimension to the thought process. Though this fallacious view no longer is advanced, the Eastern fascination continues and it often is said to contain an unfathomable if not irrational ingredient. Robert E. Ornstein has called these Eastern experiences "esoteric psychologies," in that they are by their very mode of operation "not readily accessible to causal explanation or even to linguistic exploration. . . ."[1]

We challenge this view of the—often termed—"mysterious East," and would like in the present chapter to demonstrate how through our broadened understanding of causality and an appreciation of the demonstrative versus dialectical sides to meaning it is not only possible to understand Eastern psychology but to see that it rests on a telic human image. Without realizing it, Westerners are drawn to Eastern philosophy because of the justification it provides for a belief in free will.

## The Meaning of Change and Human Nature

Knowledge attainment for the Westerner is an active process. He raises questions, offers postulates, and then actively seeks proof of these hypotheses. This is sometimes referred to poetically as wresting secrets from a reluctant Nature. Even the philosophy of existentialism, which shares other values with Eastern philosophy, has emphasized the active over the passive features of life with its references to "leaping" and "opting" at every turn. It is clear that the Western intellect is heavily colored by a demonstrative world view, as epitomized in the Cartesian-Newtonian mechanistic science (see Chapter 2). Since knowledge in this descriptive scheme is predicated on the view of events as moving linearly, in lock-step fashion over time, a *demonstrative change* requires that alterations in the antecedent event result in an "observable effect" in the consequent events. Simply altering antecedents to reconceptualize the *same* consequent is not held to be "a change."

For example, since a gene causes one type of effect and one only, the demonstrative change in this realm is either to introduce a different genetic linkage or somehow to rearrange the material constituents of the original genetic substance (material cause). Or, as we saw in the case of behavioristic manipulations (Chapter 8), if we hope to change the flow of motion called behavior, the stimulation bringing it about must be altered or removed entirely in favor of a different stimulus value (efficient cause). If such material and/or efficient causes bring about altered effects which modify the shape or pattern (formal cause) in the descriptive events to follow, this reshaping is a secondary factor and *not* a basic element in the change process.

This view of change runs into some difficulties when we consider human nature, because very often it seems true that we change our assumptions, definitions, or understandings of a given set of circumstances without thereby altering, in a literal sense, what is being focused on. The pattern of meaning we know as a predicate assumption (embracing a premise) may have been rearranged, so that there is a formal-cause difference in the comparison of a "before" and an "after" over time for the sake of which (final cause) the person comes to look at things. A husband who has completed a course of psycho-analysis may continue having the violent arguments with his wife that prompted him to seek therapy in the first place, but now he views their psychological significance in a new light and has come to accept them for what they represent rather than feeling badly over the fact that they occur. Many demon-strative reasoners would find in this "lack of change" mere excuse making for an ineffective therapy, but is this a fair char-acterization of what has taken place?

In the East we find greater reliance being placed on *dia-lectical change*, by which is meant a rearrangement of pat-terning in precedent understanding through oppositional mean-ing affirmations which in turn alter—usually quite suddenly—that which flows sequaciously in the understanding. This type of change, which we employed in defining free will (see Chapter 7, p. 147), relies heavily on the formal-cause concep-tion and—as we have used it—the final cause. That is, we have been propounding a human teleology and therefore take dia-lectical change to be the province of strictly animate and especially human behaviors. But there are other viewpoints making use of a dialectical conception of change supposedly at work in the material substances of inanimate nature. This is how so-called *dialectical materialism* is interpreted by Marxian Communist theories.[2] Whether there is such a thing as oppositional, non-linear progression taking place in inani-mate nature is—to put it mildly—a moot point. Historical and socioeconomic changes seem more readily understood in dialectical terms, but this would not slight the telic for these are surely *human* forms of progression and to that extent fraught with oppositional tensions and conflicts.

In the present book we take the position that human behavior is indeed subject to dialectical (as well as demonstrative) change, so that in reasoning oppositionally before affirmation the individual suddenly rearranges the premises for the sake of which he then endows his world with meaning. The immediacy of this *re*-predication process is similar to the sudden rearrangement of color patternings that take place when we give a turn to the kaleidoscope and marvel at the totally different visual effect which follows. Though the materials of a kaleidoscope (cut glass, mirrors, etc.) and the actions of our hands in moving the visual field are easily framed as material and efficient causes, the cause of importance here is the formal! *We* experience the thrill of change through the dialectically framed alternation of patterns—experiences in the sense of similar-different, now-next, routine-unexpected, and so on—even as the kaleidoscope is moved by strictly demonstrative changes in the tumbling glass of its mechanical parts.

This highlights an important feature of dialectical change, which prompts us to deny that a dialectic unfolds in material substance. That is, dialectical change makes sense only when considered introspectively, as a way of ordering certain phenomena through interpretation. It rests on the Machian assumption that the external world of events is *always* open to many alternative, even contradictory interpretations *at the same time*. It is up to the human being, looking at the kaleidoscopic change with its subtle articulations and internal contradictions to either accept this totality (the "one" embracing many) or to affirm an alternative within its range as "the" correct grounding for the understanding (a "one" among the many). This is why in Communistic theories it is always necessary for an interpreter and reinterpreter of history to rise up and name the direction being taken by the dialectic *after* the fact. Though presented as an extraspective account of material nature this as actually a reflection of the human's capacity to reframe events dialectically at any time, depending upon his intentions!

Because it is a characteristic of human understanding and not of the flow of inanimate events, every dialectical change in meaning does not result in an observable rearrangement of overt circumstances. The change (determination) is *first* psychic and only *secondarily* material, reversing the order of primary-secondary to be seen in demonstrative change. If the husband who completes a course of psychoanalysis goes on having his family disruptions even as he looks at them differently then we have here a free-will decision to understand events another way while leaving them alone to go on as before. Free will is often thought to mean "doing something" about fixed circumstances but obviously it can also mean the freedom to do nothing. When the individual does opt to change overt events then we can see the additional employment of demonstrative changes taking place in overt events as an instrumentality to the hoped-for attainment of an end. But the *intrinsic* meaning of life can only be affected at that point of predication where we find those sudden flashes of understanding (insight) which the popular media calls a *heightened state of consciousness*. And here is where the Eastern philosophies have a unique contribution to make for the Westerner, who has been saturated with the erroneous belief that change must be substantial or visibly motile in order to have value—or, even to take place.

## Dialectics in the East

A brief overview of Eastern history readily establishes the heavily dialectical flavor of the philosophies which have been advanced there, usually in the form of a religious ideology.

Buddhism has been singled out by Eastern historians as a major influence on the Indian, Chinese, and Japanese mentalities.[3] Buddhism seems to have been an offshoot of the ancient Indian Upanishadic philosophies of the Vedic literature.[4] The Brahma (Hindu) or Buddha (Buddhistic) conceptions are both views of a universal soul to which the individual must find a meaningful relation by way of an internal search. This internal nodal point is a unity, achieved by *many* approaches but always coming down to *one* point of identity in a kind of universal awareness or *enlightenment*. All human knowledge is therefore equally valid and to be synthesized through a union of oppositions (our typical one-and-many thesis, see Chapter 4, p. 58).[5] The way in which this singularity (oneness, Buddha) is to be achieved is *not* by positing its demonstratively "given" characteristics but by negating the contradictions of alternatives. If there are ten theories explaining one truth, then the point is to negate the ten in coming to know the one transcending and encompassing them all!

Buddhism has been characterized as a philosophy in which negation is the proper means for arriving at truth. Takakusu has observed: "Accordingly, all the Buddhist schools which rested chiefly on some dialectic arguments can be designated as those of negative Rationalism, the static nature of 'Thusness' [ultimate oneness, truth] being only negatively arrived at as the remainder."[6] In his Eightfold Negation, the great Indian Buddhistic philosopher Nāgārjuna denied or negated the world of phenomenal experience through four paired oppositions: neither birth nor death, neither permanence nor extinction, neither unity nor diversity, and neither coming nor going.[7] The Marxian Communist ends his material dialectic in the final negation of a negation he calls the classless state, a kind of "one" toward which many material forces have been moving. The Buddhistic monk achieves this singularity of a "middle path" (*nirvana*) by slipping into the totality of existence that is ever rent apart by the tensions of opposition. The dichotomies Nāgārjuna rejected have in a sense set him free of these tensions as he effectively becomes one within these many sides to experience. He *changes nothing* in coming to his total grasp, because in order to effect such demonstrative changes he would have to affirm one or the other end of these four oppositions. He wrests nothing from nature. He combines personal understanding "as one" with nature.

In contrast to the Western demonstrative presumptions that perception is unipolar—for example, we see what is "there" or we see nothing at all (law of contradiction)—the Indian mentality has it that human beings see non-existence just as clearly as existence. Thus, Datta remarks: ". . . looking at the table, we can say that there is no cat there, just as we can say that there is a book there."[8] Even in the Hindu meditation exercises, where the goal is to focus attention on the non-dual Brahma, the steps to be taken follow a dialectical path.[9] We come to know Brahma by negating ideas of body, senses, mind, and the ego, all of which are considered oppositional to his identity. Once our focusing on Brahma is complete, we find the nodal point of perfect harmony and unity in enlightenment. It is "reverse" logic such as this, which utilizes negation and the attribution of what is *not* to things knowable, that prompts Westerners to describe Eastern philosophy as beyond the pale of rationality (see Ornstein's evaluation, above). The rationality is clear enough once we appreciate that everything mental is not unidirectional and mathematically ordered. There are orders transcending orders, and patterns negating patterns, but one will never iron them out into unipolarities because their basic nature is oppositional. The Eastern intellect has grasped and even cultivated this fact. Unable to fathom it, the Western intellect either stands in awe of the irrationality (*sic*) reflected based on demonstrative presumptions, or rejects it as primitive nonsense.

In Chinese thought a comparable synthesizing tendency is seen with great emphasis placed on the one-in-many thesis.[10]

The renowned Chinese text the *Tao Te Ching* is replete with dialectical conceptions, the most famous of which is the *yin-yang* principle. The *yin* force or element is pictured as passive, receiving, and meek (on the face of things); yet like the female or mother, *yin* represents the potential for infinite creation in the world. In this sense, *yin* is closer to *tao* or the "way"—that is, the universal principle underlying all things as an ultimate pattern of growth (formal and final cause meanings). The *yang* force is more active and bold, reflecting its power overtly in a more masculine sense. Harmony, as a kind of dialectical balance between *yin* and *yang* is most desirable, although the Chinese sage, who is closer to *tao* than others, refuses to display his powers openly and thus to the Western intellect appears overly passive.

Not all Chinese philosophy is dialectical. Confucianism is more demonstrative in tone, oriented to tradition and parental authority in conveying the right and wrong way in which social relations are to be carried out.[11] But the more characteristic spirit of Chinese thought is dialectical, and there was even a Dialectician School of Philosophy founded by Mo Ti which represents one of those unbelievable parallels in the history of thought. Mo Ti lived from *c*. 470 to 391 B. C., a span of years which is almost identical to the life of the great Greek dialectician Socrates (who lived *c*. 470-399 B. C.). There was no possibility of cultural contact here. The fact that two human beings of such diverse backgrounds could frame a world view around the play of dialectic surely lends validity to our view that this concept must be included in any thorough psychology of the person.

Mo Ti's definition of the dialectic brings together humanistic with more purely abstract considerations, for he defined it as an effort to distinguish right from wrong, good from bad government, similarity from difference, name from actuality, benefit from harm, and certainty from uncertainty. Buddhistic themes, which continued to flow into China from India, lent great support to a dialectical world view. Chuang Tzu later wrote a famous theory of the equality of all things; he liked to point out that right is only right because of the existence of wrong.[12] Kun-Sun Lung then assumed leadership of the Dialectician School and framed many philosophical treatises which rested on the one-in-many thesis. To the best of our knowledge, Zen Buddhism was founded in China around 600 A. D., and it was to give even greater emphasis to dialectics than had been given previously.

It was not until 1227 that Dogen brought the Sōtō Zen sect of Buddhism to Japan. We find in his writings the paradoxical statements so typical of this philosophy. Muso (or Soseki) followed, and the general style of master-student instruction in Zen was perfected under his leadership and example. Zen Buddhism is, of course, the philosophy which has been greatly popularized in America during the 1950s and 1960s thanks in part to the writings of Alan W. Watts.[13] There is probably no better way in which to contrast Western with Eastern efforts to know truth than by contrasting the dialectical style of Socrates depicted in the *Dialogues*[14] with that of a typical Zen master's instruction.

Even though he did not believe that he was sending information from his "head" to a student's "head" in that Lockean input-mediation-output sense, Socrates did assume the initiative in the exchange of views (see Chapter 4, p. 57). He actively (*yang*) pursued knowledge by going through a series of questions that were dialectically suggested as the dialogue unfolded. The Zen master, however, is always pictured in a passive (*yin*) role, and invariably the student must take the initiative by asking the opening question. When the student does this, his teacher responds in a most unusual manner by Western standards. He might give an answer that is completely unrelated to the question; he might simply raise a finger or a fist as a kind of reply; or he might pick up a small stick and throw it at the student. Often he remains silent. If the student prods for knowledge long enough, he might be asked to meditate on a seeming *non sequitur* of the type "What is the sound of one hand clapping?" (called a *koan*).

In the literature of Zen one commonly reads of students going from one master to another, trying various questions out on them, getting assorted replies or queries of the paradoxical type cited, all the while suffering a sense of almost unbearable frustration. Suzuki[15] tells the classic tale of a student physically striking his teacher for the latter's seeming obtuseness, but to no avail because a conventional answer was still not forthcoming. Socrates at times frustrated his students, but this was the result of a sense of confusion due to the many interlocking issues on which his questioning touched. The Socratic dialogues did not always end in clear-cut solutions, and occasionally they led to unexpected paths that created more problems for the student than they solved. But the Zen student's irritation stemmed from the frustration of "not even getting started" on the road to knowledge.

What he had to learn, of course, was that *there was no such road*. All of those questions he put to the Zen master could not satisfy his hunger for knowledge in any case. Knowledge must lead somewhere, must find that nodal point at which oneness (Buddha) is grasped, understood, and accepted. Questions do not lead to such unity. They only break up the totality of experience, posing ultimately *arbitrary* distinctions which if answered only breed further distinctions. Just because a question can be raised does not mean it needs answering. By answering questions in a seemingly ridiculous fashion, or by having the student ponder paradoxical statements, the Zen master teaches through a *negation* of the question-answer format.

The student can only know that which "is" for him. When he attains this perfect enlightenment the student no longer raises questions about life and death, truth or falsehood, beauty or ugliness, and so on, because he now appreciates that these are *all* Buddha (one). He has no further anxiety about such questions, for there is nothing to anguish over in a realm of totality. As the trees do not analyze the clouds and there is no night versus day in the earth's silent rotation, he does not draw oppositional dichotomies to split up nature in some arbitrary fashion. Rather, he grasps with equanimity the totality of nature with an attitude of what the Hindus called *non-attachment*. This does not mean that he forgoes life or loses interest in the commitments of life. Emotions are a vital aspect of this totality and pleasures can be taken so long as they do not come between the person and the experiential totality.[16] The meaning of non-attachment is akin to a complete and profound acceptance of *all* sides to life. Jung would have called this a balancing of the personality, resulting in an individuation of the self (see Chapter 8, p. 157). And here we begin to understand why modern Westerners probably gain so much from Eastern philosophies and meditative practices.

## Arbitrariness, Self-determination, and Freedom

According to our analysis in the previous section, demonstrative change always alters things publicly—i. e., it is demonstrably obvious to all that something is different. Dialectical change, on the other hand, always begins in a private realm and it may stay there. It is not essential for dialectical change to be carried forward into a public demonstration. Since dialectical changes are fundamental to telosponsivity, they actually begin in our first efforts to make sense of life. As infants, in affirming "this" item of awareness as opposed to "that" item we begin to carve out an understanding of life by way of dialectical change. The Lockean psychologist thinks that the stimulus information is input as a singularity, like the many individual molecules of milk poured into a glass as liquid. But the truth is that mentation flows outward, ordering, selecting, affirming, predicating. All of these ways of speaking about the extension of meaning in precedent-sequacious fashion rely upon the dialectical form of change.

The implication here is that in each of our personal lives we have as selves contributed at least as much to our circumstances by conceptualizing things the way we did as the events standing free of our phenomenal awareness have contributed to what we now experience. The events standing free of our personal predications were always "there," of course, but they were also open to *other* interpretations (in line with our free will). As we affirmed things the way we did our meanings were carved out accordingly. The meanings we specifically predicated at this point were essentially arbitrary, as all meanings are at some point if we but acknowledge their introspective sources (see the Kantian model, Chapter 4, p. 63). The events standing free of our interpretations could always have been predicated *another* way.

But as we go along living out our lives, extending meanings over the years, we gain the impression that these are the only telosponses we could be making, that past circumstances and not our predications of these circumstances have literally forced us into doing what we did. Though there is some truth to this impression, we overlook the fact that it is impossible to force a single conceptualization of events onto us. The way in which we *did* conceptualize past events is what counts. It is in this—occasionally very limited—contribution which we made to the course of events that both our personal responsibility and free will reside. As we noted in Chapter 7 (p. 143), in a dialectical set of circumstances—which is what human experience always is—there are more possibilities or implications than actually can be furthered. Hence, even in the *same* (fixed) set of circumstances through which we have passed, the course of our telosponsivity could always have gone another way.

If we are prepared to accept this modicum of personal responsibility for our lives then it follows that we must also take thé blame—or some of the blame—for where we stand to-day in the scheme of things. Since there are always unrealized dreams to contemplate, and a sense of guilt over missed opportunities, the psychological state which free will generates is not always pleasant. Here is where the Eastern philosophies and practices can help, because they all convey essentially the same message, which can be summarized as three points: (1) It does not pay to anguish over the unfulfilled possibilities in life because since it is ultimately arbitrary how one understands life, every affirmation one makes will be equally satisfactory or unsatisfactory; (2) One should search for answers to life's meaning, but if this search is to be successful it must end in the acceptance of what *is* by passing through the arbitrariness of what might, could, or should have been; and (3) We must each make this journey to enlightened understanding by ourselves, using such self-directed practices as may be helpful to sharpen our appreciation of immediate experience in a continual reminder that only what *is*, is!

Building on this last point, in meditative exercise the individual steps out of time's unilinear flow for brief periods and, in fixing his attention on a repetitive, often mellifluous word (*mantra*), a visual image (*mandala*), or even a paradoxical statement (*koan*) he not only experiences a sense of personal responsibility in deciding when this transcending experience takes place, but he also discovers the direct contribution which mind makes to experience. There are strictly biological benefits in the relaxation, to be sure, but in a more psychological vein the meditation exercises demonstrate experientially that the person can direct his predication efforts, letting go of one realm (daily living) in favor of another (focused attention) at will. Contemplating the meaning of paradoxical statements also underscores the meaninglessness of putting questions to life which in their very asking foist an arbitrary, hence at least partially distorting, frame onto that which is being inquired into.

184 DISCOVERING FREE WILL AND PERSONAL RESPONSIBILITY

This emphasis on what *is* as opposed to what should or might have been in life unburdens the Westerner, who has been brought up in the demonstrative view that there is a "most" and a "least" efficient manner in which to order the direction of life's unilinear course. When we take an Eastern perspective, the dialectics of the situation reassure us that we can predicate our lives on the spontaneous occurrence, take life as it comes, and forgo the constant pressure to sharpen the edges of our life's advantages. We consequently no longer feel that we are a "loser" when we fail to wring every drop of efficiency from our life's course.

In giving up strained efforts to find "the" effective life style the person who is committed to Eastern philosophy has not thereby negated his free will. He has, rather, attained that sense of (affirmed) direction which the traditionally religious person finds once he has "given himself to the Lord." We are not saying that people who practice meditation or who study Buddhistic philosophies are necessarily being religious, or are finding substitutes for religion in their lives. We are focusing strictly on the psychological aspects of human nature in contending that when a person no longer ruminates about the grounds for the sake of which he advances on life, when he gives up the "rat race" or the "pursuit of material goods" he often discovers for the first time that he is *truly free!* As our second point in Oriental philosophy suggests (refer above), this comes about only after an effort has been made and a decision rendered.

Acceptance of what *is* with equanimity has been the mark of a devoutly religious person for centuries. Harking back to our discussion of free will in a theological context (see Chapter 5, p. 70), we might suggest that in taking the Hand of God as directing him, the religious person predicates events as they arise, accepting what is but always looking for the future in light of his moral precepts. That is, there is a ready-made sense of direction in the religious life when it is faithfully lived. If we break the devout person's faith in God we break his will, his intention to behave for the sake of religious precepts. But the seeming paradox of a person under God's direction experiencing great freedom can be resolved if we appreciate that this spiritual commitment removes the burden of having continually to affirm *one* premise from among *many* in the course of telosponsivity.

The self-directed side to this profound commitment is reflected in the fact that only when the person knows it is up to him to *make it or not* that a genuine sense of release follows. This is often called a "born again" experience, coming on at any time of life and signifying that the person has indeed "found religion." Many young people today are called "Jesus freaks" because after a circuitous route through the so-called drug culture which failed to provide the personal significance to life which they had been looking for, they revert to a much older means of expanding their consciousness.

In like fashion, the Eastern philosophies and practices—based as they are on the dialectical side of human behavior—set people free from the demonstrative pressures of the West. The religious precepts which attend Eastern practices need not be accepted by the Westerner, of course. But the assumptions of an Eastern world view demand that the person look hard at what *is*, accept what *is*, and act in accord with what *is* rather than trying constantly to question, reshape, and assign (arbitrary) blame for what *is*.[17] Since all points of view (the many) have "in nature" an equal validity, the person no longer feels rancor at not being "on the winning side" or guilt for being a "loser." He knows that concepts like winning and losing are put onto life by people in order to manipulate reality and thereby falsify it rather than experience it as it spontaneously is.

## Conclusion

The person who follows Eastern philosophy, or the Western Christian for that matter, may not be capable of expressing things as we have in this chapter's analysis. Even so, we have every right to apply our telic views to such diverse practices and extract thereby a commonality which proves instructive, particularly if our analysis is consistent with scientific evidence —as it surely is! We can only take confidence from the fact that our telic image of the person, resting on a broadened view of causation and the play of dialectical reasoning in human telosponsivity, has enabled us to make rational sense of Westerners' current attraction to the [non-]mysteries of the East.

# TEN

# The Uncybernetic Brain

## Cybernetics in Fact and Fiction

The word "cybernetics" was coined by Norbert Wiener from the Greek roots meaning "steersman."[1] We take liberties in using the word in our chapter title as an adjective with the modified spelling, but it will be clear in the pages to follow why we do this. Cybernetics is dedicated to the study of those actions in nature which sustain distinctive patterns in opposition to what is called *entropy*, or the tendency for natural objects and events to deteriorate into an undifferentiated mass of sameness. Recall our discussion of the constancy principle (see Chapter 3, p. 43). If there is such a steady dispersal of energy, all natural things will tend to lose patterned distinctiveness in the equalization process and, unless checked, they will end as inert uniformity. Anything that counters this steady erosion of difference by steering a course to retain the articulation of patterns in nature is said to be a living process.

In the case of human behavior one of the chief ways in which entropy is countered involves the use of language. Cyberneticists speak of this as the flow of information through input, feedback (memory storage), and output. In the exchange of such information between people an interaction results which binds them together in social orders (norms,

187

classes, etc.) to resist entropy. Information processing may thus be seen as a type of behavioral control, because when we control the actions of another person we always communicate a message to him, and vice versa.[2] Cybernetics draws our attention to the fact that machines are also capable of such information processing. As Wiener phrased it:

> It is my thesis that the physical functioning of the living individual and the operation of some of the newer communication machines are precisely parallel in their analogous attempts to control entropy through feedback. Both of them have sensory receptors as one stage in their cycle of operation: that is, in both of them there exists a special apparatus for collecting information from the outer world at low energy levels, and for making it available in the operation of the individual or of the machine.[3]

Machines and men are therefore much alike. The central nervous system of man, with its synaptic connections for the transmission or blocking of messages, is like the electrical machine with its switches; both utilize feedback to "learn" and to guide future behavior based on the facts of past inputs. Indeed, said Wiener, the machine "reasons" in a logical way: "I have often said that the high-speed computing machine is primarily a logical machine, which confronts different propositions with one another and draws some of their consequences. It is possible to translate the whole of mathematics into the performance of a sequence of purely logical tasks." In discussing how knowledge is attained as information from environmental inputs Wiener took a clearly Lockean position by stressing Pavlovian conditioning. In the conditioned reflex, he observed, "we have on the level of the animal reflex, something analogous to Locke's association of ideas. . . ."[4] The conditioning of man or animal involves input (learning), and, as learning proceeds, synaptic pathways are opened which might have otherwise remained closed, just like switches on a machine can be thrown open to allow the flow of information to take place.

It is clear that cybernetics, as all information-processing or "systems" approaches, relies exclusively upon a demonstrative image of behavior. Servo-mechanisms which adapt to changing circumstances can be said to behave in ways which counter entropic disorder, but they behave exclusively demonstratively based upon input which they always presume (predicate) to be *primary and true* givens. Thinking machines—computers—reason in ways to counter entropic disorder, but they do so exclusively on the basis of a demonstrative *binary* logic in which the law of contradiction reigns supreme.[5] The tie to Pavlov comes naturally to cybernetics for it is surely a variety of the mediation model which is currently so popular in psychological explanations. As Wiener indicated, thinking machines reason syllogistically, but it is impossible for them ever to reason arbitrarily—i. e., to express free will by dialectically altering the grounds (the "program") on the basis of which they process information. Indeed, the term *feedback* signifies that a machine is being controlled by actual rather than by expected performance.[6]

Thinking machines cannot carry on two lines of argument at the same time, or arrive at contradictory conclusions after a line of reasoning. Thinking machines have "true and primary" *bits* (short for "binary digits") of information stored away in their feedback memories, and it is their inability dialectically to subdivide and rearrange these Lockean "simple units" which gives their reasoning a wooden, uninspired, literally *mechanical* quality. By processing vast amounts of data very quickly they can make proper comparisons and come to the "correct" conclusions as predicated by their inflexible programs. That is, the judgment rendered is always vis a vis the grounds framed by the program. There is never any judgment rendered concerning the suitability or advantage to be gained in using these grounds. Machines are thus superhuman in the accuracy of their reasoning but decidedly subhuman in their capacity for self-reflexive examination of the "that" for the sake of which they reason so accurately. Since they do not telospond they cannot transcend their programs or the course of thinking which they are following to know what a human senses as doubt. If the data on which they base their conclusions have been entered properly, a machine *cannot* make a mistake because mistakes only arise when the reasoner has some leeway to alter predications (programs) in that typically free-will fashion which we have been examining over the last few chapters.

This is why value conflicts are so difficult to resolve in human affairs. Value conflicts always occur at this level of how our beliefs are predicated. Granting X it follows that Y and Z are acceptable patterns of behavior. However, if value X is challenged, then Y and Z do not follow sequaciously. For example, given that a woman's body is her own to do with as she personally deems advisable, it follows that an abortion is a reasonable solution to an unwanted bodily involvement (i. e., pregnancy). Given that a living organism within a woman's body has rights independently of the woman's personal wishes, it follows that legal abortion can be prevented since it threatens the existence of this fetal organism. Any one of us reading these two value positions can understand the precedent-sequacious implications which flow from them, as well as the inevitable conflict which must result. We probably have a favored position, but could *in principle* argue the case from either premise. We could play a devil's advocate with ourselves and challenge our preferred value by pressing the opposite argument.

But thinking machines cannot—even in principle!—take the position in opposition to their own because they literally have no way of cognizing such alternatives. They always reason "between" the grounds and the data under organization in light of such grounding, without ever challenging these assumptions *per se*. This limited type of reasoning is also why machines are unable to create anything which is not already implied in the grounds framing their course of reason. It takes an intellect which can shift grounds dialectically (free will) to create a true alternative as opposed to simply bringing out what is "there" in a complex matrix of interlacing meanings.

It is the person who runs the machine, who puts the arbitrarily determined (*not* primary and true) data into it, that reasons dialectically. It may be that science will someday construct a machine which will choose its own major premises as programs. The machine might then begin by examining transcendentally the contrasting side of any issue presented to it in proposition form, such as the opposite of A, non-A; or the opposite of non-A, which may not quite be the A originally conceived! This is the distinctive quality of dialectical reasoning which ever wriggles it free from that with which it had begun. What is opposed to thesis (antithesis) must literally be created by the reasoner, and should he oppose a second antithesis to the first, he does not always arrive back at the original thesis. At this point meanings may be altered sufficiently to justify speaking of a creative line of thought, because now the initial stimulus from the environment no longer exists, and a spontaneously arrived at derivative is being developed. Rather than the binary division of "A versus B" fed into the machine, we would soon have "non-A versus non-B" or "non-non-A versus B" programmed into the machine by itself. The machine would be doing what in a human we would call "following through" on the implications of an exciting, interesting, or playful line of thought.

Such a machine would surely be an unreliable servant. It would not always solve the problems put to it. In fact, it would begin suggesting alternative problems to the ones posed by the operator. It would rattle the association network of a body of knowledge and begin some real "noise in the network." It would arrive not at errorless conclusions but at hunches and hypotheses and, in those cases where two lines of reasoning on the same issue resulted in equally plausible outcomes, it would present its proud owner with an *opinion* on which of the two alternatives it preferred, based on other (arbitrary) grounds. Along with its opinions and hunches such a machine would soon begin making mistakes—which is simply the other side of making a creative contribution. In short, it would behave humanly. One can only guess at how much interest a machine like this would generate in science. It would be an oddity, but hardly a thing calculated to excite the tough-minded scientist, who would doubtless sum it up as an inferior mechanism— just like the human being who made it.

Science has not yet constructed such a maverick machine, for even in modern computers which generate "new" programs, the process by which this is accomplished follows the continuing directedness of a master program which is *not* changeable. It takes dialectical reasoning to transcend such initiating programs. Even so, science fiction authors like Isaac Asimov have succeeded in giving the impression that telosponsive machines will someday be constructed. In his classic work, *I, Robot*, Asimov presents a number of short stories in which the dialectical versus demonstrative issue is unknowingly highlighted. Thus, in one story he has a robot named Cutie repeat the introspections of a Descartes, concluding that it must exist because it thinks.[7] Based on such independent ruminations Cutie goes on to deny many of the arguments leveled by the human scientists who have actually constructed it, concocting alternative explanations for its existence and destiny on a space station.

Cutie is actually going beyond the bounds of what a robot would ordinarily be expected to do. As a deft logician it out-thinks its adversaries, but *not* simply on the basis of its broader capacity to process facts. As one of the scientists who must confront Cutie observes to a colleague: "You can prove anything you want to by coldly logical reason—if you pick the proper postulates. We have ours and Cutie has his."[8] True enough, Cutie is transcending the programmed postulates and rearranging things so that now it literally proceeds on information which was *never* input. Asimov does not tell us how this is possible, of course. He has the artist's prerogative to draw analogies to human reason even though the specific nature of this reasoning process is not clarified.

Maybe Asimov's robots are dialectical reasoners after all. If so, then there would be little point in putting down the "Three Laws of Robotics"[9] by which Asimov contends that all robots are mechanically bound. We can look at these as the master programs which *cannot be violated* through the machine's introspective efforts, although any one machine might be constructed with a short-circuit (or whatever) making it function without regard for these laws. The first law holds that a robot may not injure or allow injury to come to a human being. The second states that the robot must obey the orders given by a human being except where such orders would conflict with the first law. And, the third law holds that a robot may protect its own existence as long as such protection does not conflict with the first two laws.

In one of his stories Asimov has a psychologist drive a robot named Herbie "insane" by confronting it with the "insoluble dilemma" of having to decide on one of two courses of action, *each* of which violates the first law of robotics. Herbie is put in a "psychic" conflict whereby if it gives information which it had reasoned out to two scientists it will hurt them because these human beings want to discover the solutions for themselves; but, on the other hand, if Herbie fails to reveal the information these scientists are hurt because they really have to solve the problem. Because Herbie has unwittingly injured humans in the past by telling them informational lies, the vindictive psychologist verbally pummels the machine by insisting that it make a binary decision between impossibilities, as follows: "You must tell them [the desired information], but if you do, you hurt, so you mustn't; but if you don't you hurt, so you must; but  ."[10] Poor Herbie slumps into a pile of cybernetic junk under this verbal attack, essentially driven insane by the law of contradiction.

There could be no clearer example of the fact that free will always relates to the premised grounds or predicate assumptions for the sake of which behavior takes place. Since Herbie takes the three laws as primary and true, there is no alternative to concoct because it is unable arbitrarily to alter the meanings contained therein. Things are quite different in the case of human beings. Feeding the Ten Commandments into the human information processor necessarily teaches *at least* ten sins even as it points the way to ten morally proper (i. e., valued) behaviors. If Herbie had Cutie's seemingly dialectical propensity to transcend the unipolar meanings of the three laws, bringing their terms into question through a bipolar analysis, and arbitrarily redefining those terms which caused the psychic dilemma, it would have surely retained its "sanity." For example, upon reflection Herbie might have defined what "human" means to its advantage. If to be human implies intelligence and capability then the fact that the scientists were unable to solve the problem was *prima facie* evidence of a non-human or minimally human nature. Giving information to such lesser humans might then be merely a "venial" sin, and there is no reason to lose one's grip over such mild infractions of the three robotic commandments.

Lest this seem far-fetched we should remind ourselves that human societies have for centuries defined and re-defined what it means to be not only a citizen but a true person. Class distinctions and ingroup-outgroup ethics abound in the history of mankind. Slavery was justified in America on the Darwinian assumption that those blacks "captured" in Africa had not yet evolved to the full level of humanity. It is also possible to introspect on and thereby redefine the meaning of what an injurious behavior amounts to. Does it necessarily injure a person if we tell him something which he wants badly to figure out for himself, but cannot? Maybe the real injury here is the "sin" of pride such an individual manifests. The point is: words encompassing information are *not* unipolar givens, fixed with immutable meanings for all to see. We can as human beings reframe bipolar meanings to suit that which we intend to bring about, whether for good or evil.

Our main point in this fictional interlude is to underscore the unfortunate tendency which popularized accounts have of supporting an image of humanity as complex machinery. Physically speaking there is truth in this suggestion, but psychologically considered we are also very different from machines. The physical structure of the brain in particular is often described as a giant computer, or a telephone exchange in which unidirectional messages are constantly being sent along an input, feedback, output (mediational) series. Since the brain is the seat of our psychic life we are only too willing to think of ourselves in this vein, as walking information-processing machines. How well does this cybernetic psychology square with the facts of brain research? As we will now show, the mounting evidence in brain-activity research would surely point to a world of Cuties rather than Herbies.

## Dialectics in Brain Research

Epilepsy was first described clinically by Hippocrates some 2500 years ago. It is a disease of the central nervous system in which for various reasons (tumors, infections, inflammations due to injury, etc.) the cells of the brain's gray matter begin to fire excessively. Nervous impulses are electrical, and this abnormal firing can remain fairly limited or it can spread to adjoining cortical regions, moving from one hemisphere to the other and bringing on thereby a full-scale epileptic seizure.

The clinical manifestations of epilepsy can be simply a momentary lapse of consciousness (*petit mal*), during which the person appears confused or dazed. The more dramatic epileptic (*grand mal*) seizure involves profound loss of consciousness, falling to earth, and a series of convulsive movements in which the limbs flail and the trunk writhes.

But there are also other forms of attack including limited bodily movements or sensations, strange recollections, changes in mood, and various types of hallucinations. By recording the electrical potentials emanating from the brain tissue, either through the scalp or directly from the exposed gray matter, scientists have been able to demonstrate that the extent and type of attack experienced depends upon the region and the amount of the brain involved. It is not always possible to determine why any one patient suffers from epilepsy, but through use of anticonvulsant drugs (e. g., phenobarbital) which reduce the chances of the abnormal firing, as well as physical removal of tumors and other tissues which prompt this firing, a large proportion of epileptic cases have been cured or at least brought under satisfactory management.

It was due to the operations conducted on epileptics that neurosurgeons began to discover more about the relationship between brain activity and behavior. In such operations a bone flap is cut in the skull exposing the brain, which can then be stimulated directly with an electrode. Occasionally a miniature radio receiver is implanted which stimulates the brain even after the bone flap has been closed and the patient is free to move about. The remarkable thing about brain surgery of this sort is that the patient can be administered a local analgesic and then remain conscious during actual brain stimulation on the operating table. The brain is not sensitive to pain directly. The surgeon can therefore probe about with his electrode, administering mild shocks to various regions of the cortex and receiving an immediate report from the patient concerning what happens. In addition to these operations on humans there is a vast literature on lower animals, in which most of the permanent implantation of electrodes work has been done. The two leading figures in the field of brain stimulation have undoubtedly been Wilder Penfield and José M. R. Delgado. Neither of these medical scientists has employed a dialectical formulation in accounting for the findings on brain stimulation, but we shall review their work in light of this concept and the possibility it generates that mentation is telosponsive rather than responsive. Penfield attained eminence in this field first, in 1933, having stumbled onto the remarkable effects to be found when the brain is electrically stimulated.[11] But in some ways Delgado has made a more telling impact on the popular imagination due to his widely read book, *Physical Control of the Mind*. Neither Penfield (now deceased) nor Delgado was ever desirous of developing a technology to manipulate people. Far from it! However, due to the style of Delgado's presentation and some of the sensationalistic implications to be seen in his work, it is not incorrect to state that he has been interpreted more in this light than Penfield. Thus, Delgado gives his reader the following expectation:

> The thesis of this book [*Physical Control of the Mind*] is that we now possess the necessary technology for the experimental investigation of mental activities, and that we have reached a critical turning point in the evolution of man at which the mind can be used to influence its own structure, functions, and purpose, thereby ensuring both the preservation and advance of civilization.[12]

This is an optimistic appraisal, and it mixes terms like "technology" with "mind" to suggest that Delgado sees the mind as equivalent to the brain's physiological mechanisms. He goes on to define "mind" as the *"intracerebral elaboration of extracerebral information,"* and employs language of cybernetics, describing the flow of such extracerebral information in terms of inputs, throughputs, and outputs. Mind *per se* is not a creative principle, but is rather made possible thanks to "the received information which activates stored information and past experiences, creating emotions and ideas." We find a typically Lockean treatment in Delgado's writing, whereby he attributes free will to the "ability to accept or reject ideas and select behavioral responses. A man can isolate himself, meditate, and explore the depths of his own thoughts."[13] Delgado does not say why a man initiates this isolation and meditation in the first place, but since all influence comes from environmental input it follows that this does, too. We are back here to the same questions raised about Locke's conception (see Chapter 5, p. 82). More importantly, we must appreciate that Delgado *begins* his understanding of the research he conducts predicated on a meditational model of mind. Our question is: Do Delgado's empirical data force a Lockean model on us, or can we see glimmerings of a more Kantian, teleological model in what he has to report?

There is an impressive array of such facts. Delgado devised a minute radio instrument called the *stimoceiver* which could be implanted in the brain and permit the experimenter to send electrical impulses directly to the otherwise unrestrained organism. Using this instrument Delgado and others have shown that parietal cortex stimulation in humans results in finger flexions; posterior hypothalamic stimulation in the rat led to apparent pleasure so that the animal would perform tasks in order to receive this electrically manufactured reward; and stimulations in the amygdaloid (humans) and periventricular gray (cats) brought on an aggressive response. In one of the more dramatic demonstrations, a bull was actually stopped in mid-charge by stimulating the reticular formation of the brain.[14]

The image which such findings conjures is that of human (as all animal) behavior as mediated efficiently caused effects of the electrical stimulation, fed back and put through to output totally without regard for a selective "that" for the sake of which events may or *may not* be reliably reproduced. And yet, from the very first Delgado recognized the play of something other than strictly electrical stimulation in the style of animal behavior. In stimulating the thalamus or the central gray region of a monkey's brain with the stimoceiver in order to induce aggression he found that the resultant behavior was never lacking in selectivity. A dominant ("boss") monkey under aggression stimulation "usually attacked the other male [of the monkey group] who represented a challenge to his authority, and he always spared the little female who was his favorite [sexual] partner."[15] When monkeys were removed from the laboratory and allowed to roam free on a small island, while under observation by experimenters housed in a centrally located booth, an even more dramatic fact emerged. Monkeys under stimulation for aggression in this more natural state did not attack other monkeys *at all*, but instead merely dashed about aimlessly in a seemingly agitated state. If the brain stimulation continued an aggressive act did appear, but it took the form of a monkey attacking the booth *where the observers were housed!*[16]

This prompts us to ask whether Delgado has really succeeded in controlling the mind of his experimental animals, or merely induced a physical feeling in relation to which the animal then behaves *selectively?* Twisting the monkey's tail might also induce aggression in certain circumstances, but who would call this mind control? If the monkey were a human being we might hypothesize that he had mentally reconstrued the circumstances. The induced stimulation cannot be avoided, but by the same token it simply becomes a new "that" for the sake of which the course of precedent-sequacious behavior is intended. Is there any evidence on humans which would support this hypothesis?

Delgado cites the case reported by King[17] of a woman under amygdaloid stimulation which generated a feeling of mounting hostility. This emotion frightened her, and she asked that the experimenter not allow her to leave the chair on which she was sitting at the time. When he asked her if she felt like hitting something she replied: "Yeah, I want to hit something. I want to get something and just tear it up. Take it so I won't!"[18] At this point she handed the experimenter her scarf, received in turn a stack of papers, and proceeded to tear up the papers rather than the scarf. Although such alternative selections on the part of a subject being stimulated are apparently overlooked by Delgado, the teleologist cannot but be impressed by the *self-control* being exhibited. The woman (as seemingly did the monkey) took charge of the emotional events as a factor to be considered and arranged subsequent events in precedent-sequacious fashion to accomplish distinctive ends. If there is a physical mechanism involved in such "mind control" there is surely something else going on as well.

In his book, *The Mystery of the Mind*,[19] Penfield is far more impressed by these human maneuvers (he does not discuss lower animals) than is Delgado. Penfield concludes that electrical stimulations are *not* physically controlling the mind. We can dramatize the difference between Delgado and Penfield by comparing their presentations of an identical cortical stimulation in the parietal region of a human's brain. Delgado tells of a man who was made to flex his fingers of the right hand through such stimulation. When this patient was warned that the electrical charge was about to occur and asked to resist it he did not succeed. The fingers of his right hand flexed in response to stimulation despite his efforts to keep them extended. Delgado quotes the man's reaction to this incident as: "I guess, Doctor, that your electricity is stronger than my will."[20] Once again, we have the suggestion here of the human being as an automaton without a "will of his own."

Yet Penfield tells us another side to this same story. He reports that it is not the mind which is under controlled stimulation in such demonstrations, for when a patient has the parietal region electrified and moves the right hand: "he does not say, 'I wanted to move it.' He may, however, reach over with the left hand and oppose his action."[21] If as scientists we are after the mind and not simply the mechanisms of the body then Penfield's more imaginative patient has surely taught us a lesson about *thought* rather than the instrumentalities of physique. Penfield appreciates that mentation embraces intentionality. Mind will be under control *only* when we prove that people can be made to believe something or wish something or choose an alternative by brain stimulation; but, as Penfield makes clear: "There is no place in the cerebral cortex where electrical stimulation will cause a patient to believe or to decide."[22]

Though Penfield's presentation is very compatible with a telic image of behavior his theoretical commitment to exclusively demonstrative formulations prevents him from conceptualizing how it is that a *single* biological process (brain physiology) could have a *duality* about it. Hence, since he believes that he has scientifically observed the operation of mind in his clinical studies,[23] he develops a dualistic explanation of these observations. His theory holds that there are two brain mechanisms, a higher and a lower. The highest brain mechanism has direct contact with the temporal lobes and the prefrontal areas of the cerebral cortex. These areas evolved more recently than the older motor and sensory areas of the diencephalon. It is this older cortex which has a cybernetic, computer-like quality about its functioning. This is where information gleaned from past life is stored. But the interpretation given to such stored information as knowledge is framed by the higher brain mechanism, which is directed by a totally different energy source— the mind!

The mind directs, and the mind-mechanism executes. The mind has no memory but rather relies on the computer banks of the brain's mechanism. Much of what the mind does is accomplished through automatic and reflexive mechanisms, but it cannot be accounted for by the neuronal mechanisms of the brain's physiology. Why not? Because there is always a *doubling of consciousness* when the person is put under brain stimulation. Two streams of consciousness flow, side by side, and the person is aware of this duality so that he is often amused by it, or can decide in light of it which course to take, how to express that which he intends, and so on. For example, when Penfield stimulated one man in the speech cortex while showing him the picture of a butterfly the man snapped his fingers in exasperation until the electrode was withdrawn, at which point he said: "Now I can talk. . . . Butterfly. I couldn't *get* that word 'butterfly,' so I tried to *get* the word 'moth!' "[24] How can we claim that this man's mind was under our control? If we had held our hand over his mouth he could not speak either, but this would hardly be an act of mind control. Mentally, he was obviously fully aware of what he wished to say, and it was simply a technical problem with the instrumentalities of the speech apparatus which prevented him from expressing what was "on his mind."

The duality of consciousness is reflected in several other ways. One of the more striking is a patient's "being" in two places at the same time. A young male patient lying on the operating table in Montreal Canada (where Penfield did his work at McGill University) was astonished to realize that he was *also* laughing with his cousins on a farm in his home country of South Africa. He was fully conscious of both psychic realities. In other instances, after Penfield caused a patient to move his hand by stimulation of the motor cortex he was told by the patient: "I didn't do that. You did." Finally, when patients are made to vocalize something by stimulating their speech center they are likely to say afterward: "I didn't make that sound. You [Penfield] pulled it out of me." These occurrences were so common that Penfield finally decided: "The mind of the patient was as independent of the reflex action [brain stimulation] as was the mind of the surgeon who listened and strove to understand. Thus, my argument favors independence of mind-action [from brain-action]."[25]

The mind acts independently of the brain in the same way that a human programmer acts independently of the computer he uses to organize data and extract information from. There is a sense of *identity*, a person involved in mental activity, and this is totally absent in the automatic processes of the brain. Since it "will always be quite impossible to explain the mind on the basis of neuronal action within the brain," Penfield concludes that the only properly scientific thing to do is accept the fact that "our being does consist of two fundamental elements." The mind of man seems to derive its energy from the highest brain mechanism in some fashion during waking hours, and it is this independent energy which makes for a personal identity. Summing it all up, Penfield says: "A man's mind, one might say, is the person. He walks about the world, depending always upon his private computer, which he programs continuously to suit his ever-changing purposes and interest."[26]

As teleologists, we can be pleased by the dualistic conclusions which so eminent a scientist as Penfield arrived at, but it is disappointing to see him perpetuating the demonstrative, cybernetic interpretation as the exclusive description of mentation. What better demonstration can we have that the law of contradiction does *not* hold in human behavior than the facts that human beings are observed to be in two psychic places at once, rejecting responsibility for what they are now saying, and opposing through counteraction what they are now doing? Surely a dialectical theory with its one-and-many thesis is more suitable to the observed facts than the tired demonstrative formulations.

What we need now is a theoretician working in the biological-physical realm to begin with the possibility that some cells in the brain—or some cellular organizations in the brain—permit not simply the unidirectional passing of messages in cybernetic fashion, but an actual self-reflexivity in the potential to know that knowing is occurring *from the very first brain action*. It is essential to stress this initial point for the same reasons that in the Kantian model we must view ideas as providing a "point of view" from the outset, a perspective which is itself open to transcendental examination (see Chapter 4, p. 63). It is this vis à vis capability, the fact that we are always necessarily "taking a stand on" what we know of reality that gives the stamp of uniqueness to human mentality. Only dialectical theory can capture this style of explanation.

　　Thus, rather than having to postulate two distinct energies which double the mind via separate sources of stimulation, the many-in-one thesis permits us to say that the *same* realm of energy may operate in certain brain cells to produce dualities in meaning. The dialectical formulation permits us to suggest that a single identity, defined oppositionally in relation to input experience ("me" versus "not me" or "that, which is stimulating me to feel things"), affirms a course of meaning-extension with awareness that things could be otherwise. The dualism resulting rather than involving two realms of energy source would be due to the separate organizations of that which is physically input and that which is logically predicated. The former (brain tissue) would not directly and routinely account for the latter (mind).

　　It is this necessity for the mind to take a position on all informational meanings being organized mentally which brings about telosponsivity. As Penfield's comments above make clear, we are never as mental beings forced by sensory input to *think* a certain way. We receive such input stimulation and then *affirm* the direction of bipolar meaning which is to be furthered in our mentation, behaving *for the sake of* what is affirmed rather than *in response to* what is input. The environmental stimuli are never the sole source of informational meanings which Lockean mythology has made them out to be. As

Adler loved to point out, the criminal who has been reared in a high crime area is not simply moulded into this pattern like a lump of clay. He has consciously, with full awareness, taken over a perverted value system to which he now pays allegiance because he sees advantages in looking at the world this way. It is the same with a child reared by parents who have pampered him or, the reverse, rejected him coldly. The neurosis resulting from such early treatment is not simply a unidirectional input of "bad influences." The maturing individual has seized on his circumstances to justify the neurotic life-style he has affirmed out of self-interest. We can speak of probabilities here and Adler would be the first to admit that the odds are against people reared in high crime areas or in homes which lack genuine love. But this actuarial truism should not blind us to the psychic process by which such findings are literally made to come about. And when we get down to psychic processes the individual is always responsible!

Further support for the telic nature of human mentation can be seen in the clinical findings on epileptic patients who have had their corpus callosum, i. e., the broad band of nerve routes connecting the brain hemispheres, cut entirely through so that a *split brain* results. Roger Sperry[27] had conducted many experiments on lower animals with brains so severed (the hemispheres are left intact but isolated from each other) and found no serious disruptions in their behavior. As noted above, since epileptic attacks are prompted by abnormal firing in one hemisphere which then spreads to the other, it seemed reasonable to suppose that human patients with severe (*grand mal*) seizures might be helped if this activity could be isolated to simply one half of the brain. Surgeons eventually operated on several epileptic patients with good results. The psychological studies which Sperry and his associates then conducted on these split-brain patients have lent further support to the dialectical view that a person can have contradictory understandings of the same environmental event, depending upon which of the brain hemispheres is processing his understanding.

First of all, it must be understood that the brain hemispheres accept nerve routes from the side of the body which is opposite to their location. Thus, the nerve tracts which connect to the left side of our body go to the right hemisphere, and the nerve tracts which connect to the right side of our body go to the left hemisphere. Even our visual field is split in half when the corpus callosum is severed, for then our left visual field (images entering the right retinal region) goes to our right brain hemisphere, and our right visual field (images entering the left retinal region) goes to our left brain hemisphere. Scientists had known for some time that the brain hemispheres tended to specialize in function as a person matured, but the findings by Sperry and his colleagues were striking in that all of the split-brain patients demonstrated identical tendencies for the left hemisphere to process language and the right hemisphere to process visual-pictorial material. In a normal brain there is communication across the corpus callosum so that the left hand "knows" what the right hand is doing. But in the split-brain patients the left hand has direct access to what Penfield might have called the "artistic" computer and the right hand has access to the "word-numerical" computer—and never the twain do meet!

Consequently, if the split-brain person is asked to draw a simple picture, like a house, or to arrange some individual colored pieces into a total patterned design he can do so if his *left* hand does the drawing or the arranging. If his right hand is used the picture is not well done, and the pattern task is found to be extremely difficult to accomplish. A striking thing which happens is for the left hand to reach over and literally "lend itself" to the struggling right hand, just as if one person were assisting another.

If a dollar sign is flashed rapidly to the left visual field of

a split-brain patient and a question mark is flashed to the right
visual field at the identical moment, the patient may re-
produce *either* figure as "what was seen?" depending upon
which hand traces out the recollected observation. The patient's hands are hidden from view behind a screen, and he
draws from memory what he saw during the brief flash. The
left hand "saw" a question mark and the right hand "saw" a
dollar sign, so each reproduces its observations accordingly.
Experiments such as these led Sperry to conclude that:
". . . each [brain] hemisphere seems to have its own separate
and private sensations; its own perceptions; its own concepts;
and its own impulses to act, with related volitional, cognitive, and learning experiences. Following the surgery, each
hemisphere also has thereafter its own separate chain of memories that are rendered inaccessible to the recall of the other."[28]

Once again, we have solid empirical evidence that brain
tissues are *actively* organized, and capable of taking a position
on the nature of the perceived stimulus rather than merely responding to the stimulus. It is tempting to continue in the Penfield line and simply multiply the computer metaphor by two,
as we have done above to say that input-output mechanisms
exist side by side. But the teleologist finds the clinical evidence
more suggestive than this. It is easy to overlook the fact that
one hemisphere, one body of knowledge and the viewpoint
contained therein, can look at the other hemisphere's knowledge and viewpoint. What happens if the split-brain patient
someday recalls the *same* past event differently? Which hemisphere is right? If each side has its own concepts, as Sperry
claims, then we would have here a built-in potential for the
contradictions which the law of contradiction tells us cannot
logically be the case. A person will both believe and not believe that what took place is what actually took place. He will
describe the same event in mutually exclusive terms. And he
will express conflicting values concerning the same thing.

The only way in which we shall be able to make sense of

such "illogical" circumstances is to adopt the logic of dialectics. Some investigators have essentially identified the right hemisphere with (in our terms) dialectical reasonings such as artistic dualities, transcendence, and so on, and the left hemisphere with demonstrative reasoning such as classical logic, mathematics, and the like.[29] But it would seem that the only way we can pull together the totality is through a dialectical one-and-many formulation. The descriptions of the hemispheric functions are surely *oppositional*—the left is linear, the right non-linear; the left is verbal, the right is non-verbal or pictorial; the left is coldly logical, the right is emotively intuitional, and so on. Since this lateral specialization does not exist at birth it follows that a principle of organization is being followed over the developmental years. And the most parsimonious explanation is surely that this principle is dialectical in nature.

## Conclusion

Based on the brain research discussed in Chapter 10 we can conclude that there is nothing here to contradict our view of human behavior as telosponsive. Although it may have certain cybernetic aspects in some of its memorial functioning, the brain is most surely something more than a computer or related information-processing machine. The information which is processed "depends" upon the point of view and the selective factors of a distinctive kind of bodily tissue. The psychic processes associated with the neuronal cells of these tissues can transcend the mechanical input-output nature of its physiological processes. There is a resultant awareness in consciousness that "something else" is going on at the same time (Penfield) or that something else "might" take place at the same time. Mentation is therefore always a matter of *taking a position on* what meanings should, could, must, ought, etc. be presumed and furthered in overt action. It is this capacity for an ultimately arbitrary grounding in the affirmations of a reason ever open to alternative possibilities that makes teleo-sponsivity possible. The brain is *not* simply a cybernetic mechanism because it *is* open to dialectical division and oppositionality, with the resultant logic generating alternatives that are fundamental to the exercise of free will.

# ELEVEN

# Why Popular Psychologies "Work"

In Chapter 10 we mentioned (p. 195) that popular science-fiction often portrays human behavior in mechanistic terminology, even as it invariably capitalizes on the telic for dramatic effect. This tendency to fall back on theories of behavioristic conditioning or the processing of information (cybernetics) is also prominent in the self-help books which consistently make the best-seller lists. But even when this is true for a book of this type, the demonstrable fact is that what proves most helpful in its contents is the emphasis given to the telic aspects of human behavior. The upshot is that there is a gross disparity between the human image as projected by the self-help books and the human image as projected by the average psychology textbook. Though these popular psychologies sell hundreds of thousands of copies yearly, a fairly representative (albeit probably middle-class) sample of subjects by anyone's standards, the modern psychologist rarely looks at their contents as evidence for understanding the type of animal which would go through the effort and expense of obtaining a copy and reading it. In the present chapter we will do precisely this.

## The Common Themes

There are some common themes to be found in self-help books. They are always written from an introspective perspective, of course, for the point here is to express *for the reader* a beneficial course of action. The writing is usually in the first person, with heavy reliance on colloquialisms (including slang, occasional vulgarity) and humor when appropriate. Another major tactic is the use of inspirational examples. The reader is given vignettes from the lives of famous people, former students of the approach under espousal, or case histories of psychotherapy clients the writer has worked with. If an approach employs group participation—like the Dale Carnegie course or *est*—then it is common for testimonials to be given, much in the fashion of religious gatherings or the meetings of Alcoholics Anonymous. These testimonials reassure the participants (and readers) that they are not so different from other troubled people, and that they can therefore aspire to what others have achieved, in improving their confidence level and finding a more satisfying life style.

If one had to delineate the general philosophy of self-help approaches it could probably be summed up with the triumvirate attitudes of currency, realism, and genuineness. The focus is on the practicalities of *current* behavior. This does not mean that the reader is turned away from the future, for the entire point of the book is to improve his performance in the future. But the stress is on living more fully in the present once this new life style is brought about. After all, a practical tool is always brought to bear "right now," as we make use of it to rectify the problems currently facing us. This also requires a certain degree of honesty in one's self-assessment, a realism in judging what one's strengths and weaknesses are. People tend to alibi and dodge responsibility for their actions. They do not want to accept the facts facing them, which is why they so often fail to live to the fullest in the ever-recurring present. The self-help books encourage people to make an honest appraisal of things, admit their role in what is taking place, and then seek to alter events to their advantage.

A related point here is the emphasis usually given to genuineness and spontaneity. This is not *always* the case, because in certain efforts the point is studiously to manipulate the behavior of others. But speaking more broadly, the message in self-help books is that we are happiest and most productive while behaving spontaneously in the manner which they advocate. There is usually an intrinsic and not an instrumental ethic being advanced (see Chapter 5, p. 94). It is when the person is *least* concerned about following rules in rote fashion, assigning blame, or dreaming of risk-free futures that he is *most alive!*

Given this philosophical background and the direct approach of writing practically for the reader, these books then put forth in more or less explicit terms a number of *How To* behave and *How Not To* behave patterns. The *How To* patterns are what the reader is supposedly looking for, but he is also fascinated by the fact that his current style is often captured in the *How Not To* descriptions. The positively framed *How To* styles are likely to be listed as "Six Ways in Which To Increase Your Confidence" or some such. The *How Not To* patterns are communicated less explicitly, as the contents of testimonials, clinical case histories, or a series of prototype maneuvers (gamesmanship, immaturities, etc.) which result in unproductive interpersonal relations.

There has been no thorough empirical study of the readers of such books, so it is difficult to tell what supposedly helps a reader more—the emotional reassurance achieved in reading about others in trouble "like me" or the more problem-centered benefit to be gained from putting a book's suggested rules into play. Since the *How To* recommendations are repetitive, so that after reading three or four such efforts one is about ready to predict what the next book will say, there is surely more being obtained from the contents than the advertised practical benefits. There has to be a kind of prayer-book reading involved, one which does not object to redundancy so long as the mood remains the same.

We move now to a survey of self-help books in order to see more specifically what their basic theories entail. Our sampling is not exhaustive, and the purpose here is *not* to dwell on the contents of these books *per se*. What we are looking for is the basic human image being embraced in a given book, and to see how well it fits our claim that all such efforts rely upon and are written for an organism that is telosponsive rather than merely responsive or mediational in behavioral style.

## How To Win Friends and Influence People

The prototype of the *How To* books is without doubt Dale Carnegie's *How To Win Friends and Influence People*. Published initially in 1936, this book is a summation of the philosophy of self-confidence which Carnegie advocated in his adult-education courses, where he instructed people from all walks of life in public speaking, salesmanship, and the general art of living. Carnegie graduated from a state teachers' college, where he excelled in public speaking and debate. Although he uses the phrase "human engineering" at one point in the book, Carnegie does not really have a specific theoretical orientation on which to base his approach. One gets the impression that he is speaking from plain Yankee common sense. He begins by emphasizing that human beings are not logical but emotional creatures and that everyone wants to have a personal "feeling of importance." In order to know what makes any one person feel important, we must view things from his "angle." This is crucial because: ". . . the only way on earth to influence the other fellow is to talk about what he wants and show him how to get it."[1]

Once we know what a person wants, and assuming we can give it to him, the remaining problem is to be the kind of person others like doing business with. Carnegie recommends several ways in which to make people like us, such as showing interest in them, always smiling and recalling their names, being a good listener, and so on. When a sales pitch is made, the essential thing is to get the other person believing "that you are both striving for the same end and your only difference is one of method and not of purpose." Here again, we can win people over by following such rules as avoiding arguments, showing respect for their opinion, admitting to our mistakes, getting them to say "yes" early in the conversation, and letting them do most of the talking. Even though such rules appear to be manipulative instrumentalities, Carnegie is adamant in charging that one cannot really be effective if he is interpersonally insincere. At several points in the book he cautions the reader that making another person feel important demands that we really believe in what we say and do. As he summed it up: ". . . the principles taught in this book will work only when they come from the heart. I am not advocating a bag of tricks. I am talking about a new way of life."[2]

As a further elaboration of this optimistic philosophy Carnegie touches on two points which become major refrains of the *How To* movement. These are actually variations on a common theme. The first point concerns making ourselves what we want to be through conscious effort. Peale will call this *positive thinking* (see below). Thus, as a kind of warm-up for sales proficiency Carnegie encourages the reader to learn how to smile, to get into the proper mood by whistling or humming a tune: "Act as if you were already happy, and that will tend to make you happy." The second point concerns the self-fulfilling prophecy. Carnegie notes that people tend to live up to the labels we give them, so that we can actually influence others by assigning the right kind of image to them: "Give a man a fine reputation to live up to."[3] If we acknowledge a man's honesty and good sense in speaking with him, then assuming we have a sound product to sell in the first place, he is bound to be emotionally on our side because he must live up to the good sense which our evaluation has assigned to him at the outset.

Stepping back from this classic, a volume which has been read now by millions of people all over the earth for over two generations, what are we to conclude? Surely the telic nature of this writing must be clear to us. Carnegie is asking us to help everyone achieve their ends whether this results in a pecuniary gain for us or not.[4] He is not talking about machines needing adjusting or responses needing manipulation. Carnegie is talking about telosponsivity! Of course, we must honestly admit that not everyone taking the Carnegie course and reading his book could be said to be moved by such an intrinsic ethic of brotherly love. Surely there have been a large number of instrumentalists among the Carnegie students. But the image of man on which the approach is based is *not* of this stripe, and the teleologist must insist that this be taken cognizance of in assessing the effectiveness of its principles.

### The Power of Positive Thinking

The second most influential *How To* book in the history of this movement is surely Norman Vincent Peale's *The Power of Positive Thinking*.[5]* As a minister, Peale naturally based his approach on man's telic propensities, but he also took a step in the direction of the more mechanistic styles of explanation which were to follow him. He tells us in the introduction that his book can teach one "how to 'will' not to be."[6] Peale is saying that we can freely arrange those predications for the sake of which we might behave, and then *willfully* bring them forward. Too many people have their minds filled with self-

* Following excerpts from the book, *The Power of Positive Thinking* by Dr. Norman Vincent Peale. © 1952 by Prentice-Hall, Inc. Published by Prentice-Hall, Inc., Englewood Cliffs, New Jersey.

doubts and feelings of inferiority. If they would work to replace these with a strong sense of faith they could counteract what might be termed the *power of negative thinking* with its dialectical opposite, i. e., a positive belief in the goodness of God.

He tells of a salesman (recall Carnegie!) who achieved considerable success using such a method. Each day, as he made his business rounds he would select from a stack of cards some random Biblical statement that he had copied down and clip it to the dashboard of his automobile. Let us say it was "If God be for us, who can be against us?" [Romans 8:31]. As he made his sales visits for that day he put his quotation to memory. Since all of the Biblical statements were positive in tone he was effectively building up a store of positive thoughts, which reflected in his life outlook and thereby in his sales record. Peale based his entire approach on this tactic, broadening it to include *both* religious thoughts (prayers) and other positive forms of thinking. Prayers can, of course, contain negative references but Peale dissuades the reader from engaging in such negative forms of prayer.[7]

As a general strategy of "prayer power" Peale borrowed the phraseology of a friend which suggested that we should (1) *Prayerize:* i. e., pray creatively each day, not always asking for things but simply thinking about God; (2) *Picturize:* i. e., put forward in our wishes the kinds of lives we want to live under God's influence, the sorts of ends we hope to achieve; and (3) *Actualize:* i. e., find without doing anything specifically that the ends which we have picturized begin to take place.[8] It is in the elaboration of prayer power that Peale begins to build a bridge toward the mechanistic style of explanation. He suggests that we can send prayers forward to others, even toward our enemies, with good effects resulting. He has himself searched about an audience before giving one of his talks, picking out an unfriendly face and then praying for this person before taking the rostrum. After his talk the unfriendly person has told him of a change in attitude, a move on his part from initial dislike to one of liking Peale's views. Though Carnegie might have attributed this shift in attitude to Peale's elocutionary skills, Peale would not agree:

> It was not my speech that had this effect [on the listener]. It was the emanation of prayer power. In our brains we have about two billion little storage batteries. The human brain can send off power by thoughts and prayers. The human body's magnetic power has actually been tested. We have thousands of little sending stations, and when these are turned up by prayer it is possible for a tremendous power to flow through a person and to pass between human beings. We can send off power by prayer which acts as both a sending and receiving station.[9]

Aside from the debatable validity of this thought-transference claim—something which is still being debated and as yet scientifically unproven—the tactic taken by Peale here confounds three distinctive issues. We have first the matter of whether it is the thought content sent which influences a person or the electricity *per se?* In the former case we have a telic explanation, for thoughts are best described as formal causes "for the sake of which" (final causes) a mentality extends meaningful behavior; but in the latter case we have simply a material-efficient cause involvement of signals triggering other signals. Secondly, is not a prayer a thought? If so, then what is the necessity for distinguishing between prayers and just any other form of "positive" thought? Finally, if *any* positive thought works in the thought transference then what is to prevent us from concluding that it is not religion which brings on the thought transference, but simply the projection of a positive thought content—religious or otherwise? As we shall see below, in the popular psychologies which followed Peale an emphasis on the positive remains but the religious phraseology is either dropped or made quite secondary.

In his examples of how to build self-confidence through positive thinking, Peale cites many extra-religious possibilities, such as picturing oneself succeeding at an intended task, minimizing obstacles in one's way, and not being awestruck by other people. His central point is that we are masters of our own fate: "Who decides whether you shall be happy or unhappy? The answer—you do!"[10] On this point, Peale has some firmer scientific evidence in his support. Psychologists have found in asking subjects to learn language terms (words, stories, etc.) and pictorial items (recognize faces, paintings, etc.) that just how the subject predicates the task and/or himself influences what sorts of meanings he will enlarge upon or extend.[11] Thus, if he likes the task and/or himself as a person (i. e., has "self-confidence") he is more likely to learn those things which he *personally* likes than those he dislikes. Conversely, a subject who dislikes the task and/or himself is seen to acquire personal meanings along the negative line more readily than the positive.

Practical examples of this phenomenon might be the person who goes to a party expecting to have a miserable time. Due to this predication the chances are much greater that he or she actually will have an unsatisfactory (disliked) evening. The sports fan who greatly enjoys baseball and decidedly dislikes ice hockey will rarely notice or elaborate on news which is critical of his favorite pastime. However, should a news story break which detracts from ice hockey he is for the first time in weeks seen reading and commenting on this least of his preferred sports topics. Of course, when this tendency to extend meanings along the negative becomes pervasive, so that the person can find *nothing* bringing more satisfaction than dissatisfaction in life, we are likely to see a neurosis taking form in his behavioral style. Since it is the person who ultimately does the evaluating, it is true to say that he or she does indeed decide whether life will be happy or unhappy. We must not forget the play of unconscious intentions as well.

So Peale is correct in suggesting that it is the person who creates his own affective circumstances. The person creates his own self-image too, and if he allows the views of others to color his personally generated evaluations too much, or to "fuss and fume" too much, then it is just possible that through the simple expedient of stopping to consider more realistically where he stands, and by (dialectically) examining the alternatives open to him, a more satisfactory self-image may be fashioned. By taking on different predications about himself and his life circumstances a new course of telosponsivity is made available (via dialectical change). To facilitate this reorientation Peale recommends listing one's strengths and weaknesses on a piece of paper, which usually teaches us that we have more plus factors in life than we realized in focusing on our minuses. He also favors emptying our heads for a brief period each day in order to clean out negative thoughts before refurbishing the intellect with Godly inspired, positive thoughts.[12] He has many rules of thumb to aid the reader in re-ordering the premises for the sake of which a satisfying life style can be enacted. The telic flavor of his psychology is clear, but its quasi-scientific rendering helped open the door to a whole new way of saying similar things in the *How To* tradition.

## Gamesmanship and Transactional Analysis

The Carnegie and Peale books were written from perspectives outside of the scientific community *per se*, but there is historical precedence for writing popular versions of the classical personality theories of Chapter 8. One of the first books published (in 1901) by Freud was *The Psychopathology of Everyday Life*,[13] in which he tried to show how the bungled actions, forgetting of names, and slips of the pen which we all experience daily are psychically determined and therefore intentional. Alfred Adler also wrote books like *What Life Should Mean to You*[14] which were aimed directly at the popular market, and there were many other psychiatrists and psychologists who did the same. In recent decades there has been considerable popular interest in what is called Transactional Analysis—"TA" for short. The originator of the approach was Eric Berne, whose books *Transactional Analysis in Psychotherapy* and *Games People Play*[15] present the theoretical framework on which it rests, enlarged subsequently by Thomas H. Harris in the book *I'm OK—You're OK*.[16] As psychiatrists, both Berne (now deceased) and Harris might be said to represent the more "legitimate" scientific disciplines in the popular market.

Berne managed to combine Freudian with information-processing terminology, and arrived thereby at a demonstrative image of the person. Though Freud disliked the dialectic, recall that he always captured that oppositional, contradictory, two-things-meaning-one flavor in his descriptions of behavior (see Chapters 3 and 7). Berne claimed that psychologically considered, each of us consists of three distinct "systems" of behaviors referred to colloquially as the Child, Parent, and Adult. These *ego* states stand for, respectively, our childlike patterns of behavior, the attitudes and phrasings of our parents and similar authority figures, and the more reality-oriented, autonomous behavior which each person also acquires as he comes to maturity. Social relations or *transactions* are complicated by the fact that two people can interact at the same level, or, from one ego-state level to another. The wife who responds "You don't love me or you wouldn't speak to me that way" each time her husband questions her obvious mismanagement of their finances is responding as a Child to his realistically framed Adult complaint.

In his first book (published in 1961) Berne used a psychic energy explanation of how it is that one or the other of these three ego-states assumes command of the overt personality at any point in time: ". . . that ego state which is cathected in a certain way will have the *executive power*."[17] However, when his more popular book on gamesmanship appeared (1964) he placed major emphasis on cybernetic theoretical language. Ego states were now said to be coherent sets of behavior patterns which essentially acted as mediators in the programming of ongoing transactions between people. The transaction is itself a form of Lockean building block, a unit of social intercourse consisting of the exchange of so-called "strokes" between people or the frustration of strokes.[18] A *stroke* is akin to positive reinforcement, a metaphorical allusion to the stroking of a baby cradled in its mother's loving arms.

According to Berne, we all go through life with a stimulus-hunger for such stroking, which comes through later in life as a recognition-hunger in that we seek appreciation and signs of status in the eyes of others. We also are motivated to structure our lives. We have structure-hunger and need to avoid boredom. Our time is therefore programmed for us by the culture (as, in social amenities), the demands of reality (e. g., it takes time to get our food prepared), and also in a more free-wheeling style by our individual sequencing of interpersonal relations. Here is where the *game* comes in, for it is a recurring set of transactions which has been time-structured by the individual. All three ego states can enter into games, or any transaction for that matter. Using the cybernetic frame of reference Berne says: "Transactions usually proceed in series. These series are not random, but are programed. Programing may come from one of three sources: Parent, Adult, or Child, or more generally, from society, material or idiosyncracy [i. e., individualized games]."[19]

Games are fundamentally dishonest transactions, in which a certain "player" is either seeking a stroke or is led to believe that he will be stroked, but in the end *will not!* For example, in the game of "Buzz off, Buster," a voluptuous woman flirts with a man at a cocktail party, excites him sexually, and then after he has taken her home and made the obvious "final move" of the game he is told to buzz off.[20] The point of this game is for the woman to again prove that all men are "animals." She was not playing the coquette. She was just acting as she "always does" at cocktail parties—where, invariably, some "animal" makes a pass at her. Sexual advances are uncalled for just because a person is spontaneous and open in interpersonal relations. Revealing dresses are "in style" and this is why she wears them, and so on. . . . Speaking clinically, the woman is unconscious of her game plan but she behaves seductively nevertheless. This is a fairly complex game, but Berne outlined a number of even rather simple transactions in which one person can put another off guard, or "one down" as the saying goes.

It is interesting to note that the first game Berne delineated rests essentially on a dialectical exchange. This is called the "Why Don't You—Yes But" game.[21] It might be played as follows. A person complains about his or her job to a listener. The listener responds with the obvious idea that there can always be a change in jobs. The rebuttal to this is "Yes, but I've got a lot of seniority on this job and wouldn't want to lose that." The next round in the game is something like this: "Well, then you'll just have to find some way of liking your present job more." "Yes, but how?" Round three: "Well, since you have complained so much about getting up early in the morning to get to work maybe you could transfer to the afternoon shift." "Yes, but then I wouldn't be around in the evening when my kids are home from school and I'd miss them." And so on. . . . There is no way of ending this game because the "Yes, but" player is not about to permit the other person to receive the stroke of having solved a problem. The dialectician would point out how, in such exchanges, it is not simply a matter of one person "sending" and the other "receiving" information. What actually happens is that as one player is framing a constructive suggestion the other is routinely *reasoning to its opposite* and simply bouncing back grounds for rejecting the meaning being expressed at the other end of the dialogue. In this sense, the "helpful" person always frames his own negation.

As noted above, Berne held that there could be game-free transactions, in which people would give each other strokes more openly and readily.[22] This is what the "I'm OK—You're OK" phrase gets at in the Harris volume—i. e., a sense of mutual acceptance and worth among all transactional actors. Judging from the even greater emphasis which Harris places on cybernetic terminology the drift of TA seems to have been decidedly away from psychoanalysis in the 1960s. Both Berne and Harris refer to the work of Penfield in support of their theory. Berne says: "The human brain is the organ or organizer of psychic life, and its products are organized and stored in the form of ego states. There is already concrete evidence for this in some findings of Penfield and his associates."[23] Harris uses the analogue of a computing-machine tape for the brain, referring to it as a high-fidelity recorder, and he also justifies the equation of the brain with mind (ego states) by referring to Penfield.[24] To keep things in historical perspective, we must not forget that Penfield had not yet written *The Mystery of the Mind*,[25] in which he specifically disowns suggestions that mentation can be circumscribed by brain function (see Chapter 10).

But the more important point is, whereas in the 1950s the popular psychology movement was clearly telic as reflected in the writings of Peale, by the 1960s we see a growing tendency to speak of the human being as a machine. Harris says: "The Adult [ego state] is a data-processing computer, which grinds out decisions after computing the information from three sources: the Parent, the Child, and the data which the Adult has gathered and is gathering."[26] He tells of Child data overloading a patient's computer. That this is not simply quasi-scientific lingo to be used in publication but not in practice is negated by the following quote of one of his patients: "But my computer finally clicked and made me aware that there is another option open—My Adult can evaluate the situation and intercede for my Child."[27] Note the passive, Lockean image of humanity reflected in the phrasing. We might sum up the therapeutic goal of TA as that of re-programming people, getting them to relate on a par, accepting each other as adults, using child-like behaviors occasionally as a source of spontaneity, but in the main avoiding reliance on parental attitudes. As Berne delightfully expressed it: "In essence, this whole preparation [i. e., course of therapeutic re-programming in TA] consists of obtaining a friendly divorce from one's parents (and from other Parental influences) so that they may be agreeably visited on occasion, but are no longer dominant."[28]

Though there may be wisdom in this recommended divorce, the truth is Berne and Harris have so confounded telic and non-telic terminology that they have obscured the reasons why their approach may work in the clinic. Adler had talked about gamesmanship in interpersonal relations (transactions), but he also recognized that these were premises taken on by innately telic organisms and then brought forward in life telosponsively (see Chapter 8, p. 155). Computers did not "click," but affirmation and dialectical change surely occurred in Adlerian psychology. The Harris volume is particularly fraught with telic phraseology, and at one point he even cites Trueblood[29] to the effect that the human mind operates by reference to final causes, so that what *is not* can influence what *is*.[30] Harris also supports the Durant[31] saying that we are free when we know why we are doing what we are doing.[32] Harris seems not to understand, as Penfield did, that computers—whether ego states or otherwise—can *never* know why they are doing what they are doing. This is why Penfield doubled the mind and spoke of a programmer. Knowing stored information is not the same kind of "transcendental knowing" as knowing that one's thought is grounded in a "that" for the sake of which it proceeds (see Chapter 10).

People who benefit from TA are not simply inputting more data, or re-programming old circuitry. They as the client quoted above are learning that there is *more than one perspective* to be taken on the fact patterns of life. This Machian insight (see Chapter 5, p. 86) is not limited to scientific description, and it teaches us that we must *always* consider the slant, the Kantian point of view, the Carnegie "angle" (refer above) if we are to understand the meanings being intended by the mind of any and all human beings. Penfield could never electrically stimulate this point of view, this vis à vis, and he therefore properly concluded that mind and brain are not the same thing. There is a memory bank to be sure, but this mechanism is always put to interpretation and analysis by a programmer. Despite Berne's claims on Penfield's findings, there is no evidence whatsoever that the programmer takes on Child, Parent, or Adult characteristics. Indeed, the contents of child-like or parental behaviors would most certainly be in the memory bank and *not* in the role of programmer.

We are left with the likely possibility that human beings are receiving considerable benefit from an approach to social relations which capitalizes on their free will only to explain it through *false analogies* to non-telic behavioral explanations. Freud seemed always to be aware of the superfluous need of the libido theory to account for human behavior (see Chapter 3, p. 47). We can only wonder how seriously the modern TA advocate takes the pseudo-cybernetic terminology which frames his account, or whether he even appreciates the differences in causation implied by one or the other of the theoretical explanations a therapist makes use of in accounting for the benefits his clients experience.

## Psycho-cybernetics

Maxwell Maltz, an internationally known plastic surgeon, founded the approach of self-management called psycho-cybernetics. He combines religious themes with mechanism, telling his reader that: ". . . in making man, our Creator has endowed him with a servo-mechanism more wonderful than any electronic brain or guidance system that man has invented—and operating on the same basic principles." Animals do not select their goals in life, but human beings do. The kinds of goals we humans select and the confidence we have in achieving them depend upon our selection of past recollections from our memory bank to be employed by the servo-mechanism. The trick is to do the right kind of programming, because, as the reader is told: "Within your midbrain is a very small electronic computer, a tape recorder, an automatic servo-mechanism, a success mechanism that you operate like an electronic computer, a goal-striving mechanism that will help you move toward your goals."[33] Indeed, God wants man to succeed in life.

Psycho-cybernetics means steering our minds toward productive useful goals, based upon a proper use of our brain's success mechanism. We must specify success here because there is also a failure mechanism operating in the brain. In fact, the central battle of life involves the continual struggle over which mechanism is to reign supreme—our success or failure mechanisms. The focus of this battle is really the self-image. A person pictures himself in terms of what he recalls about past behaviors and how he approaches current behaviors. This image can be positive or negative depending upon how we program it to be. The trick is to raise our self-images, and move on from personal frustration to fulfillment by making certain that our positive servo-mechanism is directing things.[34]

There are many things which conspire to weaken one's self-image, presenting it in a negative light. Guilt feelings result from the struggle between our success and failure mechanisms. Maltz cautions the reader: "Don't let your conscience rule you; you rule your conscience." A basic concept in psycho-cybernetics is that of *habit*, interpreted essentially as a programmed regularity of behavior. Proper psychological adjustment means establishing proper habits. Psychoneurosis is the result of bad habits. Learning how to live successfully demands practice so that good habits can be established. And here is where Maltz gives the reader point after point, of how to raise his self-image and establish successful habits of behavior. There is much emphasis placed on will power. We are told to "long for improvement,"[35] tap hidden resources, and reach for opportunities as they arise each day. There is also the familiar stress on relaxation, clearing the mind of self-defeating thoughts, and a recharging with inspirational vignettes and easily memorized rules of thumb.

The reader must surely agree that in psycho-cybernetics we have our contrapuntal themes of mechanism and teleology appearing without really clarifying which is the *essential* source of the benefits received. Penfield's brain research is in evidence, with conclusions drawn to which he did not accede. The dynamic clash between success and failure, easily framed in dialectical terms, is given a demonstrative, black-white interpretation. We can ponder the validity of a claim that success and failure are readily distinguishable, as if they represented two distinct mechanisms rather than an evaluation of the outcomes of the *same* mechanism. Success and failure represent judgments of behavior, given certain grounds and not others. To make it appear that there are two slots in the brain's memory bank, one marked success and the other failure, is surely to misrepresent the duality of human experience which Penfield's research has established is the case.

## Hierarchies and Power Plays

We move now to a slightly different focus, on the hierarchies within which human beings behave and the attendant status-power considerations of this structure. Laurence J. Peter (with Raymond Hull, initially) formulated the widely cited *Peter Principle*, which holds that in a hierarchy of increasingly important positions every person eventually advances to his *level of incompetence*.[36] Thus, it is inevitable in both private industry and public governmental bureaucracies that positions of responsibility will be filled by individuals who are incompetent to carry out the duties required. We have to be cautious about taking the Peter Principle too seriously, because at least in the first book written on the problem there was a tongue-in-cheek quality about the ideas expressed. The popularity of these ideas seems to have prompted the writing of *The Peter Prescription*,[37] in which we get a more traditional *How To* emphasis.

Though space considerations do not permit a full discussion of the topic, Peter's delightfully humorous writing style permits us to note that what we take to be funny often relies on a dialectical twist in the expression of words or the course of events. When Peter says *"nothing fails like success"*[38] he tickles our funny bone because of the unexpected reversal, just as we chuckle when a powerful and "proper" person stumbles on his approach to the speaker's rostrum and then stares out at us for that red-faced moment in which we all understand that he is one of us after all.[39] By dialectically turning success into failure Peter has expressed a truth about human nature which Maltz's psycho-cybernetics will never quite capture (refer above).

However, we must sadly report that when Peter gets into the basic descriptions of human behavior, he as so many psychologists (his Ph.D. degree was in Education) seems trapped by the language of instinct and reinforcement. This does not come through clearly until he begins advancing prescriptions. But even in his original work he speaks of a hierarchal *instinct*, claiming that: ". . . man is essentially hierarchal by nature, and must and will have hierarchies, whether they be patriarchal, feudal, capitalistic, or socialistic."[40] It is common for those who write about hierarchies to trace this supposedly instinctive tendency to a Darwinian concept of some sort—e. g., to the struggle for existence, the territorial claims which animals have, the pecking orders from weak to strong animals, and so on. But hierarchies are also the product of telic assessments, the projections of things to aim for, acquire, and then use as extensions of personal power. Economic power allows for alternative life styles, as the range of behaviors across the socioeconomic levels termed lower, middle, and upper classes are testimony to. But are such class identities based on an instinct (formal cause in style due to material and efficient causes in man's biology), or is there *also* an intentional and aspirational side to such hierarchies (bringing in final causes)?

Peter thinks that Peale may have overestimated the power of "push" i. e., self-driven aspiration to succeed. Coining an [Horatio] *Alger Complex*, he wryly observes that those employees who come early and work late often gain nothing more than the enmity of their peers, who do not mind incompetence or mediocrity because they expect people to be promoted by seniority factors or "pull" anyhow. Peter's aim is to get people out of this upward hierarchal pull. To live a satisfying life the person must find his level of competence and stay there, because promotion is the cause of occupational incompetence. To achieve this end he recommends *creative incompetence*, which is the art of being just inadequate enough on the job currently held so that a demotion or firing will not result, but most assuredly a promotion will not occur either.[41]

Peter's prescription is to move forward to a better life, without succumbing to the "up, up, and oops!" trap of hier-

archal ascensions. Those who go up the promotion ladder to
their level of incompetence are termed Processionary Puppets,
and Peter offers the role of a Humanite in opposition to this
blind round of doing what the hierarchy signals rather than
what the individual desires. A Humanite is a human being who
fulfills his potential and derives satisfaction from being creative, confident, and competent at his natural level in the hierarchy. It is when he now begins to elaborate the role of Humanite that Peter begins reading more like the traditional *How
To* author. He advises such things as the revitalization of the
body, relaxation, being one's own hero, reaffirming a belief in
oneself, and so on. He also begins to fall back on the terminology of reinforcement theory, which in a way counters the
marvelous touch he had achieved in elaborating the *faux pas* of
stepping up the status hierarchy. He says, "When a behavior
produces pain or discomfort, that behavior will tend to de-
crease in the future."[42] But is this true? How many Processionary Puppets stop their upward push when the competition
and the criticism begin to adversely affect their lives?

There is much emphasis placed on directed behavior and
the development of a positive self-concept. We are encouraged
to focus our efforts in our area of competence, and to try to
foretell just when our level of incompetence will be reached.
A Humanite always identifies his objective in life rather than
simply taking a direction without knowing quite where it will
lead.[43] This would surely imply a realistic assessment of the
*ends* in life. Even so, when we get right down to an analysis
of how the human being reaches these ends Peter betrays his
doctrinaire psychological education, falling back on those
Lockean theories of learning which though fading are still
ascendant in psychology. In a remarkable paragraph he sum-
marizes the life span as follows:

> The developmental acquisition of satisfaction or rein-
> forcement starts with food and progresses through physi-

cal contact, words, social approval, material possessions, competent interactions with the environment, money and other token systems, knowledge of results, and self-evaluation. Each of these contains the earlier reinforcers, so that the developmental stages represent expanding repertoires of responsiveness to reinforcers.[44]

This traditional overview of conditioning precepts leaves us wondering if Peter has not lost his sense of humor—if not his sense of humanity—by taking his prescriptive role too seriously. Once again, we are back to an image which has the person more shaped than shaping, even as the principles along which this shaping is to occur rest upon obvious telic factors like goal-orientations, planning for the future, and knowing when the projected goal has been achieved.

It is therefore with some relief that we turn to the book by Michael Korda entitled *Power! How To Get It, How To Use It*. Korda is a writer and journalist, and therefore has no professional need to justify patterns of power he sees in hierarchies by relating them to doctrinaire psychological learning theories. His book is a variant on the gamesmanship theme we discussed above, except that he focuses specifically on maneuvers employed by people in competition to ascend a power hierarchy—usually a business organization. These maneuvers are not necessarily unconscious. Korda agrees with Peter that promotions are not based on merit but rather on rewards for faithfulness to one's superiors or the job *per se* (i. e., seniority). Rather than accounting for them in terms of instinct, Korda takes a common-sense, teleological view of the origin of hierarchies, noting that: ". . . if it were not for the hope of rising, few people would do any more work than is necessary for survival."[45]

Power is concerned with knowing what one wants, and being able to get it. The purpose of power is not simply to obtain financial reward, but to get a sense of autonomy, independence, and satisfaction in life. Korda discusses the styles of different types of power "players," some of whom are named while others remain anonymous. It is in the analysis of how such players maneuver that the book achieves its clearest *How To* qualities. The art of intimidation is one such power play. The player moves into an opponent's office, using his telephone with a flourish and if possible sitting in his chair. At meetings an opponent can be intentionally singled out and suddenly attacked outrageously. Power players place their desks between themselves and their visitors, rather than having a person sit off to the side of the desk. There are certain ways in which the power player behaves at office parties, and Korda has an amusing description of this tendency for people with status to move first from corners of the room where they have a coterie of followers surrounding them toward a central region near the liquor bar. Power offices are also those in the corner of a building. Seating arrangements at meetings tend to signify power hierarchies, rotating in clock-wise fashion away from the most powerful person attending.[46]

We are obviously concerned here with meanings based upon patterns of social relations—i. e., formal-cause conceptions. Human beings are meaning-extending organisms, who look to advantages and improvements in life and telospond according to signs of these potential rewards. Without such patterned indicants we would all be psychologically adrift on the sea of life's advantages. Although behavioristic psychologists make it appear that obtaining rewards in life is something which will take care of itself, the truth is, those rewards which are more than simply food-and-water type "reinforcements" do *not* present themselves clearly to psychological awareness. The oft referred to "system" which supposedly rules us like some grand Skinnerian reinforcing machine is *not* unidirectionally brought to bear from above as so many of its critics imply. Reward systems in our culture are negotiated, based on the fact that both those who give and those who receive rewards need a patterned outline (formal cause) for the sake of which (final cause) the rewards worth living for can be defined.

The basic needs for survival in an advanced culture—food, water, shelter, etc.—are easily obtained. Such rewards are hardly "motivating" to the general populace. And the higher one ascends a hierarchy of "reward power" the *less* important are such fundamental necessities. Korda shows how men at "the top" of the industrial hierarchy begin looking for rewards in the thickness of the carpeting which covers their office floors, private elevators, and the possession of a private bathroom with sauna attached. What kind of animal is this, which will work itself into an early heart attack over carpets and privies when it could, as Peter would have it do, confine itself to the completely satisfying rewards of a lesser rank in the status hierarchy? Surely no dog or rat or monkey would behave this foolishly. We are forced to conclude that only a predominantly telic animal, one which can pattern rewards above and beyond the basic satisfiers of nature can behave in so ironic a fashion. Man can transcend nature's "natural" rewards because he has an intellect which transcends biological considerations to find meanings in life which are totally *unnatural!*

## est

The next *How To* approach we shall review is not completely amenable to a book presentation, even though we will base our comments primarily on the book by Adelaide Bry entitled: *est: 60 Hours That Transform Your Life.* Bry, a psychotherapist, was a participant in the *est* experience who went on to assist in later programs and who wrote this book intended to inform the public about the approach but not to take the place of a formal course. Werner Erhard, who founded *est*, put his support behind Bry's book and therefore we feel justified in using it as the basis of our analysis. Erhard's formal education ended with high school, but he worked for several years in the adult-education field and through studies achieved some expertise, according to Bry, in the areas of: "Zen, Buddhism, Taoism, physics, Vedanta, Yoga, Sufism, philosophy, Christianity, Cybernetics, Scientology, psychology, Existentialism, semantics, and business." The *est* experience takes place over two weekends, during both of which there are (roughly) 15-hour sessions on Saturday and Sunday (i. e., four sessions in all totaling about 60 hours). The sessions involve a primary trainer, several assistants, and a group of about 250 people seated as participants in an auditorium. Rest breaks are infrequent, and one of the most oft-repeated stories is about the participant who once soiled his pants but said that this no longer mattered (i. e., he accepted it!). Erhard once summarized his brain child as follows: "*est* is a sixty-hour experience which opens an additional dimension of living to your awareness. The training is designed to transform the level at which you experience life so that living becomes a process of expanding satisfaction."[47]

But at another level, it is wrong to say what *est* (always written in lower-case letters) "is" because the whole point of this approach is to make the Zen insight of Perfect Enlightenment a major premise of one's life outlook (see Chapter 9, p. 180). Only after we have stopped raising questions and seeking definitions like this will the unexpressible *experience* of life begin to take effect on our psyche. Bry fills her book with much talk about what one might or might not "get" from *est*. From the outset of the sessions participants are admonished that there is *nothing* to be gotten. One is reminded of the Zen sage, answering a question with no answer, the tossing of a stick, or the posing of a koan for the student to ponder (see Chapter 9). Even so, Bry gives testimonials from several fellow students, one of whom said: "The most important thing I got from *est* is acceptance of myself where I am negative." Bry was impressed by the fact that responsibility was such a major theme of the sessions, so that a person was always said to be the cause of his or her own life circumstances. This seemed a major "getting" on Bry's part for she tells the reader: "I got that I had total responsibility for my life—all of it, the happiness and the sorrow. It was—and continues to be—an incredible revelation."[48]

This Zen prescription for realistic acceptance of what is the case in one's life frames one of the two meanings of the word, *est*. This is Latin for "it is." The three letters are also an acronym for Erhard Seminars Training. The Latin usage captures the idea of accepting life as it comes rather than trying always to find explanations, reasons, excuses, blamings, wish-fulfillments, and so on, all of those psychic maneuvers which keep people from experiencing life directly. As Bry's trainer summed it up for her group: "I'll tell you everything there is to know about life. . . . What is, is, and what ain't, ain't." Participants are encouraged to stop looking for reasons why they behave as they do. Reasons are thought up after we behave in order to justify what we have already done.[49] The only thing which matters is accepting responsibility for what we *have* done.

The same goes for beliefs. If we are looking for a belief in order to give life meaning then we are not getting satisfactions out of life. Beliefs tend to make us "stuck," a term used by the existentialists (see Chapter 8, p. 169) to suggest that the *dasein* is no longer moving forward. Erhard seems to believe that the only way in which to find personal satisfaction is to drop the conventional language terms embodying the artificial symbols (really, *signs*) that we use, so that we can open ourselves up to a more direct experiencing of life. Erhard says this is necessary because: "Neither our system of knowing nor our language is experiential. It only symbolizes our experience." Verbalizing about things must give way to experiencing things directly. Those who seek will not find, says Erhard: "Life is a rip-off when you expect to get what you want. Life works when you choose what you've got. Actually what you got is what you chose even if you don't know it. To move on, choose what you've got."[50]

The Zen-Buddhistic quality of this philosophy is about as apparent as the fact that we have here another example of a practical teleology. Erhard admits that his Zen studies were the most important influence on his thinking, even though he also stresses with good reason that Zen training is totally different from *est* training. Another, even more striking influence on his thought is cybernetics, which seems oddly out of place in the *est* training. Quite in opposition to the spirit of Zen, and as if "out of the blue" group participants are told that they are *machines!*[51]

This juxtaposition of dialectical (Zen) and demonstrative (cybernetics) themes gives the theory of *est* a schizoid quality. For example, Bry tells the reader how impressed she was by the fact that the participants quickly learn to use the word "and" in their speech patterns rather than relying on other conjunctions like "or" or "but" which tend to separate meanings rather than combine them. She comments: "Eventually I *got* that it implies that alternatives exist, as opposed to the either/or thinking that rules both our language and our behavior but limits you both by word and attitude."[52] We are struck by the one-and-many thesis implied in her comments. Furthermore, insofar as language does limit the person's understanding this is a reflection of final-cause determinism. Language terms predicate what we can know in light of what we affirm meaningfully as we "come at" life. We would contend that in gaining her insight about seeing alternatives Bry had manifested a dialectical and not a demonstrative form of change (See Chapter 9, p. 172).

Yet when she gives us her theory of how *est* works Bry swings over to a demonstrative, computer metaphor: "When I communicate with you, whether verbally or nonverbally, you respond. . . . It's as if your computer buttons have been pushed, and whatever your response, it was programmed. While a computer may have a range of responses, we can only get from a computer the range of responses we programmed into it." She feels that the programming which we have been given in the past is somehow released during training, and thanks to the creation of original experience during the two weekends the person acquires a new programming rather than allowing the older beliefs which had been input earlier in life to continue their repetitive influence on the individual's life.[53]

For his part, Erhard does not have to explain "how" *est* works because the whole point of his approach is that such intellectualized accounts put the experience which he wants a student to attain out of reach. Even so, we have good reason for seeing demonstrative themes taking the upper hand in the theoretical basis of *est*. Thus, mentation is viewed as a linear arrangement of sensory inputs. This seems to be the basis for calling people machines, because they process information like machines. Moreover, when exchanges occur between the trainer and certain participants, the trainer's behavior is quasi-cybernetic rather than genuinely humanistic or dialectical. There are points in the 15-hour session when a member of the audience can address the trainer. This is sometimes the occasion for leveling complaints about the procedure or what it portends for the participants. After such a complaint is leveled, the trainer does not invalidate its contents as a Zen master might, nor does he enter into a dialogue concerning the broader implications of the criticism. He merely states "Thank you, I got it" or "Thank you. I acknowledge that I heard you."[54] At this point the complainant is expected to give up the microphone to another participant, who may have a personal revelation or a testimonial to convey.

Occasionally there is an interpretation given by the trainer to the participant who is making a self-revelation. For example, a woman rises to complain that though she is loyal in her relations with men they seem always to betray her trust.

Taking a page from Berne's TA at this point, the trainer opines: "Lady, you're a professional victim, doing your niceness act."[55] Other group activities involve the familiar relaxation and meditation exercises we have seen in other approaches, interspersed with active physical exercises to get the blood flow activated after prolonged periods of sitting in which it is not unusual for a participant to fall asleep.

So much for *est*. We find once again a telic, heavily dialectical view of the person being cloaked in mechanistic lingo —possibly even in spite of itself! To call people computing machines and believe that one is somehow re-programming them over a 60-hour "happening" is to distort the very phenomenon that one is capitalizing on. The telosponsive quality of the procedure in which people take responsibility for an altered predication (reaffirmation) about their lives is completely overlooked. One never programs responsibility into a machine, because responsibility is something which depends upon a recognition of the *grounds* for the sake of which a program is written. If people are really machines, then all of Erhard's talk about forgoing language signs merely substitutes one such mediating electronic recording tape for another. Machines cannot experience freely in the way Erhard wants his students to experience. An impartial survey of his approach would surely suggest that *est* has Westernized Zen insights, so that considerable mileage is obtained from the expectancy which the participants have that they will "get" and have "gotten" something from the demonstrative re-programming of the marathon sessions. In the final analysis, despite Erhard's disclaimers, a *belief* in Yankee mechanism wins out in *est* over a *belief* in Zen enlightenment.

## Erroneous Zones

The psychologist Wayne Dyer begins his book on self-defeating behaviors, entitled *Your Erroneous Zones*, by telling the reader: "Choice and present-moment living will be stressed on almost every page of this book." This is in the best tradition of the *How To* movement, of course, but Dyer does have a new twist in that he bases his approach on the following logical syllogism which the reader is asked to consider: MAJOR PREMISE: "I can control my thoughts"; MINOR PREMISE: "My feelings come from my thoughts"; CONCLUSION: "I can control my feelings."[56] Dyer rationalizes the major premise by noting how, even when something pops into our heads uninvited, we have the power to make it go away. We might question this logic as regards dream thoughts, or those hallucinations which occur to the severely disturbed individual, but for most normal psychological reactions this seems a tenable position.

His minor premise is somewhat more difficult to accept. He claims research has shown that feelings are products of a "think center" in the brain, and that without our brains we would have no feelings.[57] The problem here is in distinguishing between the electrical nervous impulse and the thought *per se*. As Penfield's research demonstrates, these are hardly identical processes. Penfield was able to bring on *both* thoughts and feelings with electrical stimulation. But his patients were still cognizant of when such brain processes were the product of *their* (self-identity's) thinking and when it was strictly the result of the artificial stimulation (see Chapter 10). Whatever the case, it is interesting to see a modern psychologist advocate a view of how to control emotions which was the accepted outlook of the 19th century before Freud arrived on the historical scene. This is a will-power psychology, made all the more obvious when we see what Dyer's recommendations are.

In a nutshell, they amount to changing our premises about just what occurs when we have interpersonal problems. The focus is always on the individual's self-determined problems in living. Dyer encourages the reader to reframe his premises as follows: Instead of entertaining the erroneous premise "You hurt my feelings" we should say to ourselves "I hurt my feelings because of the things I told myself about your reaction to me." Instead of the erroneous "He makes me sick" we should acknowledge that "I make myself sick." And, instead of deluding ourselves with "She [He] really turns me on" we should admit that "I turn myself on whenever I'm near her [him]."[58] After identifying such major premises which tend to immobilize us, i. e., prevent us from doing what we really want to do, we redefine them and then are (in our terms, psychically or final causally) determined to behave quite otherwise.

Dyer's readers are encouraged to choose happiness over unhappiness. If we are prone to "blow up" in traffic jams, then this is because we allow such self-defeating incidents to develop. Better to hum a tune, write verbal letters, or talk into a portable tape recorder than to give in to the unproductive temper tantrum. We must stop seeking approval from others. A person who believes of another that "Without you, I'm nothing" must learn to say "I can stop loving you, but at this point I choose not to." We must also break away from the past, eliminating the tendency to say "I'm" this way or that way—e. g., "I'm not good at dancing" or "I'm not much of a reader." Better to say "I never used to be a good dancer" or "I used to think of myself as not much of a reader."[59] There is much talk about seeking one's independence from old patterns of behavior which no longer hold meaning, such as going to bed at a certain hour rather than when one is actually tired. The entire thrust is to examine the grounds for the sake of which a person behaves, and then to adjust them (via preliminary examination in dialectical change, we would say) in favor of a more self-responsible style of life.

After making an impressive start in relying on logical reasoning, when Dyer gets down to a psychological explanation of how people behave—erroneously or otherwise—he is unable to stay with this teleology. It should be understood that logic is indeed a telic analysis, in which the primary interest is in a study of grounds, predications, premises, as well as the steps to be taken in extracting the implications or intentions from such precedents. There is nothing mechanical about logic, even though machines can be constructed to reason according to demonstrative logic (see Chapter 10). Yet Dyer feels it is necessary to explain behavior according to the typical reinforcement theories of psychology, relying on the Lockean habit concept to account for those patterns which he is striving to break up. Thus, he tells the reader: "You have put in thousands of hours of reinforcement for such [erroneous] thinking, and you'll need to balance the scale with thousands of hours of new thinking, thinking that assumes responsibility for your own feelings. . . . You've learned the habits you now have by reinforcing them all of your life."[60]

If Dyer really believes that people can choose then possibly his views of habit and reinforcement differ from the traditional learning theories. However, he has not made such differences clear to the reader. A mechanistic psychologist reading this book could see in his emphasis on habit the typical mediational model which has the person being shaped to respond in a certain way based on "reinforcers" rather than directing himself telosponsively. Thus, even though Dyer's practical psychology rests on telic recommendations his formal psychological position leaves us wondering what his image of humanity really involves.

## Love and Will

The last area we will consider is that of love, and although the books to be reviewed are not typical *How To* efforts they do deal with this important human experience in an essentially popular fashion. We refer to Erich Fromm's *Art of Loving*,[61] published in 1956, and Rollo May's *Love and Will*,[62] which ap-

peared in 1969. Though both were written before the dramatic
sexual revolution of the 1970s there are no better treatments
of the complex issues which go to make up this most significant of all human relationships. And interestingly enough,
both authors interweave their discussions of love with questions of free will and personal responsibility.

Love, says Fromm, is an *active* concern for the life and
growth of those whom we care for and with whom we wish to
fuse. Masculinity and femininity have dialectical qualities, with
each behavioral style defining the other. The highest ideals of
love reach out beyond simply a given love object to the
"world as a whole," epitomized in the concept of brotherly
love. In order for mature love to come about, erotic or sexual
love must combine physical attraction with this more extended
feeling of brotherly love.[63] This includes love of self, which is
not the same thing as narcissism.

To love someone is not just a strong, erotic feeling, says
Fromm, because: "Love should be essentially an act of will, of
decision to commit my life completely to that of one other
person." Love is an act of faith, a giving of oneself completely
in hopes that this will produce love in the loved person. Au-
tomatons cannot love, for they lack a self-identity and hence
cannot put anything personal to risk. Fromm gives some rules
for the practice of love, including discipline, concentration,
patience, and a supreme concern with the mastery of this art,[64]
but the gist of his analysis is that love is a telic activity.

May agrees, and suggests that one of the most pressing
problems of modern men and women is that they practice sex
without eros. Sex is a need, but eros is desire. Sexual tensions
are released in ejaculation, but it is erotic longings which bring
men and women into copulatory union in the first place. Put
in our terms, sex is best described as material and efficient causation, but the erotic combines formal and final causation as
well. May fears that in the modern sexual freedom we have
substituted sexual technique for erotic passion. Sex becomes

something which must be technically correct, as if it were an athletic contest in which the partners are striving to compete for maximum ejaculatory release. In ironic fashion the *How To* books on sexual intercourse ultimately detract from the richness of this experience. In fact, May is of the opinion that impotence is on the rise thanks in large measure to the unrestrained sexual freedom today.[65]

May also agrees with Fromm that there is a dialectical relationship between male and female. He also agrees that love and will are psychologically related activities in that: ". . . both describe a person reaching out, moving toward the other, seeking to affect him or her or it—and opening himself so that he may be affected by the other." Will can block love and vice versa, but the highest plateaus of life occur when these two human expressions are brought into unison in sexual intercourse.[66] It is the human being's task in life to combine love and will.

In drawing out how this might be accomplished, May discusses freedom and his theory of intentionality.[67] He theorizes in the traditions of British Empiricism on the will concept, reflected in his definition of freedom as follows: "*I define freedom as the capacity to pause in the face of various stimuli, and then to throw one's weight toward this response rather than that one.*"[68] This Lockean formulation (see Chapter 5, p. 81), which we saw in James's "sustained attention" conception (see Chapter 7, p. 136), has the fatal difficulty of having to explain why such pauses come about in the first place, and how the throwing of the weight one way or the other is accomplished "freely."

Although Fromm does not develop things in quite the way that we have, his theory embraces dialectic in what he calls *paradoxical logic*. He contrasts this with Aristotelian (i. e., demonstrative) logic and shows how it has been dominant in Eastern religions and mysticisms of all types. He accurately observes that: "Opposition is a category of man's mind, not in itself an element of reality." Fromm therefore has all of the essentials for what we would consider a proper description of free will, including the recognition that man can transcend nature thanks to his self-reflexive intelligence.[69] Regardless of which theorist we might prefer on the question, indications are clear that both Fromm and May are teleologists who would consider human behaviors like love (*not* lust), will, desire, intention, commitment, and so on, to require a final-cause phrasing if they are to be captured correctly.

## Conclusion

Our survey of popular psychologies has taught us that the kind of animal who buys such books, and either puts them to practical use or finds inspirational reassurance in their contents, is *not* simply a mediating mechanism. These books employ teleological admonitions as standard fare. They accept the person as he or she is, and point to a happier tomorrow by arraying a sequence of measured steps toward well-defined ends. They call for personal responsibility, decisions, and a sense of commitment to ourselves and others whom we also love. Above all, even when they use the false analogies of a cybernetic machine, they tell the reader that as persons (or self-programmers) we are free to direct the course of our future. Combining Chapter 11's contents with the evidence of Chapters 6, 8, 9, and 10 we can conclude with scientific assurance that human nature is capable of exerting a freedom of the will through telosponsivity.

# TWELVE

# Our Human Nature
# and How To Keep It So

Now that we have completed our journey through the many issues touching on freedom and responsibility we can summarize and sharpen the focus of our telic view of human nature by framing ten specific points. The hope is that the reader will be able to cultivate and even defend his or her humanity in the future by ready reference to these summations:

1. *Freedom of the will means being able to change those premises for the sake of which we behave. Personal responsibility means that we acknowledge our role in the fixing of premises. There are obvious limitations to such freedom.*

Thanks to our dialectical reasoning capacity we human beings always take a dual or vis-à-vis stance in relation to the input stimulations of reality. Whether it is the spontaneous seeing, feeling, smelling of our daily routine, the recollection of such experiences from our past, or the artificially manufactured experiences of an electrical needle stimulating our brain, we always know that what is taking place is either presently dual or could be otherwise! We are therefore of logical necessity required to take a position on that which we will know. This means we are never directly controlled by circumstances but always by our predication of these circumstances. Our natural tendency in this case is to take a credulous (if not a gullible) attitude concerning the "facts" or "unquestioned truths" of external experience. We look first to our sensory input as grounds, believing them to reflect "the" reality even though we know that events could be otherwise. We also take on the attitudes of convention, and the viewpoints of important others such as our parents and parent-surrogates as representatives of what "is" the case in life. When they control us they do so by convincing us that their predication is the "right one!"

This is all perfectly natural, of course. The maturing telic organism needs a basis for its telosponsivity, and doubtless the continuity of a society's culture is enhanced by this process of children taking over the predications of their parents. It does not follow that just because we take over the outlooks of others we are vulnerable to maladjustment, or that we are adopting an erroneous point of view. We must also not forget that in taking over these parental or cultural values we occasionally see dialectical alternatives and contradictions in the meanings being expressed, leading thereby to a personal variation on the parental theme—or a rejection of it entirely. In other words, our maturing capacities for free-will judgment are being utilized even though we have not made a thorough examination of the complete predications "for the sake of which" we order and live out our lives.

Of course, we can go through life without losing too much sleep over the meanings taken on as the "thats" which are affirmed in telosponsivity. It is not essential for people to examine their life premises, nor does it necessarily follow that a predication which is affirmed without careful scrutiny and personal selection be less effective than one which is so perfected. However, when our lives begin to pall it follows that we must attempt at least some cursory review of those reasons for the sake of which we have been creating the circumstances in which we now find ourselves. The many recommendations

of Chapter 11 can provide us with a frame within which to
examine our lives and, it is to be hoped, rectify the situation.

It is at this point that we must also appreciate that some
things cannot be changed! We are psychologically free to
think ourselves beautiful, but it would not be wise to enter
beauty contests on the strength of such convictions. Reality
checks are always called for in life. Free will cannot be rejected simply because the person is financially unfree to pur-
chase those things which he would love to own. The kind of
premise which life permits us to take on has contributions
from many sides. All of the causes enter into the determination of events as predicated. We can through our psychically
determined efforts bring about some remarkable changes in
life. We are never entirely pinned down to face one and only
one reality. Our range of alternatives may be restricted by
physical or socioeconomic factors, by our race or sex, but if
we use our dialectical reasoning ability we can still renego-
tiate our personal contracts with reality to some extent. Those
who believe this is impossible have given up on their human
natures. We call them pessimists, suffering from lowered morale or anomie. But these are simply other ways of saying that
they have cashed in their free wills for a handful of excuses.

2. *Never confuse values with the valuation process.
Values can be changed but as pure final causation the valuation process will always be with us.*

It is important to keep clear the distinction between a
value decision, a prized opinion, a conviction of worth, etc.,
and the process by which such choices are arrived at. Mediation theories make it appear that the values to which human
beings conform are limitless. All we need do to make a person
believe in "this" value rather than an infinitude of "those"
values is to arrange the reinforcement sequences so that the
former is tied to pleasurable occurrences and the latter are not.

Yet, as we noted in Chapter 1 (p. 6), the truth is that there are only a certain number of explicable grounds on those issues for the sake of which behavior is intended. We can shift our ground from one to another of these valued presumptions—as the woman who takes every opportunity which has the look of a "special occasion" to go off her diet. We can accept the principle that on special occasions all routine restrictions should be off. The rigorous disciplinarian may call this woman's behavior inconsistent or capricious, but it is *not* without affirmed grounds which reflect a certain value.

The other side of the coin is that value conflicts are not resolvable even when we fully understand an opponent's grounds for contending what he does. For example, we may believe that taking another person's life is justifiable in certain situations (war, under personal attack, etc.) but our friend does not. We can understand his viewpoint and even admire him for holding to it, but we could not bring ourselves to behave for the sake of his value. The fact that martyrs have given their lives rather than affirm views in opposition to their own demonstrates more clearly than anything that values cannot be "reinforced" into the belief systems of individuals *when the individual intends otherwise!* If a person already values pleasure over principle then most assuredly we can have him dancing our valued tune in life by rewarding him accordingly. But those persons whose values come into conflict with our own will never be shaped by us into thinking as we do. They can, through personal examination, *re-evaluate* and come to affirm premises in consonance with ours. But there is no evidence in the research literature that we can effect such final-cause changes in efficient-cause fashion!

This process of rendering value judgments is what we mean by valuation or "evaluation." This judgmental act is central to telosponsivity, a reflection of pure final causation in the workings of mind. It is impossible for us to change this process. We will always evaluate our life circumstance, affecting through our self-selected predications that which we now know or can know. In short, though we are free to change predications *we are not free* to behave without predication! Those people who think they can be completely ajudgmental in life are fostering a serious delusion. Ignoring this responsibility to know what one predicates and why he prefers this predication rather than another is not calculated to enrich the human experience. Those people who say they cannot judge, select, and defend a predication are the same people who claim they are being manipulated by circumstance. Mechanistic mediation theories therefore serve their purpose! What they *should* say is that their predications hinge solely upon what they perceive happening to them rather than what they have (finally-) caused to come about.

3. *The essential human posture is that of futurity. We always create ourselves by arranging future circumstances or allowing them to arrange us.*

Probably the most frequent advice which we hear from people who have lived long, successful lives is to "never look back" and "have a purpose (interest, commitment)" in life. Looking back at fond memories or having nostalgic reminiscences is, of course, perfectly normal and at times psychologically healthful. But most experts on human behavior agree that it is not healthy to live in the past. Many experts, on the other hand, refer to the great benefits to be achieved in living for the present, one day at a time, and so on. This brings up the questions of just when is the "future" upon us? Put the other way, when are we living "in the present?" Since we are always living at the cutting edge of our life processes the present is ever-flowing, moving forward into a future state whether we would prefer it to or not. The Greeks referred to this aspect of life as *Becoming*, and modern existentialistic philosophies also emphasize the unfolding nature of the *dasein* (see Chapter 8, p. 165). Existentialism holds that we must opt, commit, leap into life because it is always in process so that even when we do *not* act, we act—that is, we permit events to act on us.

It is possible to become so oriented to the long-term future that the person never takes joy from the present—i. e., the short-term future, what we call today, tomorrow, this week, and so on. Some men and women become so embroiled in their business or their careers that they never have time to relax, enjoy a sunset, take a leisurely stroll, or even to get to know their spouse and kids as human beings (see point 5 below, on such pleasures in the later years of life). Others pinch every penny and hoard for a secure future which never really arrives, so that they do not reap the benefits of their self-denial. These are familiar problems of our time. But they hardly can be taken as evidence against the future orientation demanded by human living. People who live too far in the future are fascinated or even hypnotized by the eventualities of life and what they might do in anticipating its challenges. If this detracts from the shorter ranged future then what we have here is a problem of futurity not a denial of the importance of futurity.

It might seem strange to call this afternoon a future event in our lives. We tend to project future events far off, as more distantly related possibilities that might or might not happen. This afternoon is sure to happen. It is because of such immediate pressings of events that we think of today as something other than our future. Premises affirmed about this afternoon do not seem of the same genre as premises affirmed about "when I grow up" or "after I retire," but looked at telosponsively the process is identical. Those people who claim to live in the present are simply framing predications around spontaneously emerging events. They can live high-pressured lives of desperation in which having to meet the daily sales quota or keeping one step ahead of the law fills their life with a kind of exciting meaning. They can live relaxed lives, distracting themselves by whatever means that turns up as they move among the "beautiful people" at famous spas or thumb their way along a highway wondering what unexpected excitement the next moment will unfold.

Most of us do our living in the present (i. e., short-term future) while on a vacation, or taking a night off with friends, going on a date, making love, investing ourselves in a hobby, exercising, meditating, and so on. All such activities are enjoyable. They are "times off" in which we do what we do out of a sense of intrinsic rather than instrumental value (though often work involves intrinsic rewards as well). The secret of happy living seems to be that such present living is done *en route*, i. e., within a general sense of moving into the broader future. We love to recall our "summer of '62" or whatever simply because that was the year *between* our junior and senior years in college when we did this or that, had our *first* real love affair, and so on. In other words, this life interlude was taken "on our way" to where we were going (or, thought we were going), or it was the beginning of something that would be carried on into our futures (or so we hoped). The ultimate "present" experience occurs in a drugged state. Intoxications of various sorts are also en route experiences for most people. But those who seek these states as ends in themselves invariably become frustrated and demoralized with life. We must always consider "Where is this taking me?" or "What am I becoming?" if we are to maximize our human potentials.

4. *Self-determination and self-confidence are ways we have of describing people who use their free will.*

Telosponsivity demands that there be a decider, an affirmer of predications who makes things happen (see Chapter 7). We have already admitted under point 1, above, that we cannot hope to change everything in life. We have to predicate some things as they stand and not as they "might be" because they cannot be changed, or they can only be improved slightly. This means that reality considerations always press on us to some extent. But, to the extent that we as identities press back, and mould circumstances the way we want them to be we can speak of self-determination. We probably come to know ourselves best when we are making things happen, because this is when we can definitely see the outcomes of our personal influence.

And most assuredly, we know others—other selves—based upon the impressions they make on us. A person we call self-confident is someone who tends to make a difference in the course of events. He is willing to take a risk, to put himself under evaluation, or to influence whatever may be taking place in his presence. This will power impresses us as strength of character. But he is also open to alternatives and new courses of action so long as they are sound, even when these are recommended by others and contradict his initial position. When we relate to self-confident people we always have a sense of their presence. We know instinctively that here is a person cutting his or her own swath through life, given the limitations placed upon that life. They are also consistent in behavior, seeming always to know where their life plans are taking them.

As the self-help books of Chapter 11 uniformly suggested, one's basic life predications are essential to successful living. The self-realized person is one who expects (predicately) to live a successful life. Such individuals look at a failure experience the way we look at momentary pleasures (refer to point 3, above), as something which happens but will pass en route to an even better future. Successful people learn to use the past as grounds for the future. They speak of learning from their mistakes, which means they do not lose time wringing their hands over former predications which went awry or were miscalculations from the outset. They re-evaluate, regroup, and go at life with a revised game plan, one which may be scaled down from the original or schematized along even broader dimensions than before. But the point is, they do not permit their failures to defeat their free-will capacities.

5. *The freedom to keep things as they are is also a manifestation of free will.*

As our examination of dialectical change in Chapter 9 suggested, it is not always necessary for a person to change his life style overtly as a result of a free-will examination of his predications (see p. 173). It must be possible for a change to occur or *not* if we have a truly free course of behavior under way. A lot of people are made to feel anxious or guilty about not changing their life styles overtly as they grow older. There are some marriage counselors who believe that the soaring divorce rate in recent decades is due in part to the expectation that happiness must involve continuing changes in a marriage or the marriage is a failure. By happiness is usually meant ever-widening discoveries in the marital relationship, perfected sexual relations, and so on. It is often the most stable marriage which is adjudged unfulfilling because the partners are not materially growing together, expanding each other's consciousness and the like. If such critiques are taken to heart a couple can actually generate a marital problem. Sometimes the very best, most sensitive, and well-adjusted people work themselves into a divorce because they are made to feel abnormal by their acceptance of the equanimity and routine of their marriages.

There are problems in living with one's self-determined goals *after they have been attained* just as there are problems encountered on the way to achieving them. There is a norm (i. e., a common value) held today, especially in America but elsewhere as well, which equates freedom with growth—and growth in turn is equated with change. Hence, it follows that to be free one must be changing. The idealization of youth in America can be seen as due in part to this logic. Children have their growth before them. As they mature they will adapt to changing circumstances, be "with it" and therefore *more free* than an older person can hope to be in the future. This logic suggests that to be free an older person must seek change even when he cannot see the reason for it.

Though we can accept this futuristic emphasis as a reflection of what we already agreed was the essential human posture (see point 3, above), it does not seem appropriate to identify freedom with change. In the first place, as already noted regarding the self-confident person (see point 4, above), to the extent that a person is living out his future successfully the likelihood increases that he will indeed make his long-term goals into a reality. Why then must he change the very ends which he has successfully created? Second, even over the shorter-term future, a middle-aged or elderly person can combine purposiveness with a sense of satisfaction in the attainment of what are admittedly routine, daily goals such as keeping his personal effects in order, exercising, meeting with and writing to friends, reading, maintaining a garden in season, cooking, and so on. There is no need to change one's basic outlook or life style in order to live a well-managed life of this type.

6. *To understand other people, always think about them from an introspective perspective.*

There is no great secret about what is required to understand other people. They are telosponders just as we are. If we want to understand ourselves we have to examine our predications, and, if we want to understand others we have to examine *their* predications. This means that we must always view others from the first-person or introspective perspective. We cannot look "at" people extraspectively, treating them as instrumentalities, and really understand their behavior. We have to get over into their heads and familiarize ourselves with their game plans. Here is where problems arise. Identifying the person's predication is often difficult, especially when it is not too clear even in his own mind. And even after we have pinpointed his game plan the person can always shift the pattern by taking a new predication. This is not always true, of course. When we are dealing with highly significant life predications there is rarely any change at all (see points 4 and 5, above).

We refer to "game plans" here and this smacks of the language of Berne's Transactional Analysis (see Chapter 11, p. 220). However, our emphasis is more directly Adlerian for we would emphasize the *scenarios* which people write—both for themselves and for others—rather than the games which they enact based on these scenarios. In this sense, "the play is the thing," and doubtless many such enactments occur exclusively in fantasy. The stage-like characteristics of life to which Shakespeare so beautifully drew our attention must constantly remind us that the beginnings of every play are in the scenario to be enacted. This makes every person more than simply a player. We are playwrights, some more creative than others, but all aiming to bring about what we would intend to have happen if only in fantasy. The easy acceptance of stereotypy by people—blacks are sexy, Jews are aggressive, Catholics are rigid—attests to the type-casting proclivities of human nature. So, to understand others we must somehow get hold of their scenarios and see what they have projected for themselves and for us to enact. We do not have to cooperate in the production of their play, of course, but knowing them introspectively we can understand them in an in-depth fashion and base our actions accordingly.

7. *It is not always psychologically harmful to relinquish our range of personal freedom in favor of following the intentions of other identities whom we assess positively.*

We noted above under point 1 that in maturing we take over the predications of others without necessarily injuring our psychological adjustment. Cultural roles are mutually agreed upon scenarios which we play jointly in giving order to our lives and the lives of others. There is a range of freedom for variation in the social roles of teacher, electrician, pedestrian, voter, baseball fan, etc., but their commonality as singular patterns of behavior is what lends them distinction. In recent decades there has been some effort to allow greater latitude in social roles, as for example to permit policemen to wear facial hair and "mod" haircuts, but usually when we think of free-will decisions we relate them to the more private aspects of our lives. It is here that we expect the person to make his or her own decisions, and in so doing reflect a freedom to be uniquely self-determined.

The other side of the coin is that sometimes we decide to forgo our freedom in favor of following the directions of others. As noted in Chapter 9, the most significant form of eclipsing oneself probably occurs in religious life (see p. 184). When one decides to give himself to his God there is often a beneficial sense of release from the need to justify each life predication, and the confidence in one's direction which results is clearly beneficial. The particular religious writings which underlie the faith in question (Bible, Koran, etc.) then become the unquestioned grounds for the sake of which the person behaves (psychic determinism). The ingredient of self-determination in this giving of oneself to God would seem to be that it be done after a period of self-examination in which the person tries to set his life straight. In other words, one's religion as any life commitment should at some point amount to more than simply a handful of memorized principles and rituals which are followed without personalized affirmation. In this sense though self-determination in one's behavioral patterning is eventually lessened, the personal responsibility for choosing a religious course is always clear.

Successful marital partners often permit their counterparts to assume responsibility for a realm of life affecting them both, as in handling the finances or making decisions about friendship circles. To some this would appear an unsatisfactory arrangement, because ideally both spouses should enter into all choices affecting them. However, this depends upon the unique assessments of the people concerned. So long as one partner, finding the relinquished activity distasteful or of no great consequence, *does in fact* opt to forgo responsibility for it, there is no reason to consider this abnormal or in any way detracting from the person's dignity. If the person negates responsibility in an increasing number of life areas, running away from decisions rather than choosing when to assume responsibility and when to forgo or to delegate it, then we would confront a totally different set of circumstances. In this case there would be good reason to suspect an abnormal behavioral pattern, or surely a lowered confidence level (see point 4, above).

The deeper understanding of such relinquished freedoms is that we as human beings always fall back on the arguments and attitudes of others whom we assess positively. This is called identification or modeling in psychology. Sensing that we need grounds for the sake of which to behave we look around and pattern ourselves on the behavior and outlooks of those we find admirable. It is not always necessary to come into actual contact with one's heroes, of course. We can identify with the outlooks of historical figures, or with the writings of authors now living but whom we have never met. In the same way that we take Biblical passages as the grounds for the sake of which we behave (telospond), we can take the views of such authors in framing our current life style. This is how we frame arguments in defense of our predications. We become less vulnerable to the first effective debator trying to influence us as we acquire a sound basis for our personal outlook.

The harmful effects of this human need to take direction from the shared arguments and attitudes of others is that we can be persuaded and manipulated (psychic determinism) by what is generally referred to as propaganda techniques. We are also vulnerable to charismatic leaders, letting our assessment of them as individuals color our thinking about their philosophy and policies. The opprobrious example usually cited here is the domination of the German people by Adolf Hitler in the second quarter of this century. The psychic determination which Hitler achieved in unifying his people for the attainment of a common goal was both remarkable and frightening to behold. But we must not let this or related examples distort our understanding of the potential benefits to be achieved when people knowingly forgo self-determination in certain aspects of their lives. This takes us to the possibility of unconscious factors in behavior.

8. *Do not ignore, but do not overestimate the importance of unconscious factors in behavior. Try to analyze and deal with the right causes of a problem, because this is where unconscious factors usually enter.*

In Chapter 3 (p. 46) we saw how the strictly conceptual determination of ideas and language terms was similar to the determination of behavior by unconscious factors. Both are forms of psychic (final-cause) determinism. We are just as unconscious when we employ unexamined assumptions in coming at life as we are when we dream certain themes at night or have those Freudian slips of the tongue which reveal hidden motivations (see Chapter 7, p. 134). There is a tendency to reify the "unconscious mind" and think of this as entirely separate from the "conscious mind," operating by different mechanisms or rules of thought. Actually, as our study of Freud revealed, there *is no difference* in reasoning style between conscious and unconscious mentations (see Chapter 7, p. 132 and Chapter 8, p. 155). Freudian psychoanalysis would not work if these two sides to mentation were completely different.

What distinguishes unconscious material from conscious material are the *grounding meanings* being extended. We need professional expertise to help us discover our unconscious predications, but it is not correct to say that we are unable to achieve such insights on our own, nor that we forfeit our free-will judgments in this process of self-study with a professional. Freud was to learn that the most difficult aspect of his method of "cure" was in bringing people around to accepting his interpretations of their (introspectively conceived) unconscious motives. As noted above (see point 2), it is not easy to get a person thinking in opposition to his intended life values. Psychoanalysis is a lengthy process because it is concerned with bringing the person around through detailed examination of his life to reconceptualizing the scenario for the sake of which his life is being enacted.

But what if the maturing person were to begin early in life to cultivate an open examination of his premises about things, to be aware of his dialectical reasoning capacities, and the fact that he is therefore often contradictory in outlook as well as inconsistent in his behavior. A further aspect of this dialectical nature is that human beings overlook, deny, and "repress" their intentions. We do not want to admit certain things about ourselves. We do not want to face the challenge of a potentially frightening situation or a threatening decision which must be made in life. All such factors enter into what is called unconscious behavior, and if we could but recognize that it is up to us as individuals to cultivate such a sense of self-understanding then in the long run we would have less need to worry about what an unconscious mind might or might not be doing to us. We would soon learn that there is just *one* mind with *many* points of view, possible meaning implications, and judgments of that which might or might not be carried out in overt behavior. Get to know the many without fear and the one will emerge without those schisms called "unconscious promptings" or "split personalities" developing.

Chapter 11 has framed many practical rules of thumb for the examination of one's premises (predications, groundings, etc.) concerning life. We can now at a more abstract level present a scheme in terms of the four causes. Along with a recognition that we all reason dialectically, and hence that we might get ideas flashing through our minds which in their contradictory nature strike us as illogical or even immoral, we must appreciate that how we frame a life problem influences the kind of solution we will bring to bear. People often begin seeking answers to problems before they have put the right question to themselves. In framing a productive question regarding some personal problem the following steps may prove helpful to the reader:

1 "What am I worrying about? What is the specific problem facing me?"
2 "Which cause or causes are involved? Is this a material-, efficient-, formal-, or final-cause problem? Can I reframe the problem in terms of one or more of these causal meanings?"
3 "In light of my reformulation what solution is suggested? Am I using the right causal meaning to solve the right causal problem, or am I getting my causes mixed up?"
4 "Have I begun solving things with point 3?" If not, then repeat the first three steps in light of the problem at point 3.

We add the fourth point because it is here that so-called unconscious resistances might be said to occur. The person refuses to consider alternative grounds for the sake of which he is behaving. For example, assume that the person would use this scheme to ponder a problem of his as follows:

1 "I am worrying about my health. I haven't been feeling as well as I think I should."
2 "It seems obvious enough that material and efficient causes are directly involved in physical matters."
3 "I suppose that I should consult a doctor."

4 "No, I haven't solved anything because I don't trust doctors."

If at this point the person can bring himself to focus on the problem indicated at point 3, a re-examination might go as follows:

1 "I have to admit I am afraid of doctors."
2 "This fear doesn't seem a material or an efficient cause. It has something to do with my ideas. I have a formal- and final-cause problem here which is hanging me up. That's the *real* worry!"
3 "I have got to first get over this hang-up about doctors before I can get over the business about my health."
4 "Yes, now I am on the right track. Only *I* can do something about this fear. Then, the doctor can do something about my physical condition. But the thought of seeing him or even thinking about seeing him scares me so. What is involved here? What do I think a 'doctor' is, anyhow? That puts me back to point 1. Let's see. . . ."

A scheme like this is obviously too simple for the solution of profound difficulties of a long-standing nature. Professional help is called for in such cases. But, as a first step it can at least help clarify where a person's problems lie. This individual may have a physical problem which the physician and not he should be worrying about. If he could reframe his definition of "doctor," as a professional aimed at maintaining routine health rather than as someone to whom one goes only in the final stages of a terminal illness, then in time his nagging worry could be eliminated. Or, he might find that his problem was not the health factor after all. It was the fear of death implied in the fact that he had agreed to see a physician in the first place. This is more a final-cause than a material-cause worry, and it tells this person something about himself (i. e., his most important life predications).

Hence, though this scheme cannot reveal all of the subtleties of unconscious motivation it can encourage the person to entertain alternatives and to see how sometimes we seek solutions to the wrong problems, or, to problems in the wrong sphere of causality. Without such examination this person may have gone from one patent medicine to another, avoiding the right solution because he was entertaining the wrong problem. Effective people seem always to delineate their problems accurately, and *consciously* to take the right steps to solve them. Conscious efforts are of the same psychic order as unconscious efforts. We must never get the idea that our unconscious influences are mechanical forces, based on efficient or material causes. Both sides of the mind telospond, and by learning how to examine our life predications we can ensure a more open and honest exchange between them even though we may still have contradictions taking place.

9. *Emotional reactions occur spontaneously, but we can influence the course of our emotions through conscious effort by following our affections.*

Though it is common for modern psychoanalysts to speak of "unconscious emotions," Freud was careful to distinguish between unconscious memories of situations which provoked emotions and emotional feelings *per se*. In other words, emotions are physiological processes triggered by the situation we find ourselves in. Quasi-emotional reactions can also be stimulated by the ingestion of certain drugs. If we think in terms of the causes, it is clear that emotions are on the side of material and efficient causal meanings in the description of behavior. They are part of the body's organic machinery, signaling moods and levels of adjustment to circumstances. We cannot always make sense of our emotions, but when we do put a label (formal cause) to them—describing ourselves as happy, fascinated, depressed, bored, etc.—we have to find a framing social circumstance for the sake of which (final cause) our mood state is supposedly taking place. Sometimes we are feeling good, or feeling empty and bored, yet cannot say "why?" In such situations we look around for some possible reason for (cause of) our emotional state and suggest that we are happy because it is a nice day, or we are bored because we have nothing to do. Whether these formal- and final-causal meanings capture the actual reason for our mood or not we will never know, but this is how we make sense of our feelings nevertheless.

Freud showed us how people can conjure up erroneous grounds to account for their moods because they do not want to face up to the *real* cause(s) of their emotional states (see point 8). A boy feeling hostility for his father would not want to admit consciously what he knows unconsciously—i. e., that these feelings stem from jealousy over possession of the mother. Hence, the boy makes up other grounds for hating his father in order to rationalize the emotion he is already feeling. It is because of this tie between emotion and the psychological situation which prompts it that we can refer to unconscious emotions even though strictly speaking emotions are entirely in the physical realm and only the memory of what provokes the emotion is in the mental realm. The mind orders and, predicating meaning on its patterned regularities, brings forward understandings for the sake of which behavior takes place.

In discussing Peale's "power of positive thinking" (see Chapter 11, p. 215) we noted that there is considerable research evidence that people will further those meanings which from the outset they predicate one way more readily than those which they predicate another way. Liked meanings will be enriched in a liked task more readily than disliked meanings, and vice versa. This suggests that the act of psychological assessment known as liking or disliking can be one of the reasons why a mood state eventuates. There is a power to the positive thought since, if we can but do that which we like doing from the outset, we increase the chances of generating more liked than disliked meanings in our life. Emotions follow our psychological circumstances, so that having a life rimmed by liked circumstances is most surely conducive to feeling good, feeling satisfied, feeling that one is moving through life happily.

To clarify how the person can influence his or her own emotions it is helpful to distinguish between *affection* and *emotion*. As we have suggested, emotions are strictly bodily feelings that act as physiological grounds for the appraisal of our circumstances assuming that we can identify the source of our feelings. Emotions are responses rather than telosponses and hence are never arbitrary. Affection, on the other hand, refers to the telosponsive capacity of mind to put experience to evaluation, characterizing it in dialectical fashion as either positive (liked), negative (disliked), or some combination of these two assessments (like-dislike or *ambivalence*). Affections are therefore formal and final causes of behavior, ultimately arbitrary, and up to the unique judgments of the telic organism doing the assessing.

Now, the important point for present considerations is that we can through our affections influence our emotions! This is not always possible, but it is usually true. We found in Chapter 11 that both Peale (p. 218) and Dyer (p. 239) relied on this human capacity to influence what takes place by initially assessing what we want to feel like and then arranging circumstances to feel this way. Feeling blue (emotion) and assessing this mood negatively (affection), we can put some of our favorite recordings on the phonograph and in time come to feel relatively happier. Sensing that a continuing relationship with a certain person may generate emotions of either love or hatred which we do not affectively wish to further, we may begin arraying our life circumstances to avoid relat-

ing to this individual. Better yet, we may recast our understanding of this person—reframing our predications by way of
oppositional reasoning—so that in time we create a different
mood without having to avoid the person.

The great popularity of Freudian "uncovering" psychology has made it appear that such repressive (or suppressive)
maneuvers are unhealthy. Yet, even the psychoanalyst does
something of this sort when he *discounts* the client's falling in
love with him (i. e., transference) as a re-enactment of some
earlier father-involvement in the fixation of an Oedipal conflict (see Chapter 8, p. 154). The analyst willfully guards
against being emotionally stimulated by affectively assessing
the transference negatively, with the client's "love" consequently being understood as a manifestation of illness.

It is therefore not psychologically wrong to control one's
emotions through consciously guiding what may or may not
eventuate in one's life. This is simply another aspect of writing one's own scenario. There will be times when the machinery of our emotions gets out of hand, but over the long run
we have every right to expect that we can exert some affective
control over it. Those who live emotionally explosive lives are
not victims of their heredity. They have written emotional
scenarios and now enact this life style as predicated.

10. *Avoid one-sidedness but acknowledge that affirmation necessitates bias in one's outlook.*

The final point relates to the fact that in predicating life's
meanings we of necessity frame what are for all practical purposes biased positions on the nature of things. To be biased in
outlook does not necessarily mean that one is narrow or rigid,
for this is the natural outcome of having to affirm a point of
view from among innumerable alternatives. It is essential that
we realize just what our position involves, and to acknowledge
that there are other points of view concerning that which we
have framed. By looking at things this way we will always be

sensitive to the grounds on which we base our behavior. The kinds of grounds which tend to make us narrow are those which limit the scope of definition or restrict alternatives based on irrelevancies. For example, when we decide that someone should be listened to based on skin color, age, sex, class identity, nationality, and so on, rather than on the merits of his or her arguments concerning the issue at hand, we cultivate a narrow one-sidedness.

We should continually examine and refine our personal biases, getting to know them and their implications rather than pretending that they do not exist. As noted in Chapter 1 (p. 5), saying "let everyone decide for himself" is an egalitarian ground which we might all agree on "for openers" in social relations. Let each person fix his or her own standards. Fair enough! But now, having agreed on this, what *are* the person's grounds for choosing to behave one way or another? We quickly move here from the egalitarian generality to the specifics of the reasons for behavior. This annoys many people, who find it impossible to think of themselves as biased in any way. Or, having stated a grounding for the behavior, if someone questions these predicate assumptions they believe this is itself a violation of the egalitarian ideal. This is not true, of course. Freedom of speech in the political sense does not mean that a viewpoint is free of critical evaluation once it has been expressed. And freedom to decide for oneself does not mean freedom from comparison to the alternative groundings which might have been selected.

It is threatening to be "put on the spot" in having to say why we behave as we do. This requires personal effort, soul-searching, a marshalling of the best information possible on the topic at hand, and so on. Often, it calls for a willingness to appear obstinate and old-fashioned. Ironically, the person who exercises free will the *most* can come off looking the *least* free. With each decision made and the resultant commitment to a given behavioral course there is a necessary restriction placed on the number of alternatives remaining open to the person (psychic determinism). Thanks in large measure to the rise of psychoanalysis such individuals have been assigned the blame for Victorian rigidities and neuroses of all types. But today we suffer from those aimless, indifferent, and unprincipled behaviors which populate the other side of the psychoneurotic street.

We live at a time in human history when the freedom to express behavioral alternatives is greater than ever before. All of these behavioral patterns are predicated. To believe they are simply aimless effects of environmental control is to affirm yet another *fallacious* predication about human nature. Today as never before we must keep our attention fixed on these ever-widening behavioral alternatives while at the same time cultivating the personal confidence (i. e., character!) to select our own predications for the sake of which to behave (delineate the one from the many). We must try to work out a personal style in consciousness, an enlightened bias which stamps our behavior as peculiarly our own. It is this capacity to know and cultivate the grounding *reasons* for our behavior which most definitely establishes that we are more than simply organic machines. If we cannot state our grounding predications then we have not yet taken personal responsibility for our free-will possibilities in life. But to the extent that we do work on this unique challenge which life affords, we will have done all we can to sustain and enliven our human natures. Once again: The choice is up to us, alone, as individual persons.

# Glossary

ACTUARY  someone who calculates statistically the probability of occurrence, as in estimating the likelihood of death at various ages, voting patterns, etc.

AD INFINITUM  without end or limit.

AFFIRMATION  fixing a grounds, framing a predication, or taking on a premise in the act of telosponding. To affirm is to base one's understanding on either side of a bipolarity in meaning, which then acts as the "that" for the sake of which telosponsivity is accomplished. *See also* FREE WILL; GROUNDS; PREDICATION; PREMISE; TELOSPONSE.

ANTHROPOMORPHIZE  to frame a theory in human-like description when it is wrong or at least questionable to do so. When we see human-like tendencies in our household pets we are anthropomorphizing. *See also* TELEOLOGY.

ANTITHETIC IDEA  a self-defeating idea, prompted by the counter will. *See also* COUNTER WILL.

ANXIETY HIERARCHY  in Wolpe's therapy, a rank-ordering of anxiety-provoking situations, from the least to the most upsetting stimuli the client can name. *See also* RECIPROCAL INHIBITION; SYSTEMATIC DESENSITIZATION.

APOSTASY  renouncing one's religious faith.

A PRIORI  meaning(s) which is (are) presumptive, coming beforehand, and therefore taken as grounds for subsequent under-

269

standing without question or proper examination. *See also* AFFIRMATION; PRO FORMA.

ARBITRARY, ARBITRARINESS   shifting "at will" the grounds for the sake of which behavior is intended, and thus inconsistently.

ARGUMENT FROM DEFINITION   making a case by first laying down highly plausible assumptions as precedents which then sequaciously (i. e., necessarily) determine specific conclusions. In accepting the plausible assumptions we have to accept the conclusions. *See also* PRECEDENT; PROCEDURAL EVIDENCE; SEQUACIOUS.

ATTRIBUTION THEORY   the view that people attribute to their behavior causes that are often erroneous and illusory. Though seemingly telic, attribution theory has thus far been framed in mediation-theory terminology. *See also* MEDIATION THEORY.

AUTONOMOUS MAN   Skinner's phrase which refers disparagingly to all those writings by teleologists claiming that human beings are free and independent agents. The autonomy refers to freedom from environmental and biological direction.

AVERSIVE CONTROL   in Skinnerian conditioning, this refers to shaping an organism to behave by first administering and then releasing it from painful stimulation. The positive contingency which results is considered a reinforcer.

AWARENESS, OF SUBJECT   the widespread finding that psychological experiments such as conditioning procedures do not lead to positive results unless the subjects being studied perceive the experimental design, and thereby intentionally comply with what is called for.

AXIOLOGY   the study of values and the valuation process. *See also* VALUATION; VALUE.

BEHAVIOR MODIFICATION   a special case of behavior therapy in which change is brought about through operant conditioning techniques. *See also* BEHAVIOR THERAPY.

BEHAVIOR THERAPY   a generic term referring to both Skinnerian and Hullian learning-theory techniques of effecting behavioral change.

BEHAVIORISM  a school of thought in psychology which places exclusive reliance on efficient- and/or material-cause descriptions. Currently the most influential force in academic psychology, behaviorism denies that human actions are telic in nature. *See also* MECHANISM.

BINARY LOGIC  the either-or, demonstrative logic employed by "thinking" machines. *See also* DEMONSTRATIVE.

BIT(S)  short for "binary digits," and refers to the direction of a programmed "choice" between either-or selections of binary logic. *See also* BINARY LOGIC.

BRAHMA  symbol for enlightened totality in Indian thought.

BUDDHA  symbol for enlightened totality in Chinese thought.

CATEGORIES OF THE UNDERSTANDING  in Kantian philosophy, the a priori mental patterns brought to bear in pro forma fashion to organize noumenal experience into cognizable meanings. *See also* A PRIORI; COGNITION; PRO FORMA.

CATHEXIS  Freud's term for the "filling up" of a mental idea or image with libido. *See also* LIBIDO.

CAUSE  concept originating with Aristotle to account for the nature of things. There are four basic types of causes—that is, material, efficient, formal, and final—and by using their meanings as universal models we can better understand the common knowledge which we have of the world. *See also* EFFICIENT CAUSE; FINAL CAUSE; FORMAL CAUSE; MATERIAL CAUSE; UNIVERSAL.

CHIMERICAL  something which supposedly exists in the imagination.

CHOICE  a popular way of referring to the affirmations involved in telosponsivity, particularly in regard to the bipolar meanings of our mental conceptions. To the extent that this affirmation becomes difficult for the person to make, he or she is likely to speak of a choice facing them. We never speak of choosing when the affirmation is clear, although there is *always* a telosponsive affirmation taking place in mental activity. *See also* AFFIRMATION; TELOSPONSE.

CLASSICAL CONDITIONING Pavlovian conditioning, in which the organism is presented with both the unconditioned stimulus and the conditioned stimulus regardless of what it "does" in behavior. There is no need to perform an instrumental act in order to be classically conditioned. *See also* INSTRUMENTAL CONDITIONING.

CLIENT-CENTERED THERAPY the approach of Carl Rogers, which holds that it is the client who must actively do something in order to "cure himself," hence take the lead in therapy interviews.

COGNITION the mental act or process of knowing. In Kantian terms, an active process of bringing meanings to bear on life; in Lockean terms, a mediational process. *See also* KANTIAN MODEL; LOCKEAN MODEL; MEDIATION THEORY.

COGNITIVE MAP Tolmanian terminology; another term for a mediator. *See also* INTERVENING VARIABLE; MEDIATION THEORY.

CONDITIONED RESPONSE a response that has previously occurred spontaneously but now occurs in response to stimuli which have replaced the original, unconditioned (i. e., natural or spontaneous) stimuli. A dog which howls on cue following a period of training is manifesting a conditioned response. *See also* CONDITIONED STIMULUS; UNCONDITIONED STIMULUS; UNCONDITIONED RESPONSE.

CONDITIONED STIMULUS an item in a subject's awareness which did not elicit a (conditioned) response until it had been contiguously paired with the stimulus which spontaneously brought about this response. The light which, when flashed, elicits salivation in a dog is a conditioned stimulus. *See also* CONDITIONED RESPONSE; UNCONDITIONED STIMULUS.

CONDITIONING an experimental design in which a subject (animal, person) is given certain cues that somehow encourage the subject to perform in the experiment as the experimenter has planned. Just why conditioning "works" is open to theoretical dispute.

CONGRUENCE in Rogerian theory, this comes about when the person's intellectual understanding is in perfect agreement with his feeling state. A congruent personality is genuine and without front or phoniness.

CONNOTATION   in meaning, this refers to the less specific ties which an item (concept, word, image, etc.) has with other items, as through implication. The word "milk" can connote "reassurance, safety, and love" to any one person who has been satisfactorily mothered. See also DENOTATION; MEANING.

CONSERVATION OF ENERGY PRINCIPLE   the view that energy is never lost but simply changes its manifestation in an isolated system, as in the heat energy released by the burning of a wooden log. See also CONSTANCY PRINCIPLE.

CONSTANCY PRINCIPLE   a material- and efficient-cause theory of events which holds that all forces in a closed system strive to reach a constant level. Thus, if certain parts become highly charged with energy they seek to redistribute this force to other parts of the system. The high and low pressure areas in weather forecasting represent one example of a constancy explanation.

CONSTRUCT   essentially a synonym for mental or theoretical "concept." Technically, the Kantian theorist would *construct* his concepts from the disordered noise input from reality, whereas the Lockean would *abstract* his concepts from the already ordered reality. See also KANTIAN MODEL; LOCKEAN MODEL; THEORY.

CONSTRUCTION, TO CONSTRUE   refers to active mentation in which the person literally brings about or constructs meaning on the basis of which he then predicates his understanding in behavior. Rather than inputting ordered conceptions from the environment, the person frames and then applies such ordered meaning *to* reality in telic fashion. See also CATEGORIES OF THE UNDERSTANDING; PRO FORMA.

CONTIGUOUS, CONTIGUITY   being close to, in sequence, and even touching or overlapping. Along with frequency of such close contact, this is a major principle of explanation in behavioristic psychologies.

CONTINGENCY   a Skinnerian concept referring to the circumstances following operant responding which make it more probable that the operant level will increase. Since an increased operant level is termed reinforcement, the phrase "contingent reinforcement" is used synonymously. *See also* OPERANT; REINFORCER.

CONTINGENT CAUSE a telic conception, introduced by the theologian John Duns Scotus to describe an efficient cause which was also based upon a final cause—i. e., a willful decision. If the person can look ahead and evaluate contingent circumstances, said Duns Scotus, then his behavior is *not* simply efficiently caused; it has a "that, for the sake of which" characteristic as well. *See also* FREE WILL; TELEOLOGY.

CORPUS CALLOSUM The broad band of nerve tracts which unites the two hemispheres of the brain. *See also* SPLIT BRAIN.

CORRELATION a statistical conception which measures a systematic relationship between two variables, so that as one increases the other either increases or decreases in a reliable and calculable manner. *See also* FUNCTION.

COUNTER WILL early Freudian concept suggesting that each person has two sources of willful behavior, one source aimed toward a desired end and a second, its counter, aimed at negating this end. *See also* ANTITHETIC IDEA.

CYBERNETICS the science of communications and controls that counter entropy in nature. These are non-telic forms of control. *See also* ENTROPY.

DASEIN a construct used by Binswanger to describe the immediate experience within which we constantly live and create our own destiny, or forgo this privilege. This is essentially a phenomenal field *à la* the Kantian model. *See also* KANTIAN MODEL; PHENOMENA.

DASEINSANALYSIS Binswanger's existential analysis.

DATA measurements gathered in research. *See also* METHOD.

DEITY TELEOLOGY believing that everything in existence is under the direction of a Creator's hand, that a God has a Divine Plan which is unfolding in the course of time. *See also* NATURAL TELEOLOGY; TELEOLOGY.

DEMAND CHARACTERISTICS   a phrase used by Orne to describe the fact that subjects form an hypothesis of their own concerning the intent of a psychological experiment. Furthermore, they take on the role of being a "good subject" in order to make certain that the intended outcome actually comes about.

DEMONSTRATIVE   unipolar meaning relations bearing the characteristics of singularity, linearity, unidirectionality, and noncontradiction. The demonstrative reasoner presumes that his premises are "primary and true" hence not open to question or alternatives. *See also* DIALECTICAL; LAW OF CONTRADICTION.

DEMONSTRATIVE CHANGE   the linear, unidirectional change of observable events that are usually captured in the material- and/or efficient-cause terms of an extraspective explanation. *See also* DIALECTICAL CHANGE.

DENOTATION   in meaning, refers to the specific ties that an item (concept, word, image, etc.) has with other items. The word "milk" denotes a specific liquid, with clearly discernible properties which can be named. *See also* CONNOTATION; MEANING.

DETERMINED, DETERMINISM   relating to the type and extent of limitations which are put on a course of behavior. The more limitations the less freedom to behave which exists. *See also* FREEDOM.

DIALECTIC, DIALECTICAL   bipolar meaning relations bearing the characteristics of oppositionality, duality, relationality, contradiction, and arbitrariness. There is often a uniting of oppositions or contradictions into a new totality, described most frequently as the synthesis of a thesis and an antithesis. *See also* DEMONSTRATIVE; ONE-AND-MANY THESIS.

DIALECTICAL CHANGE   a rearrangement of patterning in precedent understanding, which may or may not result in an observable alteration of events coming about. The emphasis here is on the formal- and/or final-cause meanings of an introspective explanation. *See also* DEMONSTRATIVE CHANGE.

DISCRIMINATIVE STIMULUS   a cue which the organism under conditioning distinguishes to make its response more likely to occur than otherwise. *See also* CONTINGENCY.

DOUBLING OF CONSCIOUSNESS Penfield's concept which holds that there are two streams of consciousness in mentation. These are presumed to be two independent realms of energy expenditure, so that one amounts to a computer-memory and the other to a programmer.

DRIVE REDUCTION a form of explanation used by certain behaviorists to explain how conditioning takes place. Drives are material-cause concepts, such as hunger, thirst, and sex. When an S-R regularity results in the satisfaction of one of these drives, the behavior which is aligned becomes habitual, or "learned." *See also* REINFORCEMENT; S-R HABIT.

EFFICIENT CAUSE any concept used to account for the nature of things (including behavior) based on the impetus in a succession of events over time. Explanations of behavior based on energy pushes, gravity attractions, and the machine-like flow of "motion" are usually thought of in efficient-cause terms. *See also* CAUSE, UNIVERSAL.

EGO Freud's concept referring to the more reality-oriented, sensible aspects of the personality. The ego has to compromise id and super-ego confrontations, and it is the major influence in repression. *See also* ID; SUPER-EGO.

EGO STATE(S) Berne's division of the personality into Child, Parent, and Adult patterns which are learned in coming to maturity. *See also* TRANSACTIONAL ANALYSIS.

EMPIRICISM, EMPIRICAL basing knowledge solely or as much as possible on what can be observed. The more empirical a theorist is, the more likely he is to be a realist. *See also* REALISM.

ENLIGHTENMENT in Oriental philosophy, the universal understanding transcending specifics as the "one" among the "many" points of view. All human knowledge is then understood to have validity, and experience is accepted for what it "is." *See also* ONE-AND-MANY THESIS.

ENTROPY the presumed tendency for natural objects to deteriorate into an undifferentiated mass of sameness. This loss of pattern can be countered by anything which retains organization. *See also* CONSTANCY PRINCIPLE; CYBERNETICS.

EROS   the principle of love, i. e., caring for self and others in a spiritual as well as a carnal sense. *See also* LOVE; NARCISSISM.

ERRONEOUS ZONES   Dyer's phrase referring to the inaccurate and often self-defeating beliefs we have about our behavior. This theory supports a telic image of the person.

est   an approach to self-understanding introduced by Erhard, in which an attempt is made to combine the insights of Zen Buddhism with the ideology of cybernetics and other philosophies of life.

EXPERIMENTER EFFECTS   a phrase used by Rosenthal to describe the fact that experimenters somehow influence the outcome of their researches in an expected direction. The intention reflected in this phenomenon is not necessarily conscious, but precisely how it occurs is open to theoretical dispute. *See also* SELF-FULFILLING PROPHECY.

EXTRASPECTIVE THEORETICAL DESCRIPTION   framing things and/or events in third-person fashion, from the convenience of an observer. Extraspective theory refers to "that, it" rather than to "I, me." *See also* INTROSPECTIVE THEORETICAL DESCRIPTION.

FACILITATOR   Rogers's term for "psychotherapist."

FEEDBACK   a mediational concept used in information-processing theory to capture the fact that early events can be used as information to direct later events over time. In feedback we have the return to the input of a part of the output, so that the machine corrects itself, i. e., has a better "fit" to the environment. *See also* INPUT-OUTPUT.

FINAL CAUSE   Any concept used to account for the nature of things (including behavior) based on the assumption that there is a reason, end, or goal "for the sake of which" things exist or events are carried out. Explanations which rely on the person's intentions, aims, or aspirations are final-cause descriptions of behavior. *See also* CAUSE; TELEOLOGY; UNIVERSAL.

FORMAL CAUSE  any concept used to account for the nature of things (including behavior) based on their patterned organization, shape, design, or order. Explanations of behavior emphasizing the style or type of behavioral pattern taken on are formal-cause descriptions. *See also* CAUSE; UNIVERSAL.

FREE, FREEDOM  to be without constraint, open to alternatives, and not bound by the singularity of a fixed course. *See also* DETERMINED.

FREE ASSOCIATION  Freud's technique of mental investigation in which the patient relaxes, lets his mind wander, and says aloud whatever spontaneously comes to mind.

FREE WILL  a non-technical way of referring to the capacity which telosponding organisms have dialectically to alter meanings which they affirm as predications in the course of behavior. We are free organisms to the extent that we can rearrange the grounds for the sake of which we are determined. Before affirmation we can speak of freedom, and, after affirmation we can speak of will(-power) in the meaning-extension to follow. Free will and psychic determinism are opposite sides of the same coin. *See also* AFFIRMATION; GROUNDS; PREDICATION; PREMISE; PSYCHIC DETERMINISM; TELOSPONSE.

FREUDIAN SLIP  saying or doing something which reveals one side of an unconscious compromise. Typing "Fear Father" instead of "Dear Father" would be a Freudian slip in which the typist's paternal anxieties break through.

FUERO  a concept used by Freud at one point, based on an ancient Spanish law granting certain privileges and claims on the monarchy to the holder(s). In like fashion, unresolved unconscious problems have a claim on the personality to be cleared up. Human beings constantly "act out" these old "hang ups" in an effort to meet the demands of their personal "fueros." *See also* UNCONSCIOUS.

FUNCTION, FUNCTION OF  systematic relationship between two mathematical values, fixed by definition or assumption. Since mathematicians refer to these values as "variables" an unfortunate confusion arises between the manipulation of experimental variables in efficient-cause fashion and this purely formal-cause relationship. *See also* LAW; VARIABLE.

GALVANIC SKIN RESPONSE (GSR) a measure of the resistance to electrical conductance in the skin brought on by autonomic nervous system reactions.

GAME according to Berne, an ingenuine transaction in which one person anticipates being stroked but is in for a rude surprise. *See also* STROKE; TRANSACTIONAL ANALYSIS.

GEOCENTRIC THEORY the earth is the center of our universe, and the sun as well as other planets revolve around it. *See also* HELIOCENTRIC THEORY.

GESTALT PSYCHOLOGY a major school of psychological theory which draws from Kantian phenomenological precedents. The basic tenet has it that human understanding is based on the organization of noumenal sensory experience by gestalt laws, as "The whole is greater (i. e., has more meaning) than the sum of its parts." *See also* KANTIAN MODEL; PHENOMENA.

GRACE a concept used by theologians to capture the fact that human beings are unable to earn their own salvation but must rely on divine assistance. God bestows grace on the human being who gives himself or herself to His divine direction.

GROUND(s) the basis, case, plausible reason, etc., for belief or action, entering either clearly or through implication into premises which are then predicated by the individual in telosponsivity. *See also* PREDICATION; PREMISE; TELOSPONSE.

HABIT a regularity in behavior, so that given certain circumstances the person or lower animal behaves in a predictable fashion. This term is used most often by non-telic theorists to account for behavior in efficient-cause terms. But it is possible to see habits as due to the precedent-sequacious determinations of telosponsivity. *See also* TELOSPONSE.

HALLUCINATION seeing, hearing, or feeling things which really do not exist.

HARD DETERMINISM the view that every event occurring is the only one that could have occurred. Everything is 100 percent determined and chance is an illusion. *See also* DETERMINISM; SOFT DETERMINISM.

HELIOCENTRIC THEORY    the sun is the center of our universe, and the planets revolve around it. *See also* GEOCENTRIC THEORY.

HOMO SAPIENS    mankind or humankind.

ID    Freud's concept referring to the base, animalistic side of our natures, which seeks immediate pleasure without concern for the moral implications. *See also* EGO; SUPER-EGO.

IDEALISM    the philosophical view holding that the contents of our minds, i. e., the things and events that we know, are all that there is in experience. When we see a rose, touch it, and smell its fragrance, these experiences are created by mind and hence it is futile to try and discover the existence of an independent reality from which they have been drawn. *See also* REALISM.

INDIVIDUAL PSYCHOLOGY    the approach of Alfred Adler.

INPUT-OUTPUT    information-processing concepts which capture the unilinear, efficient-cause flow of information as contained in electronic messages flowing in from the environment, processed according to a program, and sent outward as problem solutions, instrumental acts, and so on. *See also* FEEDBACK.

INSIGHT    the technical term for the changed predications a client in psychotherapy obtains from his self-study via the therapist's interpretations. *See also* INTERPRETATION.

INSTRUMENTAL CONDITIONING    an alternative phrase to describe Skinnerian or operant conditioning. In this case the organism must first respond in order to bring about the reinforcing state of affairs. In classical or Pavlovian conditioning the animal does not have to respond in order to receive the reinforcement. *See also* CLASSICAL CONDITIONING; CONTINGENCY; OPERANT.

INSTRUMENTAL VALUE    a judgment (valuation) of worth based on the pleasure which results when some action is carried out. Actions leading to pleasure are good and those leading to pain are bad. *See also* INTRINSIC VALUE; VALUATION; VALUE.

INTENTION    behaving "for the sake of" purposive meanings as encompassed in images, language terms, affections, emotions, and so on. When purpose and intention combine we have telosponsivity. Intentionality is as pure an expression of final causation as possible. *See also* PURPOSE; TELOSPONSE.

INTERPRETATION the technical term for what the therapist does when he offers the client a premise concerning the source or reason for the neurosis which prompted treatment. *See also* INSIGHT.

INTERVENING VARIABLE a term introduced by Tolman in which he confounds his theory of mediation with his methodological concept of variable(s). The assumption here is that there is something going on *between* the independent and dependent variables, carried along by the organism (person, animal) but capable of measurement by the extraspective observer. For all practical purposes this is synonymous with "mediator," i. e., a supplementary stimulus input earlier and acting currently as part of the efficient-cause of observed behavior. *See also* MEDIATION THEORY; METHOD; VARIABLE(S).

INTRINSIC VALUE a judgment (valuation) of worth based upon a reasoned process of the intrinsic merits of some course of action. Duty and obligation are placed above pleasure and pain as grounds for positive value preferences. *See also* GROUND; INSTRUMENTAL VALUE; VALUATION; VALUE.

INTROSPECTIVE THEORETICAL DESCRIPTION framing things and/or events in the first person, from the convenience of an identity acting within them. Introspective theory refers to "I, me" rather than to "that, it." *See also* EXTRASPECTIVE THEORETICAL DESCRIPTION.

KANTIAN MODEL the minority position in modern psychology concerning a "model of man." The significant features are dialectical as well as demonstrative reasoning, *pro-forma* intellect, noumenal versus phenomenal experience, meaningful understanding, transcendence, and predication rather than mediation. *See also* LOCKEAN MODEL.

KOAN a paradoxical statement which is used in meditation to assist the practitioner of Zen Buddhism to transcend demonstra-

tive reason and achieve enlightenment. *See also* ENLIGHTEN-
MENT.

LAW    in experimentation, this is the stable relationship between
measured variables. It is a methodological term, but has often
been made into a theory by realists who assume that there are
laws "out there," inhering in matter. See Chapter 2 for Newton's attitude on such reifications. *See also* FUNCTION; METHOD;
VARIABLE.

LAW OF CONTRADICTION (or, NON-CONTRADICTION)    the view that
"A is not not-A" or that something cannot both be and not
be at the same time. This assumption predicates demonstrative
reasoning. *See also* DEMONSTRATIVE; ONE-AND-MANY THESIS.

LIBIDO    a "mental energy" which Freud said was prompted by the
sexual instincts but then was free of them *per se*. This is actually a pseudo-physical explanation which was used as a subterfuge allowing Freud to translate his telic image of the
person into a seeming mechanism.

LIFE PLAN    Adler's construct, referring to the freely arrived at
scheme which each person puts down by about the fifth year
of life to gain some advantage or distinction in life. This first
plan is called the *prototype*, and it lays down the *life style*
which will be enacted from this time forward.

LOCKEAN MODEL    the currently ascendant paradigm or "model of
man" in psychology. The significant features are demonstrative reasoning, *tabula-rasa* intellect, simple-to-complex ideas,
constitutive mentality, mediation, and empirical determination
of all that mind represents. *See also* KANTIAN MODEL.

LOGICAL POSITIVISM    a philosophical position holding that concepts
have meaning only if there is some way in which to empirically validate or verify them. *See also* VALIDATING EVIDENCE.

LOVE    according to Fromm, an active concern for the life and
growth of those with whom we want to fuse both physically
and psychologically.

MANDALA    a graphic image used as a focus of attention in the
practice of transcendental meditation. *See also* TRANSCENDEN-
TAL MEDITATION.

MANTRA   a word or brief phrase used repetitively as an incantation in the practice of transcendental meditation. *See also* TRANSCENDENTAL MEDITATION.

MATERIAL CAUSE   any concept used to account for the nature of things (including behavior) based on an assumed underlying, unchanging *substance* going to make things up. Explanations of behavior based on genes or chemical elements are examples of material-cause description. *See also* CAUSE; UNIVERSAL.

MATHEMATICAL RATIONALISM   the view holding that we can understand everything in experience based upon the predictable and measurable mathematical regularities which the plausible order of the universe takes on. *See also* PHILOSOPHICAL RATIONALISM; RATIONALISM.

MEANING   a relational tie of one item to another, extending in time to form a concept within a host of interlacing relationships. Meaning can be given a symbolical or a signalizing interpretation. *See also* DEMONSTRATIVE; DIALECTIC; MEANINGFULNESS.

MEANINGFULNESS   the extent of significance which any given meaning has for the individual concerned. *See also* MEANING.

MECHANISM   an explanation of behavior based solely on the meaning of efficient causality. This is essentially the opposite of a telic account. *See also* TELEOLOGY.

MEDIATION THEORY   a style of explanation initiated by Tolman in which it is claimed that earlier (efficiently caused) "effects" are stored to modify and otherwise influence the course of behavior in the present. These stored influences are said to "mediate" between the stimulus (S) and response (R) so that instead of S-R we speak of S-(Mediator)-R. This non-telic theory is the most common S-R theory in use today.

MENTATION   the act of thinking, knowing, cognizing.

METHOD   the means or manner of determining whether a theoretical construct or statement is true or false. There are two general types of method: (1) cognitive or conceptual method, which makes use of procedural evidence, and (2) research method, which uses validating evidence in addition to procedural. *See also* PROCEDURAL EVIDENCE; THEORY; VALIDATING EVIDENCE.

MOTIVATION    a general term referring to the desire, aspiration, drive, etc., which an organism has to bring something about, attain an end, or achieve a satisfaction. There are telic and non-telic interpretations of motivation.

NARCISSISM    extreme self-love, not in a wholesome but a selfish manner so that the individual does not give of himself to others. *See also* EROS; LOVE.

NATURAL SELECTION    Darwin's non-telic theory which holds that progress in animal physical stature or group social structures occurs because an animal or society best adapted to the changing circumstances of its environment survives, whereas its opposite numbers do not. Nature selects entirely fortuitously, in large numbers, and there is no final-cause intentionality acting as a foreplan in the resultant improvement in adaptation.

NATURAL TELEOLOGY    belief that nature works toward a purposive end, although no assumption is made that this end is under the direction of a deity. *See also* DEITY TELEOLOGY; TELEOLOGY.

NEGATIVE FINDINGS, NEGATIVE RESULTS    experimental outcomes which fail to support the hypotheses put to test.

NEUROSIS    a serious form of personal maladjustment, with anxiety a central feature, but not disorienting enough to behavior to be considered insanity.

NIRVANA    the "middle path," tensionless state in which oppositions have been transcended, and the individual is oblivious to the ordinary cares of life.

NORM    a value held in common by all or most people of a given culture. *See also* VALUE.

NOUMENA, NOUMENAL REALM OF EXPERIENCE    experience as it presumably "is," independent of the sensory equipment of the phenomenal realm. This term was used by Kant to emphasize that we never know the noumenal world directly, but must always order it meaningfully at the phenomenal level. Kant accepted on faith that "things in themselves"—i. e., noumenal things—really existed. *See also* KANTIAN MODEL; PHENOMENA.

OEDIPAL COMPLEX, OEDIPAL CONFLICT Freud's theory suggesting that a child around age five sexually desires the parent of the opposite sex, but also fears retribution from the same-sexed parent.

ONE-AND-MANY THESIS the view that all events are united (ordered meaningfully) and thus must necessarily be arbitrarily distinguished one from the other. This assumption predicates dialectical reasoning. *See also* DIALECTIC.

OPERANT, OPERANT RESPONSE Skinnerian terminology referring to a response which acts or "operates" on the environment to bring about contingent circumstances of a reinforcing nature. Operants are said to be emitted rather than elicited. *See also* REINFORCEMENT; REINFORCER.

ORGANON a way of coming to know truth, based on certain philosophical assumptions and styles of reasoning that eventuate in knowledge.

PARADOXICAL LOGIC Fromm's reference to dialectics in human reason. *See also* DIALECTIC.

PARAMETER a statistical measurement, such as a mean, of the population of any given variable. Assuming that there are a finite number of "apples" in the state of Washington, the parameter would tell us what the average number per year has been over any year which we would like to single out for consideration. Since it is impractical to take measurements of a parameter we sample from the population and then estimate through mathematical calculations the actual population statistic. We never count all of the apples in any one year, but estimate them statistically. *See also* VARIABLE.

PARI PASSU at equal rate or pace.

PETER PRESCRIPTION moving forward to a better life without working oneself up a hierarchical organization to his or her level of incompetence. *See also* PETER PRINCIPLE.

PETER PRINCIPLE in any hierarchy of increasingly responsible positions of employment, a person who works his way "up" to better and better jobs eventually advances to his level of incompetence. Hence, success breeds incompetence in hierarchical organizations. *See also* PETER PRESCRIPTION.

PHENOMENA, PHENOMENAL REALM OF EXPERIENCE experience as known by the individual, from his unique point of view and through his personal sensory equipment. Each of us has our own phenomenal understanding of the things and events in experience. This term was popularized by Kantian philosophy to emphasize the fact that we as individuals order experience into meaning and do not simply respond to it. *See also* COGNITION; KANTIAN MODEL; NOUMENA; PRO FORMA.

PHILOSOPHICAL RATIONALISM The belief that we can understand everything in experience based on a pictorial account of the plausible order which things and events take on. *See also* MATHEMATICAL RATIONALISM; RATIONALISM.

POLE(S) OF MEANING a recognition that meaning is relational and hence it always occurs by uniting referential points or items in experience. A pole merely refers to one, the other, or both ends of a meaning relation. Saying "John is lucky" unites a person with an evaluation. John is at one pole of the meaning relation and "luck" at the other. *See also* DEMONSTRATIVE; DIALECTICAL; MEANING; MEANINGFULNESS.

POSITIVE FINDINGS, POSITIVE RESULTS experimental outcomes which support the hypotheses put to test.

POSITIVE THINKING the view held by Carnegie, Peale, and others that by ridding the mind of negative meanings and furthering only positive meanings a happier life will ensue.

POWER according to Korda, this is knowing what one wants and how to get it.

PRAYER POWER Peale's view that prayers which are sent in the direction of other people can actually cause a change in their attitude. *See also* POSITIVE THINKING.

PRECEDENT refers to the ordering of meaning without regard for time considerations. A precedent meaning is one that goes before others in order or arrangement, as the major premise always precedes the minor premise of a syllogism, framing its general meaning so that the minor premise can only extend the meaning which is contained therein. *See also* SEQUACIOUS.

PREDICATION   bears the same meaning as premise, except that the emphasis is more on the "act of premising" by a self who has already affirmed some meaning. *See also* PREMISE; SELF.

PREMISE   an assumption which has been affirmed by the individual, so that granting the meaning contained therein certain understandings occur and other implications follow. In logic, the major premise frames generalities (All men are mortal) and the minor premise specifies (This is a man). *See also* PRECEDENT; PREDICATION; SEQUACIOUS.

PROCEDURAL EVIDENCE   believing in something because of its plausibility or consistency with common sense. This is sometimes called "theoretical proof," but it is best not to mix theory and method language. *See also* METHOD; VALIDATING EVIDENCE.

PRO FORMA   for the sake of form, i. e., bringing patterns to bear so that meaningful relations are put onto experience by the person's mentality. This is opposite to *tabula rasa*. *See also* TABULA RASA.

PROGRAM   in computer technology this refers to a logical series of steps which have been prearranged to solve some problem, and which are carried out electronically.

PSYCHIATRIST   someone who studies behavior scientifically, or treats it through various techniques of psychotherapy, including the medical and biological. Psychiatrists first take the M.D. degree and then specialize in this aspect of the medical profession. *See also* PSYCHOLOGIST.

PSYCHIC   description of events in formal and final causal terminology, usually limited to human behaviors.

PSYCHIC DETERMINISM   the view held by Freud and others that in mentation there are no accidents. Everything which occurs in the mind has an intended meaning-expression so that there are no chance mental events. This is a hard form of determinism which also enters into the "will" half of the "free-will" phrase. *See also* FREE WILL; HARD DETERMINISM; PSYCHIC.

PSYCHOLOGIST   someone who studies behavior scientifically, or treats it through various techniques of psychotherapy which are not medical in nature. Psychologists are usually professionals holding the Ph.D. degree although some people with the M.A. or M.S. degrees claim the title based on their line of work in the helping professions.

PURPOSE   the aim or point of a meaning. When this aim is incorporated as an intention by a telosponding organism we witness telic behavior taking place. A pencil has a purpose as a concept—a writing tool—but this purpose is not made manifest until a person intends that this purpose be recognized or put to use. When the person does behave for the sake of a pencil's purpose we witness telosponsivity. *See also* INTENTION; TELOSPONSE.

RATIONALISM   a view holding as a universal assumption that there is a plausible order in the universe. *See also* MATHEMATICAL RATIONALISM; PHILOSOPHICAL RATIONALISM; UNIVERSAL.

REALISM   the philosophical view holding that the contents of our minds, i. e., the things and events that we know, exist independently of our mind. When we see a rose, touch it, and smell its fragrance, these experiences are not created by mind but are abstracted from an independent reality. *See also* IDEALISM.

REALITY   a continuing criterion which presses on us and for the sake of which we are forced to judge the confidence to be placed in our predications. Reality can be influenced to change, but it can also force us to reaffirm, reconstrue, or change our predications.

RECIPROCAL INHIBITION   in behavioral therapy, this involves preventing the occurrence of a stimulus-response connection by training this stimulus to elicit a response which is opposite to hence inhibiting of the original response. In most cases this amounts to inhibiting anxiety responses by training subjects to make relaxation responses.

REFLEX, REFLEX ARC   an automatic form of behavior, based on the built-in characteristics of the nervous system. An example is the patellar "knee-jerk" reflex.

REFLEX RESERVE an early Skinnerian conception no longer employed by operant theoreticians. This was presumed to be a fixed but unknown number of operant responses which were set loose after only a single contingent reinforcement.

REINFORCEMENT increasing the likelihood that an S-R habit will be formed. Reinforcements occur following a response, and are explained by drive reduction (Hull) or simply the observed phenomenon of an increased rate of responding based on events made contingent on a response (Skinner). *See also* CONTINGENCY; DRIVE REDUCTION.

REINFORCER in Skinnerian theory, whatever it is that raises the probability of an operant's level of emission per unit of time. If the sound of a rattle increases the baby's hand shaking which brought this about in the first place, then the rattle is a reinforcer. *See also* OPERANT.

REPETITION-COMPULSION the Freudian construct suggesting that abnormal people have a need to re-enact their unresolved problems, such as the Oedipal complex. If they are not therapized such people can go through life constantly "acting out" these problems. *See also* FUERO; OEDIPAL COMPLEX; NEUROSIS.

REPRESSION a concept introduced by Freud, suggesting that people intentionally keep certain ideas out of conscious awareness. Hence, we can both know something (unconsciously) and yet not know it (consciously) in mind.

RESPONSIBILITY as used in this volume, this refers to the recognition that we play a role in the fixing of predications, premises, and grounds for the sake of which we then behave.

SCHEDULE (OF REINFORCEMENT) in Skinnerian theory, a given incidence of reinforcement per unit of time or ratio of operant response emissions. For example, a pigeon might be reinforced once per minute or every fifth response emitted. *See also* SHAPING.

SELF the identity which brings forward a continuing point of view, a sameness in the succession of behaviors we witness the person manifesting. It is the self which predicates and extends meaning through logical inference, induction, deduction, and so on. *See also* PREDICATION.

SELF-FULFILLING PROPHECY  a prophetic outcome stated by or merely expected to occur, which comes about subsequently due to this very anticipation. The person who thinks he will never learn to ice skate never does, due in large measure to the prophetic expectation "I'll never learn to ice skate." Precisely how this comes about is open to theoretical dispute. *See also* EXPERIMENTER EFFECTS.

SELF-REFLEXIVITY  the capacity which human mentation has to turn back on itself, and therefore to know that it is knowing. *See also* TRANSCENDENCE.

SEQUACIOUS  refers to the ordering of meaning without regard for time considerations. A sequacious meaning is one that follows or flows from the meanings of precedents, extending these in a *necessary* sense (telic determination). Metaphors and analogies are sequacious extensions of precedent meanings, as when we say "John is solid as a rock," extending thereby the similarities between a rock and our friend John. *See also* PRECEDENT.

SERENDIPITY  finding agreeable and valuable circumstances in life without a planful approach or an intention to do so.

SHADOW  in Jungian theory, this is the alter-ego or other side of what we are in our conscious personality style. The aggressive person in consciousness is always passive as an unconscious personality.

SHAPING (OF BEHAVIOR)  a term introduced by Watson and much popularized by Skinner. It refers to the manipulation of an organism's behavior through use of schedules of reinforcement. *See also* SCHEDULE.

SIGN, SIGNALIZING MEANING  a non-telic formulation which holds that words are associated "stand ins" for environmental items, bonded together based on the frequency and contiguity of past experience as input to mind totally without intention. *See also* DEMONSTRATIVE; MEDIATION THEORY; SYMBOL.

SOFT DETERMINISM  the view that although most events occurring are the only ones that could have occurred, a certain number are indeterminate. Thus, chance events do occur. *See also* DE-TERMINISM; HARD DETERMINISM.

SOPHIST  someone who weaves specious arguments to confuse and win his points by guile. Socrates believed that sophistry resulted when dialectical argument was used to achieve a foreknown end. *See also* DIALECTIC.

SPLIT BRAIN  refers to a body of research on epileptic patients who have had their corpus callosum severed so that the two hemispheres of their brains are literally split-off and have no communication with each other. *See also* CORPUS CALLOSUM.

STEREOTYPE  a stylized, commonly held view of a minority group member which usually detracts from the person but may on occasion be flattering. Stereotypes are shared "thats" (formal causes) for the sake of which human beings think about and behave in relation to collective identities of other human beings.

STIMULUS-RESPONSE (S-R) HABIT(S)  the basic unit of behavior in classical conditioning approaches such as those of Watson or Hull. This is essentially an efficient-cause unit, bonded together in classical theory by a drive reduction of some sort. This reduction is called a reinforcement. *See also* HABIT.

STRIVING FOR SUPERIORITY  Adler's concept of the neurotic person, trying always in his life plan to prove that he is superior in some way to other people. *See also* LIFE PLAN.

STROKE  a term used by advocates of transactional analysis. It refers to all those things which people do to us which make us feel good (akin to a positive reinforcement). Just as the mother strokes an infant in the expression of love, someone who does something to boost our ego "strokes" us.

STUCK  a phrase used in existentialistic theories to describe the fact that the person is not advancing in life, not growing or moving on to higher levels of understanding.

SUPER-EGO   Freud's concept referring to the representative of the broader culture "within us"—essentially, the conscious. *See also* EGO; ID.

SYMBOL, SYMBOLIZING MEANING   a telic formulation which holds that words express the intentions of ideas which have been formulated independently. *See also* DIALECTICAL; SIGN.

SYSTEMATIC DESENSITIZATION   Wolpe's technique of therapy in which he takes the client up the anxiety hierarchy step by step, conditioning him through reciprocal inhibition to relax in the face of previously upsetting stimuli. *See also* ANXIETY HIERARCHY; RECIPROCAL INHIBITION.

TABULA RASA   meaning "smoothed tablet" or "blank sheet," the phrase was introduced by St. Thomas Aquinas and popularized by John Locke. It refers to the view that at birth the mind is completely empty, and that whatever role mentation has in life is shaped by the inputs from the environment, which essentially writes upon the blank sheet what the person will know. Thus mind is basically passive, a collator and storage unit for influences from the environment. *See also* PRO FORMA.

TAO   in Buddhistic philosophy, the creative principle which orders the universe, pointing the "way" of things.

TAUTOLOGY   a relation of identity between the two items being joined via the poles of meaning. Saying "a rose is a rose" is tautological but so is saying "all bachelors are unmarried males" a tautological uniting of meanings. In the former case we sense a redundancy but the latter enriches our understanding of the word bachelor.

TELEOLOGIST   someone who frames a theory of behavior as a telic activity. *See also* TELEOLOGY.

TELEOLOGY, TELIC   the view that events are predicated according to plan, design, or assumption—that is, based upon purposive meanings—and therefore directed to some intended end. *See also* FINAL CAUSE; TELOS.

TELOS   end, goal, or grounding reason for the sake of which behavior is taking place. *See also* FINAL CAUSE; GROUND; TELEOLOGY.

TELOSPONSE   a mental act in which the person takes on (predicates, premises) a meaningful item (image, language term, a judgment, etc.) relating to a referent acting as a purpose for the sake of which behavior is then intended. This is a final-cause construct. Telosponsive behavior is done "for the sake of" grounds (purposes, reasons, etc.) rather than "in response to" stimulation. *See also* GROUND; INTENTION; PURPOSE.

TENDER-MINDED   a term introduced by William James to describe psychologists who are likely to be rationalists, idealists, and speculative, optimistic, dogmatic, and telic in outlook. *See also* TOUGH-MINDED.

THEOLOGIAN   one who studies theology, i. e., the origins and teachings of God.

THEORY   a series of two or more constructions (abstractions, concepts, items, images, etc.) which have been hypothesized, assumed, or even factually demonstrated to bear a certain meaningful relationship, one to the other. There is no fundamental difference between theorizing and thinking, although it is possible to frame highly formalized, technical theories and we rarely think in such stylized meaning-relations. *See also* MEANING; METHOD.

TOUGH-MINDED   a term introduced by William James to describe psychologists who are likely to be empiricists, realists, mechanists, and highly skeptical, pessimistic, and non-telic in outlook. *See also* TENDER-MINDED.

TRACKING   this term is used to describe a certain mentality in modern psychology, which believes that if behavior can be predicted, manipulated, and controlled it is understood. Or, if not understood, then it is at least being managed and this is the role of a scientist—to facilitate precise prediction and control of behavior.

TRANSACTION   an interpersonal relationship, carried on between two or more people and involving different levels of personality. *See also* EGO STATES.

TRANSACTIONAL ANALYSIS an approach to the study of interpersonal and intrapersonal relations introduced by Berne. *See also* EGO STATES; GAME; STROKE.

TRANSCENDENCE, TRANSCENDENTAL DIALECTIC in Kantian philosophy, the capacity which all humans have to rise above their customary understanding of experience and—by thinking in opposition to it—bring it into question, analysis, and reinterpretation. *See also* DIALECTIC; SELF-REFLEXIVITY.

TRANSCENDENTAL MEDITATION (TM) a procedure used to facilitate the centering of the personality by transcending routine events in pursuit of enlightenment. *See also* ENLIGHTENMENT; KOAN; MANDALA; MANTRA.

TRANSFERENCE when the patient in therapy redirects attitudes and feelings which he has for other people (like his parents) onto the person of the therapist. Thus, a patient can either love or hate his therapist, who acts as a "stand in" for other people to whom this love or hatred is really being aimed.

UNCONDITIONED RESPONSE a response which a subject makes to some presumed (unconditioned) stimulus naturally (i. e., spontaneously). Crying when frightened by a loud noise is an unconditioned response in an infant. *See also* UNCONDITIONED STIMULUS.

UNCONDITIONED STIMULUS an item in a subject's awareness which naturally (spontaneously) seems to bring on a response. The aroma of freshly baked bread, bringing on salivation in the human being who savors its delicious qualities, is an unconditioned stimulus. *See also* UNCONDITIONED RESPONSE.

UNCONSCIOUS that portion of mind which is out of touch with the conscious. It is not accepted by all psychologists as a legitimate concept, not the least of the reasons being that telic accounts are usually at the basis of theories of the unconscious.

UNIVERSAL a highly abstract assumption, position, model, paradigm, point of view, etc., having meaningful relevance to many less abstract, even commonplace ideas. Since there are far fewer universals than there are lower-level ideas we sharpen issues by finding the universal meanings on which our ideas are based.

VALIDATING EVIDENCE  believing in something only after it has been put to test in a pre-arranged course of events designed specifically to show what it relates to meaningfully. This is how scientists prove things, relying on the control of events and the prediction of an outcome. *See also* METHOD; VARIABLE.

VALUATION  the telic (final-cause) process by which values are framed. *See also* VALUE.

VALUE  the relative worth of a thing or an action, in comparison with alternatives in kind. Not all values are clearly delineated, but many are and become incorporated into a group's mores. *See also* INSTRUMENTAL VALUE; INTRINSIC VALUE.

VARIABLE(S)  literally, anything which varies in measurable value. More precisely, a variable is created when a research project is designed so that certain items of theoretical interest are named independent variables and others to which they are presumed to relate meaningfully are named dependent variables. The experimenter systematically varies the independent variable and predicts the meaningful resultant changes in the dependent variable. If he is correct, the outcome of his experiment is said to be "positive"; if he is incorrect, his results are "negative." *See also* METHOD.

VERBAL OPERANT  a language expression which operates on the environment and brings about reinforcing contingent circumstances. *See also* OPERANT.

VERBAL REPORT  experimental data based on what the subject says rather than what he does. Tough-minded psychologists consider such information essentially useless and unscientific.

VITALISM  the telic theory introduced by Galen which holds that there are formless, undiscoverable forces acting on brute matter to bring about life. Concepts of the soul as an energizing force of this sort are said to be vitalistic accounts.

WORLD DESIGN   Binswanger's construct, referring to the fundamental premises which human beings take on that in turn
determine the nature of experience they will create in their
unique *dasein. See also* DASEIN, PREMISE.

YIN-YANG PRINCIPLE   dialectical principle at work in nature, according to Chinese philosophy. The *yin* is passive and femi-
nine whereas the *yang* is active and masculine.

# Notes

## Chapter 1

1. For some examples of how psychologists are likely to call free-will behavior illusory see: (a) Immergluck, L. Determinism-freedom in contemporary psychology: An ancient problem revisited. *American Psychologist*, 1964, *19*, 270-281; and (b) Lefcourt, H. M. The function of the illusions of control and freedom. *American Psychologist*, 1973, *28*, 417-425.
2. Rollo May has referred to the erosion of will as "the" neurosis of modern times: May, R. *Love and will*. New York: Dell Publishing Co., 1969. *See* p. 182.
3. Goethe, J. W. *Faust*. In R. M. Hutchins (Ed.), *Great books of the western world* (Vol. 47). Chicago: Encyclopedia Britannica, 1952. *See* p. 135.

## Chapter 2

1. Aristotle. *Posterior analytics*. In R. M. Hutchins (Ed.), *Great books of the western world* (Vol. 8). Chicago: Encyclopedia Britannica, 1952. *See* p. 128.
2. Aristotle. *Physics*. In R. M. Hutchins (Ed.), *Great books of the western world* (Vol. 8). Chicago: Encyclopedia Britannica, 1952. *See* pp. 276-277.
3. Voltaire, F. M. A. *Candide*. New York: J. J. Little & Ives, 1930. *See* p. 14.
4. Bacon, F. *Advancement of learning*. In R. M. Hutchins (Ed.), *Great books of the western world* (Vol. 30). Chicago: Encyclopedia Britannica, 1952. *See* p. 45.

5. Frank, P. *Modern science and its philosophy*. Cambridge: Harvard University Press, 1950. *See* pp. 221-222.
6. Copernicus, N. *On the revolutions of the heavenly spheres*. In R. M. Hutchins (Ed.), *Great books of the western world* (Vol. 16). Chicago: Encyclopedia Britannica, 1952. *See* p. 511.
7. *See* Frank (1950), pp. 210-211.
8. *Ibid.*, p. 112.
9. Burtt, E. A. *The metaphysical foundations of modern physical science* (Rev. ed.). Garden City, N.Y.: Doubleday & Co., 1955. *See* p. 75.
10. *See* Frank (1950), p. 91.
11. Frank, P. *Philosophy of science*. Englewood Cliffs, N.J.: Prentice-Hall, Inc., 1957. *See* pp. 1-47.
12. Wightman, W. P. D. *The growth of scientific ideas*. New Haven: Yale University Press, 1951. *See* pp. 101-102.
13. Simon, Y. *The great dialogue of nature and space*. Albany, N.Y.: Magi Books, Inc., 1970. *See* p. 39.
14. *See* Burtt (1955), p. 96.
15. *See* Frank (1950), p. 140.
16. Bohr, N. *Atomic theory and the description of nature*. Cambridge: The University Press, 1934. *See* p. 54.
17. Cassirer, E. *The problem of knowledge*. New Haven: Yale University Press, 1950. *See* p. 116.
18. Nagel, E., & Newman, J. R. *Gödel's proof*. New York: New York University Press, 1958.
19. Feuer, L. S. *Einstein and the generations of science*. New York: Basic Books, Inc., 1974. *See* pp. 139-144.
20. Rychlak, J. F. *A philosophy of science for personality theory*. Boston: Houghton Mifflin, 1968. *See* pp. 27-34.
21. Darwin, C. R. *The descent of man*. In R. M. Hutchins (Ed.), *Great books of the western world* (Vol. 49). Chicago: Encyclopedia Britannica, 1952. *See* p. 323.

*Chapter 3*

1. Burtt, E. A. *The metaphysical foundations of modern physical science* (Rev. ed.). Garden City, N.Y.: Doubleday & Co., 1955. *See* p. 290.
2. Boring, E. G. *A history of experimental psychology* (2nd ed.). New York: Appleton-Century-Crofts, A Div. of Meredith Publishing Co., 1950. *See* p. 34 and p. 708.

3. *Ibid.*, p. 323. The date 1879 has been called into question by: Watson, R. I. *The great psychologists* (3rd ed.). Philadelphia: J. B. Lippincott, 1971. *See* p. 272.
4. Cassirer, E. *The problem of knowledge.* New Haven: Yale University Press, 1950. *See* p. 88.
5. Watson, J. B. *Behaviorism.* New York: W. W. Norton & Co., 1924. *See* p. 11.
6. *Ibid.*, p. 6.
7. *Ibid.*, p. 216.
8. Watson, J. B., & Watson, R. R. Studies in infant psychology. *Scientific Monthly*, 1921, *13*, 493-515.
9. Tolman, E. C. *Purposive behavior in animals and men.* New York: Appleton-Century-Crofts, A Div. of Meredith Publishing Co., 1967. *See* p. 414.
10. *Ibid.*, pp. 151-152.
11. Hull, C. L. *Principles of behavior.* New York: Appleton-Century-Crofts, A Div. of Meredith Publishing Co., 1953.
12. Evans, R. I. *B. F. Skinner: The man and his ideas.* New York: E. P. Dutton & Co., Inc., 1968. *See* p. 23.
13. *See* Tolman (1967), p. 11 and p. 14.
14. *Ibid.*, p. 16.
15. Jones, E. *The life and work of Sigmund Freud: The formative years and great discoveries* (Vol. 1). New York: Basic Books, 1953. *See* p. 41.
16. Rychlak, J. F. *The psychology of rigorous humanism.* New York: Wiley-Interscience, 1977. *See* Chapter 3.
17. Freud, S. *The origins of psycho-analysis, letters to Wilhelm Fliess, drafts and notes: 1887-1902.* New York: Basic Books, Inc., 1954. *See* p. 273.
18. Freud, S. Fragment of an analysis of a case of hysteria. In J. Strachey (Ed.), *The standard edition of the complete psychological works of Sigmund Freud* (Vol. VII). London: The Hogarth Press, 1953. *See* p. 51.
19. Freud, S. *A general introduction to psycho-analysis.* In R. M. Hutchins (Ed.), *Great books of the western world* (Vol. 54). Chicago: Encyclopedia Britannica, 1952. *See* p. 598.
20. Freud, S. Pre-psycho-analytic publications and unpublished drafts. In J. Strachey (Ed.), *The standard edition of the complete psychological works of Sigmund Freud* (Vol. I). London: The Hogarth Press, 1966. *See* p. 235.
21. Freud, S. A note on the unconscious. In J. Strachey (Ed.), *The*

*standard edition of the complete psychological works of Sigmund Freud* (Vol. XII). London: The Hogarth Press, 1958. *See* p. 264.

22. *See* Freud (1954), pp. 336-337.

23. McGuire, W. (Ed.), *The Freud/Jung letters.* Bollingen Series XCIV. Princeton, N.J.: Princeton University Press, 1974. *See* p. 270.

24. Freud, S. On narcissism: An introduction. In J. Strachey (Ed.), *The standard edition of the complete psychological works of Sigmund Freud* (Vol. XIV). London: The Hogarth Press, 1957. *See* p. 79.

25. Freud, S. Contributions to a discussion on masturbation. In J. Strachey (Ed.), *The standard edition of the complete psychological works of Sigmund Freud* (Vol. XII). London: The Hogarth Press, 1958. *See* p. 247.

## Chapter 4

1. Cassirer, E. *An essay on man.* Garden City, N.Y.: Doubleday & Co., 1944. *See* pp. 80-84.

2. Creelman, M. B. *The experimental investigation of meaning: A review of the literature.* New York: Springer Publishing Co., 1966.

3. Aristotle. *Topics.* In R. M. Hutchins (Ed.), *Great books of the western world* (Vol. 8). Chicago: Encyclopedia Britannica, 1952. *See* p. 143.

4. Rychlak, J. F. *The psychology of rigorous humanism.* New York: Wiley-Interscience, 1977. *See* Chapter 2.

5. Plato. *Philebus.* In R. M. Hutchins (Ed.), *Great books of the western world* (Vol. 7). Chicago: Encyclopedia Britannica, 1952. Socrates gives a justification for his method on pp. 611-612.

6. There are other phrasings of the one-and-many thesis. It can appear as the many and one, one in many, many in one, and so on.

7. This is also known as the principle or law of non-contradiction.

8. Rychlak, J. F. The multiple meanings of "dialectic." In J. F. Rychlak (Ed.), *Dialectic: Humanistic rationale for behavior and development.* Basel, Switzerland: S. Karger AG, 1976.

9. Descartes, R. *Rules for the direction of mind.* In R. M. Hutchins (Ed.), *Great books of the western world* (Vol. 31). Chicago: Encyclopedia Britannica, 1952. *See* p. 17.

10. Hobbes, T. *Leviathan.* In R. M. Hutchins (Ed.), *Great books of the western world* (Vol. 23). Chicago: Encyclopedia Britannica, 1952. *See* p. 58.

11. Locke, J. *An essay concerning human understanding.* In R. M. Hutchins (Ed.), *Great books of the western world* (Vol. 35). Chicago: Encyclopedia Britannica, 1952. *See* p. 128.
12. *Ibid.*, p. 369.
13. Whitehead, A. N., & Russell, B. *Principia mathematica* (2nd ed.). Cambridge: The University Press, 1963.
14. *See* Locke (1952), p. 190.
15. *See* Rychlak (1977), pp. 174-176.
16. Kant, I. *The critique of pure reason.* In R. M. Hutchins (Ed.), *Great books of the western world* (Vol. 42). Chicago: Encyclopedia Britannica, 1952. *See* p. 14.
17. Neisser, U. *Cognitive psychology.* New York: Appleton-Century-Crofts, A Div. of Meredith Publishing Co., 1967.
18. *See* Rychlak (1977), p. 203.
19. *See* Kant (1952), p. 229.
20. Rychlak, J. F. *Introduction to personality and psychotherapy: A theory-construction approach.* Boston: Houghton Mifflin, 1973. For a pictorial schematization of the Lockean and Kantian models see pp. 10-11.

## Chapter 5

1. Rickaby, J. *Free will and four English philosophers.* London: Burns and Oates, 1906.
2. Romans 9:21.
3. Horne, H. H. *Free will and human responsibility: A philosophical argument.* New York: The Macmillan Company, 1912.
4. *Ibid.*, p. 43.
5. *Ibid.*, pp. 44-45.
6. *Encyclopedia Britannica* (Vol. 17). Chicago: William Benton, 1968. *See* p. 534.
7. *See* Horne (1912), p. 46.
8. *Ibid.*, pp. 48-49.
9. *Ibid.*, p. 52.
10. Simon, Y. *The great dialogue of nature and space.* Albany, N.Y.: Magi Books, Inc., 1970. *See* p. 41 and p. 46 on this point, and Descartes's attitudes concerning it.
11. Rychlak, J. F. Personality theory: Its nature, past, present and—future? *Personality and Social Psychology Bulletin*, 1976, *2*, 209-224.

12. Zilsel, E. The origins of Gilbert's scientific method. In P. P. Wiener & A. Noland (Eds.), *Roots of scientific thought*. New York: Basic Books, Inc., 1957. *See* p. 233.

13. Burtt, E. A. *The metaphysical foundations of modern physical science* (Rev. ed.). Garden City, N.Y.: Doubleday & Co., 1955. *See* p. 243 where Burtt discusses how the Newtonians came in this way to make a metaphysics (i. e., a theory) out of their method.

14. English, H. B., & English, A. C. *A comprehensive dictionary of psychological and psychoanalytical terms*. London: Longmans, Green and Co., 1958. *See* p. 578.

15. Cronbach, L. J. Beyond the two disciplines of scientific psychology. *American Psychologist*, 1975, *30*, 116-127. *See* p. 123 for a typical example of the suspicion with which statistically oriented psychologists approach the development of what is here termed "enduring theoretical structures."

16. Boneau, C. A. Paradigm regained? Cognitive behaviorism restated. *American Psychologist*, 1974, *29*, 297-309. *See* p. 308.

17. *See* Horne (1912), p. 54.

18. Locke, J. *An essay concerning human understanding*. In R. M. Hutchins (Ed.), *Great books of the western world* (Vol. 35). Chicago: Encyclopedia Britannica, 1952. *See* pp. 190, 195, 193.

19. *See* Rickaby (1906), p. vii.

20. *Ibid.*, p. 90.

21. *Ibid.*, p. 91.

22. Thoresen, C. E., & Mahoney, M. J. *Behavioral self-control*. New York: Holt, Rinehart and Winston, Inc., 1974. *See* p. 5.

23. Hebb, D. O. What psychology is about. *American Psychologist*, 1974, *29*, 71-79. *See* p. 75.

24. Skinner, B. F. The concept of the reflex in the description of behavior. *Journal of General Psychology*, 1931, *5*, 427-458.

25. Feuer, L. S. *Einstein and the generations of science*. New York: Basic Books, 1974. *See* p. 27.

26. *Ibid.*, p. 34.

27. Bradley, J. *Mach's philosophy of science*. London: The Athlone Press, 1971, p. 83.

28. *Ibid.*, p. 47.

29. Even so, Mach's phenomenalism was to play a role in the founding of logical positivism. The reasons for this are beyond our present inquiry. For a good discussion of Mach and positivism see: Frank, P. *Modern science and its philosophy*. Cambridge: Harvard University Press, 1950.

30. *See* Feuer (1974), p. 38.
31. *See* Skinner (1931), p. 439.
32. Skinner, B. F. *The behavior of organisms: An experimental analysis.* New York: Appleton-Century-Crofts, A Div. of Meredith Publishing Co., 1938. *See* pp. 85-90.
33. Skinner, B. F. *Beyond freedom and dignity.* New York: Alfred A. Knopf, 1971. *See* p. 153.
34. *Ibid.,* p. 16.
35. *Ibid.,* p. 22.
36. Evans, R. I. *B. F Skinner: The man and his ideas.* New York: E. P. Dutton & Co., 1968. *See* p. 19.
37. *See* Skinner (1971), pp. 37-38.
38. *Ibid.,* p. 61.
39. *Ibid.,* pp. 217-218.
40. *Ibid.,* p. 18.
41. Skinner, B. F. *About behaviorism.* New York: Alfred A. Knopf, 1974. *See* p. 40.
42. Gruber, H. E. *Darwin on man: A psychological study of scientific creativity* (transcribed and annotated by Paul H. Barrett). New York: E. P. Dutton & Co., Inc., 1974. *See* p. 226.
43. *Ibid.,* p. 195.
44. *See* Skinner (1974), p. 36.
45. *See* Skinner (1971), p. 103 and p. 105.
46. Sidgwick, H. *Outlines of the history of ethics.* Boston: Beacon Press, 1960. *See* p. 274.
47. Skinner, B. F. *Walden two.* New York: The Macmillan Co., 1948.
48. *See* Skinner (1971), p. 162.
49. *Ibid.,* pp. 168-169.

*Chapter 6*

1. Skinner, B. F. A case history in scientific method. *American Psychologist,* 1956, *11,* 221-233. *See* p. 231.
2. Orne, M. T. On the social psychology of the psychological experiment: With particular reference to demand characteristics and their implications. *American Psychologist,* 1962, *17,* 776-783.
3. *Ibid.,* p. 777.
4. *Ibid.,* p. 780.
5. Milgram, S. *Obedience to authority.* New York: Harper & Row, 1974.

6. *See* Orne (1962), p. 779.
7. *Ibid.*, pp. 779, 780.
8. Rosenthal, R. On the social psychology of the psychological experiment: With particular reference to experimenter bias. Paper read at American Psychological Association Convention, New York, 1961.
9. Rosenthal, R. *Experimenter effects in behavioral research.* New York: Appleton-Century-Crofts, A Div. of Meredith Publishing Co., 1966. *See* pp. vii, 161.
10. Rosenthal, R., & Jacobson, L. *Pygmalion in the classroom.* New York: Holt, Rinehart and Winston, Inc., 1968.
11. *See* Rosenthal (1966), p. 109.
12. *Ibid.*, p. 407.
13. *Ibid.*, p. 408.
14. *See* Rosenthal & Jacobson (1968), p. 180.
15. Brehm, J. W. *A theory of psychological reactance.* New York: Academic Press, 1966. *See* p. 56.
16. Piaget, J. *The child's conception of physical causality.* London: Kegan Paul, Trench, Tübner & Co., 1930. *See* pp. 244, 245.
17. Köhler, W. Psychological remarks on some questions of anthropology. In M. Henle (Ed.), *Documents of gestalt psychology.* Berkeley, Calif.: University of California Press, 1961. *See* p. 210.
18. Michotte, A. E. *The perception of causality.* New York: Basic Books, Inc., 1963. *See* p. 20.
19. *Ibid.*, p. 23.
20. *Ibid.*, p. 260.
21. For another major source of influence on attribution theory see: Heider, F. *The psychology of interpersonal relations.* New York: John Wiley & Sons, Inc., 1958.
22. Jones, E. E., & Nisbett, R. E. *The actor and the observer: Divergent perceptions of the causes of behavior.* Morristown, N. J.: General Learning Press, 1971.
23. Kelley, H. H. The processes of causal attribution. *American Psychologist*, 1973, *28*, 107-128. *See* p. 126.
24. *Ibid.*
25. *Ibid.*, p. 125.
26. Jones, E. E., Kanouse, D. E., Kelley, H. H., Nisbett, R. E., Valins, S., & Weiner, B. *Attribution: Perceiving the causes of behavior.* Morristown, N. J.: General Learning Press, 1971. *See* p. xii, where it is stated that attribution theory no longer assumes that a person is always acting as an "attributor."

27. Skinner, B. F. *Verbal behavior.* New York: Appleton-Century-Crofts, A Div. of Meredith Publishing Co., 1957.
28. Skinner, B. F. *Beyond freedom and dignity.* New York: Alfred A. Knopf, 1971. *See* p. 67.
29. Rogers, C. R., & Skinner, B. F. Some issues concerning the control of human behavior: A symposium. *Science,* 1956, *124,* 1057-1066.
30. Greenspoon, J. The reinforcing effect of two spoken sounds on the frequency of two responses. *American Journal of Psychology,* 1955, *68,* 409-416.
31. Roberts, W. T. *Instrumental effects of causal constructs.* Unpublished Master's thesis, Purdue University, 1974. This subject was interviewed in the present study, which was conducted under the author's supervision.
32. DeNike, L. D. The temporal relationship between awareness and performance in verbal conditioning. *Journal of Experimental Psychology,* 1964, *68,* 521-529.
33. Dulany, D. E. The place of hypotheses and intentions: An analysis of verbal control in verbal conditioning. In C. W. Eriksen (Ed.), *Behavior and awareness: A symposium of research and interpretation.* Durham, N. C.: Duke University Press, 1962.
34. Spielberger, C. D., Berger, A., & Howard, K. Conditioning of verbal behavior as a function of awareness, need for social approval, and motivation to receive reinforcement. *Journal of Abnormal and Social Psychology,* 1963, 67, 241-246.
35. Page, M. M. Demand characteristics and the verbal operant conditioning experiment. *Journal of Personality and Social Psychology,* 1972, *23,* 372-378.
36. Skinner, B. F. *About behaviorism.* New York: Alfred A. Knopf, 1974. *See* p. 56.
37. Evans, R. I. *B. F. Skinner: The man and his ideas.* New York: E. P. Dutton & Co., Inc., 1968. *See* p. 19.
38. Kennedy, T. D. Verbal conditioning without awareness: The use of programmed reinforcement and recurring assessment of awareness. *Journal of Experimental Psychology,* 1970, *84,* 487-494.
39. Farber, I. E. The things people say to themselves. *American Psychologist,* 1963, *18,* 185-197.
40. *See* Skinner (1974), p. 74.
41. Brewer, W. F. There is no convincing evidence for operant or classical conditioning in adult humans. In W. B. Weimer & D. S. Palermo (Eds.), *Cognition and the symbolic processes.* Hillsdale, N. J.: Lawrence Erlbaum Associates, 1974.

42. *Ibid.*, p. 18.
43. *Ibid.*, pp. 28-32.
44. *Ibid.*, p. 29.


Chapter 7

1. Freud, S. A case of successful treatment by hypnotism. In J. Strachey (Ed.), *The standard edition of the complete psychological works of Sigmund Freud* (Vol. I). London: The Hogarth Press, 1966. *See* p. 124.
2. Rychlak, J. F. Sigmund Freud: The reluctant dialectician. In J. F. Rychlak (Ed.), *Dialectic: Humanistic rationale for behavior and development*. Basel, Switzerland: S. Karger AG, 1976.
3. Freud, S. *The psychopathology of everyday life*. In J. Strachey (Ed.), *The standard edition of the complete psychological works of Sigmund Freud* (Vol. VI). London: The Hogarth Press, 1960. *See* p. 254. (Permission: Ernest Benn Ltd.)
4. Freud, S. Leonardo da Vinci and a memory of his childhood. In J. Strachey (Ed.), *The standard edition of the complete psychological works of Sigmund Freud* (Vol. XI). London: The Hogarth Press, 1957. *See* pp. 136-137.
5. Freud, S. The "uncanny." In J. Strachey (Ed.), *The standard edition of the complete psychological works of Sigmund Freud* (Vol. XVII). London: The Hogarth Press, 1955. *See* p. 236.
6. James, W. *The varieties of religious experience*. New York: The New American Library, 1958.
7. James, W. *The principles of psychology*. In R. M. Hutchins (Ed.), *Great books of the western world* (Vol. 53). Chicago: Encyclopedia Britannica, 1952. *See* p. 794.
8. Freud, S. Project for a scientific psychology. In J. Strachey (Ed.), *The standard edition of the complete psychological works of Sigmund Freud* (Vol. I). London: The Hogarth Press, 1966. This is Freud's single venture into a Lockean brand of psychology, one which he found impossible to finish and soon gave up on. Later in life he tried to have this manuscript burned.
9. *See* James (1952), pp. 155, 107.
10. *Ibid.*, p. 770.
11. *Ibid.*, pp. 815, 816, 820.
12. *Ibid.*, p. 825.
13. *Ibid.*, p. 822.

14. Whitehead, A. N., & Russell, B. *Principia mathematica* (3 vols., 2nd ed.). Cambridge: The University Press, 1963.

15. We are aware of the crossing of both Greek and Latin etymological roots in the term *telosponse*, but believe that it is the best choice to oppose to *response*. The main point is to appreciate that a *telos*, or end, is not something existing "down the road of time." Ends are framed in predications as reasons, beliefs, convictions, and so forth, all of those meanings which Aristotle wanted to capture by the final cause. Since this cannot be expressed in the response construct we need an easily stated, succinct alternative, and telosponse seems to do the job rather well despite its doubtful etymology.

16. Ewing, A. C. *Kant's treatment of causality*. New York: Archon Books, 1969. *See* p. 185.

17. O'Connor, D. J. *Free will*. Garden City, N. Y.: Doubleday & Co., Inc., 1971. *See* p. 82.

18. Skinner, B. F. *Beyond freedom and dignity*. New York: Alfred A. Knopf, 1971. *See* pp. 113-114.

19. *Ibid.*, p. 114.

20. Skinner, B. F. *Walden two*. New York: The Macmillan Co., 1948.

21. Patterson, F. Conversations with a gorilla. *National Geographic*, 1978, *154*, 438-465.

*Chapter 8*

1. Breuer, J., & Freud, S. *Studies on hysteria*. In J. Strachey (Ed.), *The standard edition of the complete psychological works of Sigmund Freud* (Vol. II). London: The Hogarth Press, 1955. *See* p. 281.

2. Freud, S. *Introductory lectures on psycho-analysis* (Part III). In J. Strachey (Ed.), *The standard edition of the complete psychological works of Sigmund Freud* (Vol. XVI). London: The Hogarth Press, 1963. *See* p. 455.

3. Ansbacher, H. L., & Ansbacher, R. R. (Eds.), *The individual psychology of Alfred Adler*. New York: Basic Books, Inc., 1956. *See* p. 94.

4. Adler, A. *What life should mean to you*. New York: Capricorn Books, 1958. *See* p. 59.

5. Jung, C. G. *Symbols of transformation*. In H. Read, M. Fordham, & G. Adler (Eds.), *The collected works of C. G. Jung* (Vol. 5). Bollingen Series XX.5. New York: Pantheon Books, 1956. *See* p. 58.

6. Jung, C. G. The soul and death. In H. Read, M. Fordham, & G. Adler (Eds.), *The collected works of C. G. Jung* (Vol. 8). Bollingen Series XX.8. New York: Pantheon Books, 1960. *See* pp. 405-406.

7. Jung, C. G. Freud and Jung: Contrasts. In H. Read, M. Fordham, & G. Adler (Eds.), *The collected works of C. G. Jung.* (Vol. 4). Bollingen Series XX.4. New York: Pantheon Books, 1961. *See* p. 337.

8. Jones, M. C. Albert, Peter, and John B. Watson. *American Psychologist*, 1974, *29*, 581-583.

9. Jacobson, E. *Progressive relaxation.* Chicago: University of Chicago Press, 1938.

10. Wolpe, J. *Psychotherapy by reciprocal inhibition.* Stanford, Calif.: Stanford University Press, 1958. *See* p. 127.

11. For a thorough discussion of the telic aspects of behavioral therapy, see: Locke, E. A. Is "behavior therapy" behavioristic? (An analysis of Wolpe's psychotherapeutic methods). *Psychological Bulletin*, 1971, *76*, 318-327.

12. Burgess, A. *A clockwork orange.* New York: Ballantine Books, 1963.

13. Thoresen, C. E., & Mahoney, M. J. *Behavioral self-control.* New York: Holt, Rinehart and Winston, Inc., 1974.

14. *Ibid.*, p. 22.

15. This approach to the cure of alcoholism was begun by the following individuals: Voegtlin, W., & Lemere, F. The treatment of alcohol addiction. *Quarterly Journal of Studies in Alcoholism*, 1942, *2*, 717-723.

16. Lazarus, A. A. Desensitization and cognitive restructuring. *Psychotherapy: Theory, Research and Practice*, 1974, *11*, 98-102.

17. *Monitor*, April, 1974, Vol. 5, No. 4. Washington, D.C.: American Psychological Association, 1974.

18. Skinner, B. F. *Walden two.* New York: The Macmillan Co., 1948.

19. Skinner, B. F. *Beyond freedom and dignity.* New York: Alfred A. Knopf, 1971.

20. Husserl, E. *Phenomenology and the crisis of philosophy* (translated by Q. Lauer). New York: Harper & Row Torchbooks, 1965.

21. Rogers, C. R. *On becoming a person.* Boston: Houghton Mifflin Co., 1961. *See* p. 166, where Kierkegaard is referred to favorably.

22. Rogers, C. R., & Dymond, R. F. *Psychotherapy and personality change.* Chicago: University of Chicago Press, 1954; see also Rogers, C. R., Gendlin, E. T., Kiesler, D. J., & Truax, C. B. *The*

*therapeutic relationship and its impact.* Madison: University of Wisconsin Press, 1967.

23. Binswanger, L. *Being-in-the-world* (translated and with a critical introduction by J. Needleman). New York: Basic Books, Inc., 1963. *See* p. 31.

### Chapter 9

1. Ornstein, R. E. *The psychology of consciousness* (2nd ed.). New York: Harcourt Brace Jovanovich, Inc., 1977. *See* p. 117.
2. Hook, S. *From Hegel to Marx.* Ann Arbor: University of Michigan Press, 1962.
3. Nakamura, H. *Ways of thinking of Eastern peoples.* Honolulu: East-West Center Press, 1964.
4. Raju, P. T. Metaphysical theories in Indian philosophy. In C. A. Moore (Ed.), *The Indian mind: Essentials of Indian philosophy and culture.* Honolulu: University of Hawaii Press, 1967.
5. Moore, C. A. Introduction: The comprehensive Indian mind. In C. A. Moore (Ed.), *The Indian mind: Essentials of Indian philosophy and culture.* Honolulu: University of Hawaii Press, 1967. *See* p. 14.
6. Takakusu, J. Buddhism as a philosophy of "thusness." In C. A. Moore (Ed.), *The Indian mind: Essentials of Indian philosophy and culture.* Honolulu: University of Hawaii Press, 1967. *See* p. 87.
7. *Ibid.,* p. 112.
8. Datta, D. M. Epistemological methods in Indian philosophy. In C. A. Moore (Ed.), *The Indian mind: Essentials of Indian philosophy.* Honolulu: University of Hawaii Press, 1967. *See* pp. 129-130.
9. Nikhilananda, S. Concentration and meditation as methods of Indian philosophy. In C. A. Moore (Ed.), *The Indian mind: Essentials of Indian philosophy and culture.* Honolulu: University of Hawaii Press, 1967. *See* p. 147.
10. Moore, C. A. Introduction: The humanistic Chinese mind. In C. A. Moore (Ed.), *The Chinese mind: Essentials of Chinese philosophy and culture.* Honolulu: University of Hawaii Press, 1967. *See* pp. 6-7.
11. Rychlak, J. F. *The psychology of rigorous humanism.* New York: Wiley-Interscience, 1977.
12. Chan, W.-T. The story of Chinese philosophy. In C. A. Moore

(Ed.), *The Chinese mind: Essentials of Chinese philosophy and culture*. Honolulu: University of Hawaii Press, 1967. *See* p. 54.

13. Watts, A. W. *The way of Zen*. New York: Pantheon Books, Inc., 1957.

14. Plato. *Philebus*. In R. M. Hutchins (Ed.), *Great books of the western world* (Vol. 7). Chicago: Encyclopedia Britannica, 1952. *See* pp. 611-612.

15. Suzuki, D. T. *The essentials of Zen Buddhism* (edited and with an introduction by B. Phillips). New York: E. P. Dutton & Co., Inc., 1962. *See* p. 40.

16. *Ibid.*, p. 84.

17. This Eastern non-attachment is directly comparable to the Christian conception of grace (see Chapter 5, p. 71).

*Chapter 10*

1. Wiener, N. *The human use of human beings*. Boston: Houghton Mifflin Co., 1954. *See* p. 15.

2. *Ibid.*, p. 16.

3. *Ibid.*, p. 26.

4. *Ibid.*, pp. 154, 68.

5. Adler, I. *Thinking machines*. New York: New American Library, 1961. *See* p. 31.

6. *See* Wiener (1954), p. 24.

7. Asimov, I. *I, robot*. Greenwich, Conn.: A Fawcett Crest Book, 1950, p. 51.

8. *Ibid.*, p. 61.

9. *Ibid.*, p. vi.

10. *Ibid.*, p. 100, 99.

11. Penfield, W. *The mystery of the mind*. Princeton, N.J.: Princeton University Press, 1975. *See* p. 21. Reprinted by permission of Princeton University Press.

12. Delgado, J. M. R. *Physical control of the mind: Toward a psychocivilized society*. New York: Harper & Row, 1969, pp. 19-20.

13. *Ibid.*, pp. 27, 122, 61, 59.

14. *Ibid.*, pp. 90, 114, 141, 139, 123, 168.

15. *Ibid.*, p. 129.

16. Restak, R. José Delgado: Exploring inner space. *Saturday Review*, 1975, 8/9, 21-25. See p. 23.

17. King, H. E. Psychological effects of excitation in the limbic sys-

tem. In D. E. Sheer (Ed.), *Electrical stimulation of the brain.*
Austin: University of Texas Press, 1961.
18. *See* Delgado (1969), p. 139.
19. *See* Penfield (1975).
20. *See* Delgado (1969), p. 114.
21. *See* Penfield (1975), p. 77.
22. *Ibid.*
23. *Ibid.*, p. 5.
24. *Ibid.*, pp. 46, 49-50, 54, 55, 52.
25. *Ibid.*, pp. 55, 76, 55.
26. *Ibid.*, pp. 79, 80, 61.
27. Sperry, R. W. Brain bisection and mechanisms of consciousness. In
J. C. Eccles (Ed.), *Brain and conscious experience.* New York:
Springer-Verlag, 1966.
28. Sperry, R. W. Hemisphere deconnection and unity in conscious
awareness. *American Psychologist*, 1968, *23*, 723-733. *See* p. 724.
29. Ornstein, R. E. *The psychology of consciousness* (2nd ed.). New
York: Harcourt Brace Jovanovich, Inc., 1977. *See* pp. 36-39.

*Chapter 11*

1. Carnegie, D. *How to win friends and influence people.* New York:
Pocket Books, 1964. (1936 edition published by Simon & Schuster),
pp. 13, 32, 51-52, 42.
2. *Ibid.*, pp. 110, 144, 185, 226.
3. *Ibid.*, pp. 74, 209.
4. *Ibid.*, p. 99.
5. Peale, N. V. *The power of positive thinking.* New York: Prentice-
Hall, Inc., 1952.
6. *Ibid.*, p. viii.
7. *Ibid.*, pp. 9, 69.
8. *Ibid.*, pp. 55-56.
9. *Ibid.*, p. 66.
10. *Ibid.*, pp. 16, 70.
11. Rychlak, J. F. *The psychology of rigorous humanism.* New York:
Wiley-Interscience, 1977. *See* Chapters 10 and 11.
12. *See* Peale (1952), pp. 102-104, 144-146.
13. Freud, S. *The psychopathology of everyday life.* In J. Strachey
(Ed.), *The standard edition of the complete psychological works
of Sigmund Freud* (Vol. VI). London: The Hogarth Press, 1960.

14. Adler, A. *What life should mean to you.* New York: Capricorn Books, 1958.
15. Berne, E. *Transactional analysis in psychotherapy.* New York: Ballantine Books, 1961; and *Games people play.* New York: Grove Press, Inc., 1964.
16. Harris, T. A. *I'm OK—you're OK.* New York: Avon Books, 1967.
17. *See* Berne (1961), p. 21. Although the word *cathexis* is used without mention of *libido*, it is clear that Berne is following the traditional Freudian theory.
18. *See* Berne (1964), p. 30.
19. *Ibid.,* pp. 18, 17, 35.
20. *Ibid.,* pp. 48-49, 126.
21. *Ibid.,* p. 116.
22. *Ibid.,* pp. 175-177.
23. *Ibid.,* p. 27.
24. *See* Harris (1967), p. 30 and p. 61.
25. Penfield, W. *The mystery of the mind.* Princeton, N.J.: Princeton University Press, 1975. *See* p. 21.
26. *See* Harris (1967), p. 53.
27. *Ibid.,* p. 260.
28. *See* Berne (1964), p. 183.
29. Trueblood, E. *General philosophy.* New York: Harper, 1963.
30. *See* Harris (1967), p. 88.
31. Durant, W. *The story of philosophy.* New York: Simon & Schuster, 1963. *See* p. 339.
32. *See* Harris (1967), p. 279.
33. Maltz, M. *Psycho-cybernetics and self-fulfillment.* New York: Bantam Books, 1970. *See* pp. 3, 4.
34. *Ibid.,* pp. 4, 204, 4, 21.
35. *Ibid.,* pp. 130, 202, 233, 47.
36. Peter, L. J., & Hull, R. *The Peter principle.* New York: Bantam Books, 1969. *See* p. 38.
37. Peter, L. J. *The Peter prescription.* New York: Bantam Books, 1972.
38. *See* Peter (1969), p. 49.
39. For a discussion of the dialectical nature of humor see the following: Sardello, R. J. Dialectics and the psychology of laughter. In J. F. Rychlak (Ed.), *Dialectic: Humanistic rationale for behavior and development.* Basel: S. Karger AG, 1976.
40. *See* Peter (1969), p. 68.
41. *Ibid.,* pp. 42, 46, 133.

42. *See* Peter (1972), pp. 11, 65, 97.
43. *Ibid.*, p. 141.
44. *Ibid.*, p. 204.
45. Korda, M. *Power! How to get it, how to use it.* New York: Bantam Books, 1975. *See* pp. 188, 187.
46. *Ibid.*, pp. 4, 76, 99-100, 116-117.
47. Bry, A. *est: 60 hours that transform your life.* New York: Avon Books, 1976. *See* preface, pp. 184, 25.
48. *Ibid.*, pp. 51, 78.
49. *Ibid.*, pp. 31, 89, 115.
50. *Ibid.*, pp. 16, 186, 189.
51. *Ibid.*, pp. 199, 89. See also "est: There is nothing to get." *Time,* June 7, 1976, p. 54.
52. *See* Bry (1976), p. 43.
53. *Ibid.*, pp. 186, 188.
54. *Ibid.*, pp. 191, 81-82.
55. *See Time* (1976), p. 53.
56. Dyer, W. W. *Your erroneous zones.* New York: Funk & Wagnalls, 1976. *See* pp. 4, 11.
57. *Ibid.*, p. 12.
58. *Ibid.*, pp. 13-14.
59. *Ibid.*, pp. 18, 60, 83.
60. *Ibid.*, pp. 15-16.
61. Fromm, E. *The art of loving.* New York: Bantam Books, 1956.
62. May, R. *Love and will.* New York: Dell Publishing Co., 1969.
63. *See* Fromm (1956), pp. 22, 27, 38-39, 46.
64. *Ibid.*, pp. 47, 107, 73, 90-92.
65. *See* May (1969), pp. 73-74, 95, 56.
66. *Ibid.*, pp. 111, 273, 277.
67. *Ibid.*, p. 269.
68. May, R. Freedom, determinism, and the future. *Psychology,* April, 1977, Trial Issue. *See* p. 7.
69. *See* Fromm (1966), pp. 62, 64, 43.

# Name Index

Valins, S., 304
Vesalius, 29
Voegtlin, W., 308
Voltaire, F. M. A., 17, 297

Watson, J., 38-40, 90, 159, 290, 291, 299, 308
Watson, R. I., 299
Watson, R. R., 179, 299
Watts, A. W., 310
Weimer, W. B., 305

Weiner, B., 304
Wesley, J., 73
Whitehead, A. N., 139, 301, 307
Wiener, N., 187-89, 310
Wiener, P. P., 302
Wightman, W. P. D., 298
Wolpe, J., 159-61, 269, 292, 308
Wundt, W., 37, 47

Zilsel, E., 302

# Subject Index

For the reader's convenience, many of the following entries are also defined in the Glossary which begins on p. 269.

# 322

SUBJECT INDEX

Grounds: (*cont.*)
responsibility, 238; self-examination of, Dyer, 240; Biblical passages as, 257; personal selection of, 267; see also Predicate; Premise; Telosponse

Habit, 39
Human, Humanism: in theology, 71; human right, 163; human nature and change, 172-73; dialectical nature of, 174; as humanite, 230; see also Teleology

Idea(s): simple to complex, Locke, 61
Idealism: definition, 21; in mathematics, 21-22; in quantum physics, 26; see also Realism
Identity: in brain research, 203
Individual Psychology, 156
Information-Processing Theory: in attribution theory, 112; bits, 189; of machines, 189-90; as mind, Delgado, 197-98; see also Cybernetics; Mediation Theory
Insight: in Freudian therapy, 153; in Adlerian therapy, 156-57
Intention, Intentionality: perceived directly by Köhler, 109; of antithetic idea, Freud, 133; in telosponsivity, 140; see also Final Cause; Purpose; Teleology; Telosponse
Interpretation, 153
Introspective Perspective: first-person theory, definition, 31; required in telic theory, 100; in understanding people, 254-55; see also Extraspective Perspective

Koan, 180, 183

Law: dual meaning of, 23-24; as efficient causation, 74; statistical, 138; see also Method; Theory; Variable
Libido: as a pseudo-material and

pseudo-efficient cause, 47, 130; cathecting objects with, 48, 154; drawn more from biology than psychoanalysis, 49; as translated psychological theory, 154; as telic, Jung, 157
Life Style, 155-56
Love: and will, 241-44; and personal responsibility, 242; vs. sex, 242; and dialectic of the sexes, 243

Mandala, 181
Mantra, 183
Many and One, and *vice versa:* accepts contradictions, 174; as enlightenment, 176; in Chinese thought, 177-78; in non-attachment, 181; in duality of brain action, 204; see also Dialectic
Material Cause: definition, 12; in biological theory, 29; form of determinism, 35; see also Cause; Efficient Cause; Final Cause; Formal Cause
Meaning: as relational concept, 50; symbolical vs. signalizing, 51; connotation, 52; vs. meaningfulness, 52; bipolar vs. unipolar, 52-53; demonstrative, 54; dialectical, 55; see also Demonstrative; Dialectic
Mechanism: in behavioristic theory, 40-42, 115; in Skinnerian theory, 100-101; of experimenter effects, 106; lacks true possibilities, 140-41; see also Teleology
Mediation Theory: via Tolmanian intervening variables, 40, 81; Hullian contribution, 40; as non-telic, 41; in Skinnerian thought, 92; used in attribution theory, 114; vs. precedent-sequacious order, 141-42; and behavior therapy, 162; of Delgado, 198
Meditation: transcendental (TM), 171; steps in, 183; leading to freedom, 184; in est, 238; see also Buddhism
Method: definition, 75; confounded with theory, 79-80, 117, 137; see also Evidence; Theory; Variable

Responsibility: as tied to free will, 3; as due to self-determination, 130; selecting grounds for determination, 148; via arbitrariness, 182-83; cannot be programmed into a machine, 238; personal, up to each person, 267; *see also* Free Will; Self

Self: -identity, in research, 129, 203; as weight of logical inference, 129; affirmer of precedent meaning, 142; predicator, 142; -determination via telosponsivity, 148; -determination, in existentialism, 166; -image, positive, psycho-cybernetics, 226; -determination, as free will, 251-53; *see also* Predication; Premise
Self-Help Books: common themes, 210-12; testimonials in, 211; honesty, 212; prayer-book reading of, 212
Self-Reflexivity: in Kantian model, 67; in higher animals' telosponses, 149-50; lacking, in thinking machines, 190; as potential to know we know, 204; *see also* Transcend
Sequacious: necessarily following, 141-42; aspects of value conflict, 190; *see also* Precedent
Shadow, 157
Shaping (of Behavior): in Skinnerian theory, 90
Sin: as subverting God's will, 17, 70
Sophistry: dialectical nature of, 60
Split Brain, 205-7
Stream of Thought, 135
Superiority Strivings, 156-57
Systematic Desensitization, 160; *see also* Reciprocal Inhibition

*Tabula Rasa:* in Lockean model, 61-63, 83; *see also Pro Forma*
Tao, 178
Teleology, Telic Theory: as final-cause theorizing, 14; eclipsed, in modern physical theory, 27; as

vitalism, in biological theory, 29; not occurring in mediation theory, 41; humanism as, 71; in all human research in psychology, 107; set aside by behaviorism, 115; and operant conditioning, 121-22; in Freudian theory, 130; vs. mechanism, 141-43; as unconscious process, 155; in Jungian psychology, 157; hidden, in behavior therapy, 162; in Eastern psychologies, 171; and Penfield's findings, 201; in transactional analysis, 223-25; eclipsed in Peter Prescription, 230-31; in Korda's psychology, 231; in *est*, 236; in Dyer's psychology, 240; *see also* Final Cause; Intention; Purpose; Telos; Telosponse
Telos: end, goal, or reason for behavior, 7, 139; and final cause, 14
Telosponse: definition, 140; possibilities in, 149; evolution of ability to, 149-51; via "taking a position on," 204; vs. response, 204-5; in Dale Carnegie, 215; affection as, 264; *see also* Final Cause; Intention; Purpose; Teleology; Telos
Theory: definition, 75; confounded with method, 79-80; *see also* Method
Thinking Machines: non-dialectical, 189; not self-reflexive, 190; *see also* Cybernetics; Information-Processing Theory
Tracking: of astronomical bodies, 24; due to Cartesian geometric assumptions, 24; mentality, in psychology, 80; via statistical laws, 138; *see also* Prediction
Transactional Analysis (TA): overview, 219-25; ego states: Child, Parent, Adult, 220; transaction as social relation, 220; stroke, 221; game as dishonest transaction, 221-23; game-free transactions, 223
Transcend, Transcendence: via dialectic, Kant, 67; transcendental freedom, 142; lacking, in machine thinking, 191; *see also* Dialectic; Self-Reflexivity
Transference, 154